WHY THE TORIES WON

WHY THE
TORIES WON

TIM ROSS

WHY THE TORIES WON

The Inside Story of the 2015 Election

TIM ROSS

Biteback Publishing

First published in Great Britain in 2015 by
Biteback Publishing Ltd
Westminster Tower
3 Albert Embankment
London SE1 7SP
Copyright © Tim Ross 2015

ISBN 978-1-84954-947-9

10 9 8 7 6 5 4 3 2 1

A CIP catalogue record for this book is available from the British Library.

Set in Sabon and Meta by Adrian McLaughlin

Printed and bound in Great Britain by
CPI Group (UK) Ltd, Croydon CR0 4YY

MIX
Paper from
responsible sources
FSC
www.fsc.org
FSC® C020471

CONTENTS

Part 4: THE ELECTION

ACKNOWLEDGEMENTS

This book owes a huge debt to the generosity, patience, encouragement and attention of many people. There is time and space to acknowledge only a few of them here, though I am enormously grateful to everyone who helped with this project.

The foundation of this story is the material that has come from hundreds of interviews and conversations with original sources – the large majority of whom asked to remain anonymous. Without them, and the secretaries and advisers who timetabled meetings with them, there would be no story to tell. Among those who agreed to be named in the book, I am especially grateful to the following: Nick Clegg, Nigel Farage, Boris Johnson, Lynton Crosby, Grant Shapps, Bob Roberts, Tom Baldwin, James Stewart, Alan Sendorek, Craig Elder, Martin Boon and James McGrory.

I am lucky to work with some of the most talented journalists in the country and am grateful to my editors at the *Telegraph*, colleagues at Westminster and friends for their ideas and support. I especially want to thank Craig Woodhouse, Thomas Penny, Tom Everest, Ian Collins, Peter Dominiczak, Kate Mayer, Ian MacGregor, Ben Riley-Smith,

Christopher Hope and Steven Swinford. Frank Prenesti, Stephen Hall and Brendan Carlin spent long hours on French trains commenting on drafts and improved the text hugely.

The team at Biteback Publishing have been brilliant. Iain Dale's early interest was the essential spur to embark on the book, and Olivia Beattie's superb editing skills and deep knowledge of politics have been invaluable.

Without the support of my family, however, there would be no book at all. My parents carefully read early drafts of the manuscript and made numerous vital observations. By far the greatest debt is owed to my wife, Amy. She read every word, improved many and provided endless encouragement throughout, while somehow keeping our two small boys happy and still dimly aware of their father's existence.

Every effort has been made by the editors and the author to iron out the wrinkles in order to get this story out into the world while it still holds interest. Any imperfections and errors that remain are mine.

EXIT

At 10 p.m. on 7 May 2015, a handful of numbers shocked Britain. The exit poll for the 2015 general election was so far from what every pollster and pundit had been predicting that none of the main party leaders could believe it.

Like millions of others across the country, the leaders were watching on television at home in their constituencies, with their families and closest aides. Ed Miliband turned to his advisers to ask if the exit poll was wrong. David Cameron hoped it was right but dared not quite believe that it was. A dumbfounded Nick Clegg reached for a packet of cigarettes.

Instead of a 'knife-edge' election, with perhaps a dozen seats separating the two main parties, the exit poll forecast the Conservatives would win 316 seats, only ten short of an overall majority. Labour were trailing far behind on 239. In Scotland, the SNP were predicted to take all but one of the fifty-nine seats north of the border in an unprecedented landslide, while the Liberal Democrats were on course to hold just ten of the fifty-seven seats they won in 2010.

Inside Conservative headquarters in Westminster, jubilant campaign staff erupted. Perhaps only Lynton Crosby, the

Tories' Australian election strategist, and a handful of his colleagues who had been conducting seat forecasts in secret for months, were not astounded. As the first results were declared, showing swings to the Tories in crucial marginal seats, Crosby told his team that the exit poll was wrong: they were going to win a majority. By the morning, he had been proved right.

The scale of the shock that the Tory majority delivered can be measured in its impact on the party's opponents and other figures in the story. In the months before the election, both Labour and the Conservatives were making plans for ruling without a majority in their own right. Both, as it happens, were also preparing for the possibility of a second election later in 2015. But in the space of an hour on the morning of Friday 8 May, Ed Miliband, Nick Clegg and Nigel Farage had all resigned. Labour initiated an inquiry into what went wrong. The polling industry launched an investigation into how they failed to see the majority coming. UKIP descended into a spiral of infighting, with Farage ultimately reversing his resignation and seeing off an attempted coup. Meanwhile, Jeremy Corbyn, a radical left-wing underdog, emerged from the shadows to succeed Miliband as Labour leader.

This book is an attempt to understand how the Tories managed to pull off such an unexpected victory, in defiance of political history and every reputable opinion poll and professional expert who had offered a view. What techniques did the Conservatives use? Who was responsible for their success? Did they always know that they would win? What impact did the extraordinary failure of so many opinion polls have on the contest? Why did so many journalists, academics, pollsters, civil servants – and politicians from all parties – fail to see what was coming?

In order to answer some of these questions, this book relies on the first-hand accounts and personal testimonies of individuals drawn from the backroom offices to the very top of all the main parties. Some agreed to provide interviews on the record, but the vast majority – many of whom remain active in politics – needed to talk anonymously in order to be free to give their most candid reflections. Their generosity – through hundreds of conversations, interviews, phone calls and emails – has made it possible to piece together the inside story of the 2015 election. In the endnotes, the term 'private interview' is used to attribute quotations and other information stemming from formal but anonymised interviews with sources, many of whom played extremely senior roles in the election campaign. References listed as 'private information' in the endnotes refer to other material for which the confidential sources cannot be revealed.

This story needed to be written quickly, before the election-night shock faded too far from the public consciousness. It also had to focus on the battle for No. 10, which was only ever between David Cameron and Ed Miliband. While the Scottish political landscape was radically redrawn on polling day, with the SNP sweeping Labour and Liberal Democrat MPs from the map, the Tories won their majority entirely in the south. This essential fact means that the book does not dwell in detail on how the SNP won its landslide. That important story will be told by others.

The effect of the political earthquake in Scotland, however, was to send tremors south of the border that were felt in the homes of Liberal Democrat voters in Devon, Somerset and Cornwall, and those tempted to back Nigel Farage in

Kent, Essex and Lincolnshire. Ultimately, the surge of the Scottish National Party provided an essential context for the Conservatives to launch their most damaging attacks on Ed Miliband.

In tracing the reasons for the Tories' success in England, this book examines in some detail what happened to Ed Miliband's campaign. The Conservative victory was also Labour's abject defeat, as Miliband returned to Westminster with fewer MPs than even Gordon Brown managed at the height of his unpopularity, and amid a global financial meltdown, in 2010.

It also deals with the fate that befell the Conservatives' coalition partners, the Liberal Democrats. Killing the Lib Dems, in what has been nicknamed the 'black-widow strategy', above all else enabled David Cameron to return to No. 10 to rule alone. The destruction of Nick Clegg's party in England was every bit as dramatic as the Scottish National Party's near clean sweep in Scotland, and, in terms of the results, it was ultimately more important for determining the outcome of the election.

The first part of this book seeks to explore the reasons why the Conservative campaign proved to be such an effective election machine. Of critical importance is the character of Lynton Crosby and the team he assembled around him. Through these characters and their stories, the book then traces the Conservatives' strategy to fight the election through the national media in the 'air war'; on the streets in 100 target seats; and, for the first time in Britain, in a major operation through social media and digital communications. The book then looks behind the scenes at the pivotal moments of the campaign, through the eyes of those who fought it. The final section describes the drama of the election itself and its bloody aftermath.

History is frequently written by the winners and this book tells the story of the Conservative victory. But it seeks to be fair to all sides. It would be misleading to see the Tories' election success as inevitable, or their campaign as flawless. The truth is that there were many mistakes and even moments of crisis behind the scenes. Cameron and his team would rather forget how they were plagued with doubts at key points in their campaign. Some details of their story will embarrass senior figures, while others may prove controversial. Miliband's bid for power clearly faltered, but he inspired considerable loyalty and affection among his senior team. Even Lynton Crosby would acknowledge that the Labour leader held his party together exceptionally well. This book sought contributions from all the major parties. Nothing would have been possible without the generous responses of so many individual sources who gave up their time to share their personal accounts of the general election of 2015.

The techniques and tactics that the Tories used look certain to be scrutinised by others hoping to emulate their success. Yet the Conservative victory also raises questions about what it means to fight a professional election campaign in the twenty-first century, and whether the British political system itself is in trouble. The 2015 election was an extraordinary moment in the story of British democracy. For anyone who cares about that story, it essential to try to understand why the Tories won.

PART 1

THE TORIES

CHAPTER 1

COALITION

S teve Hilton was in the mood for dancing. It was 3 a.m. in Stockholm, in February 2012, and the temperature was -12°C. European leaders, including Hilton's boss, David Cameron, were in the middle of a two-day summit on social reform. But the Prime Minister's director of strategy paced the ice-bound streets dressed in a short-sleeved blue polo shirt and jeans, searching for another nightclub that was open and willing to let him in. The world did not yet know it, but Hilton, a charismatic and visionary Tory who had been Cameron's close friend and political inspiration for years, had had enough. Less than two years into a five-year parliament, he was so disillusioned with life in government that he had resolved to leave. The causes of Hilton's frustration were complex. He felt Cameron should be doing more to give power away, reducing the dominance of government in society and putting more control into the hands of the people. Yet the Prime Minister seemed too willing to wait, to compromise on the agenda that they had mapped out together for governing through the Tories' 'Big Society' programme, on which the party had fought the 2010 election.[1]

Lingering disappointment at the outcome of that contest may also have played its part. At least one reason Cameron was not able to be the Prime Minister that Hilton wanted him to be was because he was forced to govern in coalition. Hilton was sure about what he wanted to do in government, but the Conservative campaign had failed to convince the country to give them a Commons majority with which to enact their plans. According to those who worked on the 2010 election campaign, a damaging clash of personalities between Hilton and Cameron's communications director, Andy Coulson, was partly to blame. Relations between the two were so bad that they barely spoke. Cameron was adamant that the pair needed to work together effectively in order for his campaign to succeed, so he made them share a single office inside the Conservatives' headquarters at Millbank Tower. But veterans of the Tory campaign speak with horror about what went on, blaming shambolic disorganisation for the party's failure to win a majority. According to one Conservative who witnessed the 2010 operation, nobody was clearly in control. 'You knew that you would come in on any given day of the week and you'd not have a flipping clue what you were going to be doing,' the Tory says. 'There was a real "them" and "us" culture,' another party insider recalls. 'Coulson wouldn't speak to the press office. There was a big war going on between Coulson and Hilton. Cameron put them in an office together and told them, "There can't be a cigarette paper between you." But they obviously weren't getting on.'[2]

While many staffers were dismayed at the tensions and disunity that undermined their chances, some saw the funny side, notably the Tories' favourite jester, Boris Johnson. 'Boris came in and gave a pep talk to the troops,' a former 2010 campaign insider says. 'He rode a scooter up and down the office and when he had finished, he took one step into Hilton and Coulson's room and said, "This smells like the rhino enclosure at the zoo."'[3]

The Stockholm summit in February 2012 – officially called the Northern Future Forum, gathering north European and Scandinavian leaders – was designed as a sort of super-charged brainstorming conference for prime ministers looking for ideas. Hilton was instrumental in establishing the event and the trip to Sweden was to be one of his last foreign assignments as Downing Street's director of strategy. When he left two months later, in April 2012, observers concluded that he took with him Cameron's guiding sense of what he was in power to achieve. As the Tories languished ten points behind Labour in the polls, the Prime Minister, it was often said, had lost his muse.

Coulson had quit No. 10 the previous year at the height of the phone-hacking scandal, which had already cost him his previous job as editor of the *News of the World* in 2007. The public was sickened to learn that among the hacking victims was the murdered schoolgirl Milly Dowler. Others included celebrities such as Jude Law and Sienna Miller, and politicians including the former Home Secretary Charles Clarke. The scandal demanded a radical response. Rupert Murdoch closed the *News of the World*, after 168 years of printing, in the summer of 2011. David Cameron announced a public inquiry led by Lord Justice Leveson.

In 2014, Coulson was convicted of plotting to hack phones and sentenced to eighteen months in jail. His co-defendant, Rebekah Brooks, the former editor of *The Sun* and News International chief executive, was cleared. It emerged during the trial that Coulson and Brooks, both of whom were close to Cameron, had conducted a secret six-year affair. The hacking scandal prompted questions over the Prime Minister's judgement. Ed Miliband accused him of bringing a criminal into No. 10.

The departures of Coulson and Hilton left Chancellor George Osborne as the sole survivor of the trio who ran the 2010 campaign. He, too, would come close to disaster during the course of 2012. The Conservatives had been within touching distance of Labour in the polls, until the Chancellor got to his feet to deliver the Budget at 12.30 p.m. on Wednesday 21 March. Most of the significant announcements had been trailed in the media in the days leading up to the Budget, leaving little new material for journalists to report on the day. Instead, the focus fell on smaller changes, including what became known as the Pasty Tax, a plan to charge VAT on hot savouries, which had previously been exempt. This would have put up the price of pasties and sausage rolls by 20 per cent. Other proposed reforms affected caravans, churches and charities.

Osborne and Cameron encountered strident opposition from Cornish bakers, Tory MPs, the media and the high-street chain Greggs. Under intense questioning from the Treasury select committee, Osborne was forced to confess that he had no idea when he had last eaten a Cornish pasty, leading to accusations that he was clearly 'out of touch' with the real world. Cameron tried to limit the damage by professing that he loved pasties and had eaten a 'very good' one recently from the West Cornwall Pasty Company outlet at Leeds railway station. Unfortunately, almost immediately, it transpired that no such pasty shop existed at Leeds station at the time when the Prime Minister claimed to have eaten the takeaway.

Ed Miliband enjoyed it all so much that he celebrated by

reheating a phrase from the BBC political satire *The Thick of It*, which instantly stuck. Across the despatch box during Prime Minister's Questions, Miliband told Cameron:

> Over the past month we have seen the charity tax shambles, the churches tax shambles, the caravan tax shambles and the pasty tax shambles, so we are all keen to hear the Prime Minister's view on why he thinks, four weeks on from the Budget, even people within Downing Street are calling it an 'Omnishambles' Budget.

As a measure of how enduring this description of the 2012 Budget turned out to be, the *Oxford English Dictionary* named 'Omnishambles' as their word of the year. Politics paused during the summer, when London hosted the Olympic and Paralympic Games, which were widely seen as triumphantly successful events. But the truce did not apply to Osborne. When he appeared at the Olympic stadium, the crowd of 80,000 spectators booed.

Death and taxes

When the coalition was formed, George Osborne and David Cameron were determined to cut taxes, an instinct common to almost all Tory politicians. However, they were far less dogmatic about precisely which taxes should be reduced first. This turned out to have unfortunate consequences for their relations with the Tory grassroots and right-wing MPs in the years that followed. Nick Clegg had already written a plan to raise the personal allowance, the earnings threshold at which working people have to start paying income tax. Cameron and Osborne looked at the Lib Dem plan and thought, 'We want to cut tax – we might as well do that.'

For much of the 2010–15 parliament, however, Tory right-wingers wanted tax breaks first and foremost for marriage. These were often the same MPs who intensely disliked the idea of extending marriage to gay couples, a move that Cameron saw as symbolically important but strategically painful. Many MPs – including a number of senior ministers – also wanted Cameron to move more quickly to cut the tax burden on the middle classes. The *Daily Mail* was one of the papers to point out prominently how hundreds of thousands of middle-class professionals were being dragged into higher tax bands because Osborne had kept the thresholds at the same level while incomes increased.

Some of these frustrations over tax – and same-sex marriage reforms – can be traced back to a lingering resentment among Tories at the decision to enter into coalition with the Lib Dems in 2010. In private, and sometimes in public, Conservative MPs would complain that Cameron and Osborne were hopelessly out of touch, and call for the coalition to break up. Some would also whisper that Cameron was not really a winner. How could he have failed to beat Gordon Brown, the most unpopular Prime Minister in decades, a man who had bottled his chance of winning an election that was never called in 2007 and who was presiding over a massive economic crisis in 2010? Cameron was not the man to steer them to a majority in 2015, the malcontents grumbled. A number of more resolute critics sent letters of no confidence in their leader to Graham Brady, the chair of the 1922 Committee, whose role it was to keep these letters under lock and key unless and until he had received the required number to trigger a leadership election. In at least one painfully awkward conversation,

Cameron personally requested that a known opponent of his leadership withdraw the letter of no confidence, during a private, one-to-one meeting in the Commons in 2013. 'I might do it next year,' the MP replied. 'That's not soon enough for me,' Cameron said.

With cuts to the army adding to the disgruntlement of Tory traditionalists, it is little wonder that the party leader did not want Conservative membership figures to be published. When they were eventually released, they showed that Tory membership had almost halved since Cameron became leader, falling from 254,000 in 2005 to 134,000 by September 2013.

Selections and defections

Political parties have permanently roving eyes for the right kinds of celebrity endorsements, including, occasionally, recruiting actors and TV personalities to stand for Parliament. As they prepared for the 2015 election, Cameron and his team had their sights on several promising Tory supporters who they hoped would one day be added to the party's team sheet. James Cracknell, the double Olympic gold medallist, and the television presenters Kirstie Allsopp and Jeremy Paxman were among the highest-profile individuals to be linked with the Conservatives, but never became candidates. Karren Brady, the vice-chairman of West Ham United Football Club, had made a number of star appearances at the party's autumn conference, but ruled out standing for election. Cameron made her a Conservative peer instead in September 2014.

At one point, the Prime Minister personally asked Andrew Strauss, the former England cricket captain, to consider standing as a parliamentary candidate. It was not such a bizarre idea as it might at first appear, as the two men had met several times and appeared to be fans of each other's work. In 2011, Strauss had helped raise £25,000 for the Conservatives after offering himself as an auction prize at a fundraising event. Then, during the England *v.* India Test match at the Oval on Friday 19 August 2011, Strauss invited Cameron into the England dressing room, where the Prime Minister toasted the performances of Kevin Pietersen and Ian Bell, who had both scored centuries. Cameron was so thrilled at having made a speech to the England team mid-way through a Test match that he spent the car journey home phoning his friends to tell them what he had done.[4] On 29 August 2012, Louise Mensch, the 'chick lit' author, formally stood down as the Conservative MP for Corby in order to spend more time with her family in America. On the same day, Strauss announced he was retiring from cricket, after fifty Tests as England captain. The coincidence immediately sparked speculation on Twitter and in the newspapers that Strauss could be lined up to deliver the key marginal seat for the Tories. Conservative sources played down the rumour at the time, insisting that it was too late to select him as their candidate for the by-election that Mensch's departure caused, which they ultimately lost to Labour. But No. 10 had noted the idea.

When, on 19 July 2013, Cameron was making one of his semi-regular trips to watch England play against Australia (he was a left-arm bowler in his youth and remains a keen fan), he saw Strauss and seized his chance. In a typically blokeish and awkward exchange, in the MCC President's box during a break in the Test match, the Prime Minister approached Strauss and made his pitch. 'So when are you joining us?' Cameron asked. According to one witness, 'Strauss just looked completely flustered and unprepared for the question, mumbled something about having a lot of commentary and media and things he was working on and it didn't go any further.'[5]

No. 10 was always on the lookout for new talent from whichever quarter it could be found. After Nick Clegg sacked Jeremy Browne, one of his most right-wing MPs, as a Home Office minister, Grant Shapps, the Conservative co-chairman, tried to get him to switch to the Tories. According to one account, Shapps sidled up to Browne in the Commons shortly after he was demoted in 2013 and asked him: 'Shall we go somewhere quiet where we can talk?' Browne is said to have answered bluntly: 'No.'

Two leaders

By autumn 2013, prospective parliamentary candidates had been chosen for all of the Tories' forty 'attack' seats – those target constituencies the party hoped to take from its rivals, chiefly Labour and the Lib Dems. The party had also begun to recruit in earnest for Team 2015, the army of volunteers who would be asked to travel around the country to knock on doors and campaign for the Tories in the run-up to the election. Grant Shapps, the party's co-chairman, whose personal project Team 2015 had become, was proud that he had already recruited a 'secret army' of 3,000 volunteers to be taken by bus to canvass in the Tories' target seats.

The autumn conference season in 2013 was dominated by one theme: Ed Miliband's pledge to freeze household energy bills. His advisers had astutely noted that their conference, in Brighton at the end of September, would come at the beginning of the annual period in which the 'big six' gas and electricity companies announce their price structures for the winter ahead. These usually provoke a public outcry over soaring bills, with warnings that more pensioners and hard-pressed families will be forced to make the choice between 'heating or eating'.

The result was that energy prices were rarely out of the headlines, giving Labour an ideal platform on which to hawk their latest election promise and denounce the 'cost of living crisis' that George Osborne and David Cameron were failing to address. Privately, Tory MPs and ministers were dismayed at how their side was failing to respond. The party was 'on the back foot' for a month, giving ample time for Labour's policy to take root in voters' minds. Eventually, towards the end of October – after Sir John Major unhelpfully suggested a windfall tax on energy firms – Cameron announced some measures to 'roll back' the green taxes that increase consumer bills. He made the announcement at Prime Minister's Questions, only telling Nick Clegg of his plan thirty minutes beforehand, despite the fact that the Energy Department was under Lib Dem control. Even senior Tories were left in the dark, with negligible briefing before their broadcast interviews to explain the new policy.[6]

The episode added grist to Labour's argument that Miliband was more 'in touch' with ordinary families' lives than Cameron and his 'Cabinet of millionaires'. Public polling and focus groups for both sides revealed that the image of a wealthy, Eton-educated Prime Minister did not endear Cameron to the nation's hearts. He was ahead on trust to manage the economy, but behind Miliband when it came to being trusted to help families with the cost of their everyday lives. For much of the parliament, prices of household goods were rising faster than people's wages, causing a 'squeeze' for many families in the middle-income bracket, which the Labour leader tried to exploit. Though this could be easily portrayed as an old-fashioned socialist class war, there were signs that it was effective. For much of 2012, after the 'Omnishambles' Budget in March, and into 2013, Labour enjoyed a ten-point lead over the Conservatives in most polls.

Cameron knew the difficulty he had with his own image but rarely seemed troubled by it. He would confess to friends that since it was obvious that he was 'considerably posher' than the vast swathe of the electorate, it would be pointless to pretend to be otherwise. 'So, I went to Eton,' he would say. 'I can't pretend I grew up in a shoebox in the middle of the M6.'[7] He was also relaxed about the fact that he lacked a defining policy for his time in office, telling friends that such a legacy was not necessarily a good thing: 'Blair lacked definition until Iraq and now he is fucked.'

Labour strategists had been aware since 2010 that their leader, too, would require significant work in order to turn him into a winning brand in the eyes of the electorate. Weird, geeky, even too ugly to be Prime Minister: the terms used in the media to describe Ed Miliband rarely gave his side licence to gloat.

In the winter of 2013, minds began to focus on the general election. The major parties were putting their campaign teams together and preparing for a dry run during the European Parliament elections that were being held in May 2014. Lynton Crosby, the Australian election strategist, had taken charge of the Conservative election machine. For Tory MPs, as they peered over their shoulders to see the shadow of Nigel Farage looming ever closer, the priority was to address public concerns over immigration. Voters spontaneously raised the issue with

MPs in many marginal seats, complaining that only Farage seemed willing to speak about their concerns. Nigel Mills was one of those who saw the threat of UKIP. His Amber Valley constituency was eleventh on Labour's target seat list and could have fallen to Labour if UKIP had made inroads into his slim majority. At great risk to his own standing within the party, Mills led a rebellion over the government's immigration Bill, demanding an extension of limits to the right of Romanian and Bulgarian migrants to move to the UK. These limits were to expire from 1 January 2014. Cameron was forced to delay the Bill in order to avoid defeat.

For other MPs, the European Parliament elections of 2014 looked as if they would be a moment of intense danger for Cameron, who many colleagues feel is not personally committed or confirmed in the Tory Eurosceptic faith. Cameron had to be forced, through a series of back-bench rebellions, to promise an in/out referendum on Britain's membership of the EU. One Tory MP said: 'If the Euros are disastrous for us, there could be repercussions for the leadership. Would it be too late to change leader before the election? No.'

UKIP

By early 2014, Cameron knew that he had to get down on bended knee to woo UKIP voters, a position that had not always come naturally to the Tory leader. For the best part of a decade, he failed to shake off remarks made in 2006, when he infamously dismissed UKIP as a party of 'fruitcakes, loonies and closet racists' on LBC radio. With eighteen months to go until the general election, such outbursts were banned. In private, Cameron referred to UKIP supporters as 'my little purple friends'. They were no longer the enemy but increasingly, in Cameron's eyes, the key to winning a majority.

The European Parliament elections in May 2014 seemed to confirm the seemingly unstoppable rise of UKIP. During the campaign, Nick Clegg decided to debate with Nigel Farage on live television, putting himself in the role of the champion of the 'In' campaign, while the UKIP leader was well known as a populist, charismatic advocate of leaving the EU. Even Clegg himself accepts that he did not do well, and his party came fifth in the national share of the vote, on just 7 per cent, losing ten of its eleven MEPs. Farage's success in the debates also damaged Cameron. The Tories were beaten into third place, behind Labour and UKIP, which topped the poll with 27 per cent of the vote, taking its tally of MEPs from thirteen to twenty-four.

The Tories were given another reason to worry about UKIP. Not only were the 'people's army' taking votes from the established party of the right, they were also taking their MPs. In the course of 2014, first Douglas Carswell, the MP for Clacton, and then Mark Reckless, the MP for Rochester and Strood, announced they were defecting to join Farage and would seek to win their seats at by-elections. For Conservative election planners, by-elections were precisely the kind of high-profile, resource-intensive nightmare they could do without. One senior source said: 'We need another by-election like we need a hole in the head.' The Prime Minister declared twenty-four hours after Reckless defected that he wanted the MP's 'fat arse' to be kicked off the Commons benches at the by-election.[8] But Carswell and Reckless delivered a double headache for Cameron, winning their seats as new UKIP MPs.

Perhaps the most alarming feature of the defections for the Tories, however, was the fact that they'd had no idea that either was coming until the MPs were on stage in front of UKIP audiences announcing the news on live TV. This stood in dramatic contrast to the Conservatives' own defector, Amjad Bashir, a UKIP MEP who switched to the Tories in January 2015. This, too, was meant to have been a top-secret operation. But hours before the news was due to break, a whiff of the story had reached UKIP, who then put out a spoiler statement, suspending Bashir over what it called 'grave' allegations about financial and employment issues. The Tories' prize had been tarnished by a brutal UKIP media operation before they could take it out of the trophy cabinet.

Security

UKIP had already proved its ruthless streak by announcing Mark Reckless's defection the day before the Conservatives' crucial pre-election party conference was due to begin in Birmingham. The news dominated the opening of the conference and created an atmosphere of panic among MPs and Cameron's aides, who worried that Farage was preparing to unveil another defector just before, immediately after, or even in the middle of his leader's conference speech. In the end, no such announcement came and Cameron was able to dominate the news bulletins with dramatic election pledges to cut income tax for middle-class workers and to provide more tax breaks for the low-paid. The underlying subtext for the whole conference was that the Tories were the party of security and stability. The implicit question to the electorate was: who do you trust to keep you safe? The Conservative rhetoric of security was all the more powerful coming at a time of multiple international – and existential – threats. Vladimir Putin stoked the civil war in Ukraine, while RAF warplanes bombed terrorist fighters in Iraq, and a British-educated terrorist nicknamed 'Jihadi John' horrified the world by beheading western hostages in the name of the so-called Islamic State.

In September, fears over national security – and identity – played a central part in the debate over the referendum on Scottish independence. A shock opinion poll in the *Sunday Times* eleven days before the vote gave Alex Salmond's pro-independence 'Yes' campaign a clear lead, causing panic in No. 10 and spurring all the main Westminster parties to flood Scotland and beg the country's four million voters to stay. Cameron himself was said to be distraught at the prospect of presiding over the break-up of the Union after 300 years.

In the end, Scotland voted by 55 per cent to 45 per cent against becoming an independent country. The aftermath of this result, and the spectacular surge in the popularity of the Scottish National Party on the wave of patriotic fervour that the referendum had unleashed, was to become the single most decisive factor in shaping the general election to come. David Cameron felt overwhelming relief. A few days later, however, Cameron embarrassed himself with the kind of gaffe that an experienced Prime Minister ought to avoid. During a private conversation at a public event with the former New York Mayor Michael Bloomberg, he was caught on camera revealing how happy the Queen had been when he told her that Scotland was safe. 'She purred down the line,' he said. Not for the last time, Cameron's breezy manner, in a casual moment, had got him into trouble.

CHAPTER 2

THE WIZARD OF OZ

Omnishambles

Lynton Crosby was adamant. He did not want to work with David Cameron.

It was autumn 2012 and the Australian election strategist had not forgotten that a few months earlier the Prime Minister and his unpopular Chancellor had nearly ruined his reputation. Crosby was furious with them for jeopardising his chances of winning a second term for Boris Johnson as the Mayor of London. For weeks leading up to the mayoral election, he feared that the mid-term mess that Cameron and George Osborne were making of running the country would fatally handicap his candidate's campaign, allowing Ken Livingstone, the former Labour mayor, to sneak back into City Hall.[9]

The election was taking place at the height of the coalition's unpopularity. Six weeks before the vote, Osborne had delivered the 'Omnishambles' Budget, making the Conservative Party a national joke over policies to tax pasties and caravans. Labour had taken a ten-point lead in the national polls, while Ed Miliband was celebrating a successful night of local election results across England. Over lunch on a blustery spring day a few weeks before London went to the polls, Crosby was clear that the idea of working with Cameron was out of the question. He is even said to have believed that Osborne should be sacked. 'If we lose, it will be their fault,' Crosby confided to his friends. 'They've got no idea what they're doing.'[10]

On election night itself, 4 May 2012, Crosby feared that victory had slipped away. At 7 p.m. he had 'more or less written off' Johnson's chances and was depressed, according to those who were with him at the time. But Johnson won. In so doing, he defied the opinion polls, and the political landscape of the time, to retain power in Labour-dominated London. Victory was not merely the result of the unique public appeal of the candidate known simply as 'Boris'. It was, by Johnson's own reckoning, in no small part due to Lynton Crosby, who executed the kind of highly focused and disciplined campaign for which he has become known.

In the months that followed his re-election, Johnson lobbied Cameron repeatedly, urging him to recruit Crosby to take charge of the Conservative Party's campaign for the 2015 general election. Dozens of MPs joined the clamour for the man who ran Johnson's campaigns in both 2008 and 2012. Cameron, it seems, was open to persuasion. He despatched Andrew Feldman, the Conservative Party co-chairman, and George Osborne to woo Crosby.

But, despite Johnson's victory, the Australian was still reluctant. He remembered being blamed for the Tory election defeat of 2005, when he ran Michael Howard's unsuccessful campaign against Tony Blair. More importantly, Crosby had serious doubts about David Cameron's motivation and appetite for the job of Prime Minister. 'How do I know it's not just some fucking frolic for a rich bloke to do?' he asked friends.[11]

In the end, Feldman, Osborne and, ultimately, Cameron himself persuaded Crosby that it would be worthwhile, and in November 2012 he agreed to take on the role part-time. In addition to a hefty fee – reported to have been in the region of £500,000 – Crosby demanded total control over the Conservative campaign. Having been heavily criticised in 2005, he wanted to make sure he was in control in 2015 so that at least he would not be blamed for anyone else's mistakes. To Tories who questioned the new hierarchy, and few dared to do so to his face, Crosby had a crisp response: the election is a campaign for the chance to run a democracy; the campaign itself is not a democratic process. Someone had to be in charge – and it was Lynton Crosby. He also had a job to do on coaching David Cameron himself. Over the months that followed his appointment, Crosby set about 'breaking' the somewhat diffident and laid-back Prime Minister, whom he had witnessed making a mess from afar, and 're-making' him in the mould of a national leader who would command authority and respect. By the time of the election, Crosby was pleased to see his candidate had grown into the role.

For David Cameron, it would prove to be a price worth paying. Crosby's remarkable stewardship was to be the decisive factor in the Conservatives winning a shock majority in 2015. One source close to the Prime Minister has described the Australian as a 'genius'.[12] Another senior Tory figure says: 'It was Lynton's show. Everyone else was pretty secondary. He had that strength of character and personality. He just carries authority and doesn't mess around. If it had not been for him, we probably wouldn't have won.'[13]

Australia

Born in Kadina, South Australia, in 1957, Lynton Crosby has described himself as 'just a Methodist farm boy from the middle of nowhere'. His father sold the family farm when Crosby was a child and moved the family into the town of Kadina, where they started a craft shop.[14] His devoted parents were both loyal supporters of the right-wing Australian Liberal Party. As a precocious schoolboy, Crosby took on his left-wing teachers in classroom debates about politics and joined the Liberal Party aged eighteen. He even raised money for the party by staging musicals, and remains an avid theatre-lover. After studying for a degree in economics at the University of Adelaide, he went to work for the party, taking on a succession of roles.

In 1982, he tasted electoral defeat first-hand as a candidate, turning, in his words, a marginal Liberal seat into a safe Labor one. 'In hindsight,' he told the Australian newspaper *The Age*, 'I wouldn't have voted for me.' Crosby took a number of roles in the oil industry before returning to politics in the 1990s, at a time when the Liberal Party was struggling. He won attention for his work at a regional level and was made deputy director and later national director of the Liberals in time for the 1996 general election, which, under John Howard's leadership, the party won. With Crosby's help – and that of his future business partner, the pollster Mark 'Tex' Textor – Howard won successive elections and remained Prime Minister until 2007. Crosby's successes earned him his nickname, the Wizard of Oz.

His reputation as a political magician who had revived the fortunes of the flagging right in Australia saw Crosby hired to save Michael Howard's struggling Tory campaign

in the British general election of 2005. Although Howard
failed to oust Tony Blair, he did significantly cut Labour's
majority. The Tories won thirty-two more seats in 2005 than
at the previous election in 2001. Tory insiders from the time
report that Crosby was drafted in too late to make a decisive
difference to Howard's chances, only starting work a few
months before polling day. But he did inject a much-needed
late burst of life into the campaign.

Not everyone was a fan. Plenty of commentators – a breed
of journalist whom Crosby has grown to despise – objected to
what was termed the 'dog whistle politics' that the Howard
2005 campaign deployed. Crosby's message at the time
focused on attacking Labour's record on immigration, crime,
school discipline and deadly hospital superbug infections. 'Are
you thinking what we're thinking?' was the Tory slogan for
election billboards. It appeared at the bottom of handwritten
posters with messages such as 'It's not racist to impose limits
on immigration'.

It was a slogan that effectively urged voters to reject the
political correctness 'gone mad' that the right believed New
Labour was enshrining into the law of the land. It was also
an attempt to make an intimate appeal to voters' private
thoughts, to sway their hearts rather than their heads. Crosby's
method was to point up a well-chosen selection of threats
that had the potential to generate fear – killer infections,
hordes of migrants, and marauding gangs of youths. While
Howard's campaign under Crosby's direction may have been
unfairly caricatured as 'nasty', it hardly amounted to a positive
vision for Britain. However, when Blair returned to No. 10,
with a significantly reduced majority, he declared that he
had heard the voters' message on immigration and on anti-
social behaviour. He promised to 'bring back a proper sense

of respect in our schools, in our communities, in our towns, in our villages'. The message Blair said he had heard was one crafted carefully by Lynton Crosby.

London

Crosby set up the London arm of his company, Crosby-Textor, with Mark Fullbrook, to become CTF Partners in 2010. The venture required Crosby and his wife Dawn – who have two daughters and four grandchildren in Australia – to divide their time across two hemispheres of the globe.

When he was appointed as a consultant to David Cameron's campaign in autumn 2012, Crosby's critics feared he would fail because they remembered his unsuccessful 'core vote' strategy from 2005. Lord Ashcroft, the Tory grandee and former party treasurer, said his opposition to the appointment was 'nothing personal' but warned that the party must be able to appeal to the wider electorate beyond traditional Tory voters. 'To win a majority, we need to attract people who thought about voting Conservative in 2010 but decided against it, not just keep existing Tories on board,' Ashcroft wrote on the influential website ConservativeHome.com.[15]

Crosby's methods had been controversial in Australia, too. Particularly contentious was his use of so-called 'wedge' politics – messages that will split groups away from an opponent's party by exploiting issues that generate powerful emotional responses, such as race, tax or migration. In the 2001 federal election campaign in Australia, John Howard's win was partly thanks to a row over refugees and asylum seekers. Howard's government refused permission for the *Tampa*, a Norwegian boat carrying shipwrecked Afghan asylum seekers, to enter Australian waters, in defiance of international maritime law. Howard later passed a law ensuring that the Australian government would have the final say over who entered the country. Then, one month before polling day, a boat carrying more migrants was intercepted. Howard claimed the migrants were throwing their children overboard in order to force the authorities to rescue them. An inquiry that followed found no evidence to support the claim, but Howard still won the election.[16]

In the 2015 general election, his wedge of choice would be to exploit the divisions between Scotland and England in the aftermath of the independence referendum. The tactic would prove highly effective. The style of messaging Crosby uses has earned the nickname 'dog whistle' because it is designed to act subliminally. The intention is to make potential supporters sit up and listen to coded messages while avoiding causing offence to others, in the way that a dog whistle is not audible to humans but will agitate the canine world. 'Are you thinking what we're thinking?', Michael Howard's 2005 slogan, fits neatly with this description. Crosby himself has put it better than anyone: 'In politics, when reason and emotion collide, emotion invariably wins.'[17]

Pigs and cats

While the politics of wedges and whistles seeks to persuade voters through coded emotive messages, Crosby's own workplace methods are far more direct. In the office, he can be blunt to the point of rudeness and spares almost nobody's blushes when it comes to making his views known. He gets away with it because he possesses the kind of exceptional personal qualities of charm, charisma and energy that have made him an accomplished leader of political campaigns.

He explains his guiding ethos in classical terms, quoting the ancient Greek philosopher Solon: 'When giving advice, seek to help not to please.' Crosby has said: 'This is more than an excuse for us to be direct with people. It is a guide to what we see as our commitment to help our clients and add value to their affairs, and not simply make them feel good.'[18]

Although he jokes and swears freely, it would be wrong to characterise Crosby as a crude Aussie cross between Dennis Lillee and Crocodile Dundee. But his political candidates can certainly attest to his directness. Boris Johnson, during his first mayoral campaign in 2008, had to give a speech to a group of councillors at the end of a long week. He had not bothered to prepare and tried to deliver the speech off the top of his head. As he walked out of the room, Johnson thought to himself that it had gone adequately and he had probably got away with it. Then his phone buzzed. It was a text message from Crosby. 'Crap speech, mate,' it said.[19] Johnson's misreading of the strategist was not unique. Another colleague who has worked closely with Crosby says: 'Trying to really understand Lynton is a fool's errand. I used to say my favourite waste of time was trying to understand what Lynton Crosby was thinking. You just stand back and wonder sometimes.'[20]

David Cameron and George Osborne have marvelled at Crosby's gift for memorable maxims involving vivid animal analogies. These include such statements as 'It's time to scrub the barnacles off the boat', meaning that unnecessary distractions that will slow down your progress must be ruthlessly purged. Critical to his election planning was the maxim that 'You can't fatten a pig on market day', so it is best to begin marketing your messages before it is too late. If your political opponent is making all the running, it could be time to 'throw a dead cat on the table'. Boris Johnson explained:

> That is because there is one thing that is absolutely certain about throwing a dead cat on the dining room table – and I don't mean that people will be outraged, alarmed, disgusted. That is true, but irrelevant. The key point, says my Australian friend, is that everyone will shout, 'Jeez, mate, there's a dead cat on the table!'; in other words, they will be talking about the dead cat, the thing you want them to talk about, and they will not be talking about the issue that has been causing you so much grief.[21]

Needless to say, Crosby seasons his arguments with comments like these while sitting around the boardroom meeting table, in the most powerful company imaginable. Each of the rules above was deployed at some point during the Conservative 2015 campaign.

The pink cardigan

Boris Johnson hired Crosby at the end of 2007 because his attempt to unseat Ken Livingstone as Mayor of London in the election the following year was in trouble. Senior Tories knew that Johnson was 'getting a hell of a kicking' and needed to go 'up a gear' if he was to have any hope of winning, so they turned to Crosby.[22] His remit was to bring discipline to the unruly Johnson campaign – and for the Australian, nothing came more naturally than enforcing an iron will. After he was hired, Crosby is said to have warned Johnson to do as he was told or 'we'll cut your fucking knees off'.

For the general election of 2015, Crosby's supremacy was unquestioned. The Chancellor briefed journalists that the Wizard of Oz was in charge. As one party official says: 'Osborne and Cameron built the firm, and Lynton was leading the campaign.'

Crosby's overriding preoccupation for political campaigns is to deliver 'message discipline'. This means honing the election 'messages' until they lodge in people's minds, and then repeating them remorselessly. Individual slogans will be tested in polling and focus groups before they are released upon the world. But once a message has been settled upon, Crosby insists his candidates display 'discipline' by keeping to his script. The temptation to comment on distracting media stories or interventions from opponents that do not fit with Crosby's settled narrative is not tolerated. 'Without discipline, you don't have a message,' one of Crosby's colleagues says.

A senior Tory who worked with him on the 2015 election says Crosby's all-round knowledge of every facet of political strategy stood out:

> He knew about all parts of campaigning and would get involved. He understood literature and was looking at MPs' local literature and saying, 'No, yes, that works, that doesn't' and understanding the point. He knew about fundraising, he knew about media, he knew about campaigning, he knew about politics. I don't think there's anyone else next to Jim Messina [President Obama's former strategist, who also worked for the Tories in 2015] in the world who does that.

He also based his observations ruthlessly on evidence. After 'seek to help rather than please when giving advice', this was the second key Crosby principle. 'Polling was the science behind it all,' one Tory official says.

> In 2010, the feeling was the campaign was based on what people thought. Lynton's whole thing was everything should be scientific and tested – 'This is what the polling says'… Sometimes people are in denial about that. People said the 'long-term economic plan' message was boring, but it was the key to victory.

If all this makes the Tories' election supremo sound like a machine, he is far from it, personally at least. The myth that has grown up around him is of an alpha male who dictates terms to politicians and will not suffer fools. But, in person, he is surprisingly softly spoken, affable and willing to talk to virtually anybody. The result is a character who manages to command authority, as well as great loyalty and affection among those who work for him.

It is a common enough claim that a good boss knows everyone's name, from the intern to the chairman, but so many different people say it of Crosby – including those who have worked with him at different times and on different campaigns – that it must be true. He would also make a genuine effort to get his teams to gel. Even during the doomed 2005 election, Crosby made sure that every Friday in the campaign, the entire Tory Party's central staff came together for a motivational meeting.

On both of Johnson's mayoral campaigns, Crosby initiated humorous awards for Tory staff who had excelled themselves during the day, again to boost morale. Johnson explains:

> Lynton is a fantastic guy and he is brilliant at mobilising the campaign troops and making everybody feel

involved. He just loves it and it's infectious. It becomes
a great war. In my campaigns there would be a thing
called the pink cardigan, which he would dish out. Every
day somebody who did something particularly heroic,
like posing in a chicken suit next to Ken Livingstone,
would get the pink cardigan as a badge of honour.[23]

Crosby took many of these attributes and techniques into
the 2015 campaign, motivating his team to work long hours,
and demanding of everyone the highest possible standards. At
the same time, his calmness and focus made him a reassuring
presence inside the Conservative 'war room', even at times of
crisis. 'He built such a strong team,' says one 2015 campaign
insider. 'If there was any division, ever – and I can't recall
any – Lynton really knocked it out of the organisation. They
were long days, hard days. Some of them were dark days,
but with that guy you'll get through it all.'[24]

The flipside of being so approachable, however, is that he
expects to be approached. 'His big thing is that he doesn't
like being surprised,' one former colleague says. 'If you know
there's a problem and don't tell him, and you've been sitting
on it for a while, he won't accept that.'[25] When occasionally
campaign staff made mistakes, Crosby would take the
individual into an office and say, 'Quick word, mate?', rather
than deliver a public dressing-down. 'He would let people
know if they hadn't delivered. That didn't happen often. He
is pretty realistic about what we could and couldn't achieve.'
When an irritating article appeared in the press, for example,
he would say: 'That's fucking shit, mate. Who is this fucking
correspondent?'[26]

Crosby made a point of talking to every Tory MP. He
would regularly visit Parliament to give presentations to the

potentially troublesome 1922 Committee of backbenchers
and would pick up the phone to any MP who called. 'His
was a reassuring voice and that helped stop them speaking
out,' one source says. He would attend and run election
'away days' with all the Conservative MPs and present his
latest findings and strategy messages to gatherings of the
Tory Cabinet ministers. His main point was that everybody
needed to maintain discipline in their public statements. MPs
could not afford to be commentators on political events; they
were participants, he told them. Even those restive Tories
who felt that Nick Clegg had too much power over Cameron
were persuaded to behave. 'The fact that Lynton would pick
up the phone or speak to anyone when they called really did
calm things down,' one Tory aide recalls.

Those MPs who insisted on behaving like commentators
rather than protagonists in the election contest were given
short shrift. On at least one occasion, an errant Tory who
had openly criticised the leadership checked their messages
and found one from Crosby which said: 'That's not fucking
helpful, is it?' Another senior Conservative aide says:

> In 2010 there was confused messaging and differing
> camps. You needed to have a single figure in charge. Once
> a decision was taken, Lynton was very much the man in
> the driving seat. He was brilliant. It was a real privilege
> to see him at close hand. He is very astute politically. He's
> incredibly robust and plain speaking, which is valuable
> in the heat of a campaign. You're not left in any doubt
> about what you should or shouldn't be doing.
>
> But he is also a really good team leader. Morale was
> high and everyone was very loyal to him. He is pretty
> blunt but he treats people really well and he's funny.

> You need to have a leader in CCHQ and Lynton did
> that really well.

Where others could not cut through the layers of advisers to reach Cameron, or persuade him to take a particular course, Crosby had the magic touch. 'It's a total nightmare to get the PM to sign off on things,' one Tory says. 'But you could say to Lynton, "We need to do this." He would say, "Yeah, mate" and tell the PM to do it and it would get done.'

Cameron

Crosby's influence went far beyond running a happy ship inside CCHQ, testing the party's messages and enforcing discipline in the ranks. He designed and executed the election strategy that resulted in the Conservatives destroying their coalition partners. The 'decapitation' of the Liberal Democrats allowed the Tories to win enough seats to form a majority, giving Cameron his longed-for prize: the platform to govern alone. For Nick Clegg and his party, the outcome could not have been more brutal. Some Lib Dems regard Cameron as unspeakably ruthless for the way he treated their party. But they have got the wrong man. Until Crosby's arrival, Cameron did not regard the Lib Dems as worth worrying about. Indeed, he believed he would still need Clegg's help to form a government right up to the moment that the polls closed on 7 May. But one senior Downing Street figure explains that Crosby's entire focus was to destroy the Lib Dems: 'The genius of Lynton Crosby's campaign was being able to spot that the route to victory was through the Lib Dem marginal seats in the south-west, and then to actually deliver it.'[27]

Two months after the general election, on a warm evening in the middle of July, the London arm of Crosby's company, CTF Partners, held a summer party to celebrate their first five years 'and the next five years of a Conservative government'. The hundreds of guests gathered at the Science Museum in Kensington included Cameron and most of his Cabinet ministers, Tory staff, journalists, Boris Johnson and the former Australian PM John Howard. In his speech, Cameron thanked Crosby for the colourful language he had brought to work with him at Conservative headquarters and for being 'a thoroughly good bloke'. Crosby, he said, had handled Conservative Campaign Headquarters with 'this incredible charm and mesmerising ability to bring people together'.

'But, of course, most of all what I want to thank you for is the incredible work that you did to secure our election victory, and Lynton, we owe you an enormous debt of gratitude,' Cameron said, to applause and cries of 'Hear, hear' from the guests.

> Lynton, you always had faith. You always believed we could do it. In fact, of all the people in the room, you were always the most confident that it would break, and that it would break the right way, if we stuck to the plan and if we stuck to the strategy. And that is exactly what we did.[28]

CHAPTER 3

WAR ROOM

Matthew Parker Street

A five-minute walk from Parliament lies the Conservative Campaign Headquarters – known to all inside the party as 'CCHQ'. Arranged over the basement and ground floor of No. 4 Matthew Parker Street, Westminster, this was the nerve centre from which Lynton Crosby ran the election campaign.

Crosby's 'war room' itself was an open-plan office at street level, where work was conducted in a high state of secrecy. The blinds were permanently drawn to keep out prying eyes of photographers with long lenses, and any Labour spies. In the middle of the room was 'the power pod', at which sat Crosby and the heads of the Tory ground campaign, communications, digital and research departments. There was never any question of who was in charge. With David Cameron often hundreds of miles away, touring the country, Crosby's reign inside the war room was absolute. 'He could have had his own office but he sat in the middle,' one insider says. Crosby was always available and accessible to his staff and senior colleagues. 'He would talk to anyone, from the intern to the Prime Minister, and he'll call everyone "mate".'[29]

The location of the party's new offices also helped. Previously, the Conservatives had been headquartered at the Millbank Tower complex. Although this was where New Labour was born as an election-winning machine, and an address that propelled Tony Blair into office on the back of a landslide, Millbank was just far enough from Parliament to be awkward. A 10–15-minute walk was enough distance for gaps to open up between the party's full-time election operation and its MPs and ministers in Westminster and Whitehall. The move in February 2014 to Matthew Parker Street, just five minutes from Parliament, contributed to smooth party relations. 'Psychologically, having an office in the heart of Westminster, in the centre as opposed to Millbank, was good for MPs,' a senior CCHQ staff member says. 'We had a flow of MPs coming in and we could get to Parliament more quickly and No. 10 more quickly.'[30]

Inside the war room, work went on around the clock. The day began early. Crosby called the first meeting of his senior team in the Thatcher Room – which contained a large portrait of the late former Prime Minister – for 5.45 a.m. each day. Although painful to some, the early starts would give the Tories an important advantage over Labour. One senior staff member says: 'It made a real difference to how the day ran because by 6.15 a.m. any problems were ironed out.' In terms of the day's media schedule, key 'lines' – the slogans and arguments the party was putting forward that day – would be agreed before the main run of morning broadcast interviews began, on BBC Radio 4, 5 Live and the sofas of the breakfast television studios. 'It just made everything easier. There was no panic,' according to one of Crosby's senior team.[31] At the meetings, Crosby would be given summaries of the campaign activities in target seats from Stephen Gilbert, the campaigns director; Team 2015 activities from Paul Abbott, the chief of staff to Grant Shapps; media coverage and plans for the day from the head of communications, Giles Kenningham; the 'grid' of forthcoming announcements and events from Adam Atashzai, a No. 10 aide; and an update on digital campaigning from the creative and digital directors, Tom Edmonds and Craig Elder.

At 6.30 a.m., Crosby would convene a second meeting, at which the team would be joined by Craig Oliver, the No. 10 communications director, and Ed Llewellyn, Cameron's friend and chief of staff. Coffee and fruit would be served with the occasional croissant for variety as the senior strategists firmed up their plans for the day over breakfast. A more substantial meal was available in the basement kitchen area, where some early risers would compete to arrive first in order to claim the freshest porridge.

Then, at 7.30 a.m., the third meeting of the morning took place, at which Crosby's team would be joined by David Cameron and George Osborne, either in person or by telephone when they were away on the campaign trail. The Prime Minister and the Chancellor would listen to the proposals, make their own contributions and formally agree to Crosby's plan.

A few hundred yards up the road, at Labour's headquarters in Brewer's Green, Ed Miliband's team had not yet turned up for work. The first meeting of the day did not start until 7.45 a.m., two hours after Crosby had begun setting his team's priorities for the day. One Labour insider says the explanation is simple: Miliband was not much of 'a morning person'.[32]

According to some witnesses, Crosby chaired proceedings even when the Prime Minister was in the room. Others say

Cameron took charge of all the meetings he attended. One Tory official says Crosby's status as an Australian outsider was sometimes very evident: 'Most people call the Prime Minister "Prime Minister". He just said, "David..."'[33]

Koalas and kangaroos

Inside the Conservative war room, staff were left in no doubt about the focus of their endeavours. When he was appointed co-chairman of the party in 2012, Grant Shapps installed a countdown clock on the wall at CCHQ, ticking down the minutes and hours to polling day. The device certainly focused minds. During the final weeks before the election, the Tory IT department came in overnight to install a digital version of the Shapps clock on the home screen of every computer in the room. When they arrived for work the next morning, CCHQ staff were appalled. 'Overnight this clock appeared on everybody's computer, ticking down to the election. It was so stressful and made everyone so anxious that they had to change it back again,' one staffer recalls.[34]

The computerised clock was a rare blip in the otherwise careful and effective way Crosby managed his team. He worked hard at maintaining morale, knowing that he was asking people to work punishingly long hours at a frenetic pace, and that it would only get worse as the days drew nearer to the election. In order to cheer up his team, the music-loving Crosby adopted an unofficial campaign song. He chose 'One Vision' by Queen and would frequently release the tension of the day by turning up the volume and playing it out across the room from the speakers on his computer. One colleague recalls:

Suddenly, this song would erupt in the middle of the afternoon. You'd just have to end your phone call and sit back as you couldn't do any work with this deafening music going on. People were working incredibly long hours, slogging our guts out – on six- or seven-day weeks – and it all helped keep morale up.[35]

Later, Crosby would play the role of entertainer of his own troops on election night, bringing in a bugle to blow as a hunting horn whenever the Tories claimed a particularly prized scalp.

Crosby also recognised that joking around, while good for morale, would not be enough on its own. Just as he had instigated the 'pink cardigan' awards for heroic work by staffers on Boris Johnson's mayoral campaigns, Crosby made sure that every day at the 5 p.m. meeting of all staff in the war room, he would praise individuals for their outstanding efforts. This time, troops were awarded a cuddly koala or a furry toy kangaroo. The prizes were given out, to applause and general appreciation from their colleagues, to staff who had found a great anti-Labour story, a valuable campaign idea, or had just dressed up in an Alex Salmond mask to pose for a picture next to Ed Miliband. 'He was throwing them around all the time by the end of the campaign. Koalas and kangaroos were flying all over the place in the final week,' one member of staff recalls. 'We were trying to work out where he got them all from. Maybe he got a massive box when he went back [to Australia] at Christmas.'[36]

Crosby liked to keep his colleagues on their toes and was ready to use a variety of means to do so. 'You never knew when you were going to get hit on the head by a blue stress ball,' one CCHQ insider says. 'He loved throwing those things about and he was quite a good shot.'[37]

War footing

When the Tories moved into the new building, they made another important change. CCHQ's entire operation was overhauled to put it onto a war footing. The two men officially in charge of CCHQ were the party's co-chairmen, Andrew Feldman, a businessman and friend of Cameron's since his Oxford days, and Grant Shapps, the MP for Welwyn Hatfield. Lord Feldman can best be described as a reluctant Tory chairman. He initially became involved when Cameron was first considering running to become party leader after the defeat of Michael Howard in 2005. Though Feldman encouraged his friend and tennis partner to stand, he did not expect to be taking on such a mammoth role in running the party in the years ahead. But Cameron, who first worked with Feldman when they were both members of the college ball committee at university, needed his friend's help sorting out the Conservatives' finances. When he became leader in 2005, Cameron discovered the party was £28 million in debt and asked Feldman to help fill the hole. By the time Feldman's ten-year fundraising effort had made it to the 2015 election, it had amassed more than £250 million.[38]

With Shapps, who replaced Baroness Warsi as co-chairman in 2012, Feldman set about transforming the party's structures and preparing the troops for battle. He was instrumental in persuading Crosby to lead the team. Feldman also reshaped the organisation of the Conservative Party's paid army of political officers. With national membership in decline, the number of grassroots activists, who would be required to get out and work the streets in the months and days leading up to polling day, was dwindling alarmingly. In 2010, only a quarter of the party's staff were out 'in the field', with three-quarters working in London. By 2015, Feldman had shifted this balance to 50/50.[39]

Feldman has said he learned a lot from the failure to win a majority in the 2010 election. 'We spent too much on the wrong things, such as posters, and there were too many voices in the room,' he said. Instead, he focused his party on a list of eighty key seats, half of which were defensive marginals – which the Tories had to fight to hold – with the other half being 'attack' seats, to take from Labour and the Lib Dems. Over time, a few more Lib Dem seats were added and the so-called 40/40 strategy became more like a 50/50 plan.

For Shapps, the opportunity to take over the role of co-chairman was too good to miss. He had been a junior minister at the Department for Communities and Local Government, but now had the chance to attend the Cabinet and stamp his ideas on the party's election bid. The 40/40 strategy was already in place when he arrived and he supported it as a sensible use of resources. His major concern, however, was where the Tories would find their troops to knock on doors in these key areas.

In 2010, and at previous elections, the Conservatives had suffered from the fact that they lacked an army where they needed one most. Their loyal activists were all located in safe Tory seats, while the marginals upon which the fate of the election would rest were critically short of campaigners. With this in mind, Shapps designed what was to become a key feature of the Conservative ground war: Team 2015, a ready-made army of volunteers who would be taken in buses from wherever they lived to wherever the election needed to be fought.

The decisions over which constituencies should be the focus of the party's energies were made by Crosby, working closely with an unsung hero of the Tory campaign. Stephen Gilbert, the director of campaigning, was in charge of the party's professional, paid campaigners in the target seats. As a former election agent, Gilbert knew first-hand what his teams 'on the ground' would be required to do. He was so central to the effort that Cameron had to allow him to leave No. 10, where he worked as the PM's political secretary, to focus on the swing seats campaign. Gilbert, a quiet character who has worked for the party for twenty years, was rewarded by being made deputy chairman, and given a peerage, after the election.

White House

In February 2013, Crosby, Feldman, Shapps and Gilbert boarded a plane to Washington, DC, in search of another star signing for their team. Jim Messina had masterminded President Obama's 2012 re-election operation and was being lined up to work as a consultant to David Cameron's 2015 effort. The Tories were especially keen to tap Messina's knowledge of 'ground' campaigning tactics, using social media to target messages at key voters, and digital engagement – which meant mining the potential from the 1.5 million voters' email addresses that the party had gathered by the time of the election.

According to a senior Tory figure who was involved in the negotiations, it was clear that Obama would not stand in Messina's way. 'We knew Obama was broadly supportive of Cameron, which left the door open to an unusual Conservative–Democrat tie-up,' the figure said. 'Traditionally, the Republicans would have been our sister party, but recently, with the rise of the Tea Party and their less-than-progressive social stance, they have seemed far less to be our natural bedfellows.'[40]

Messina's appointment was confirmed in August 2013. Crosby's team was almost complete. One other foreign star of the backroom effort played a role that was every bit as essential as Messina. Mark Textor, Crosby's business partner, is regarded by political anoraks as among the most talented pollsters in the world. His contribution to the Conservatives' success cannot be minimised. Although he was based in his native Australia for most of the lead-up to the campaign, 'Tex' – as he is widely known – was constantly refining and analysing data sent back to him by Crosby's team from focus groups and polls.

Around the same time, in the spring and summer of 2013, Crosby persuaded two dynamic young digital specialists to join his operation. Craig Elder and Tom Edmonds had worked for the party during the 2010 election campaign and left to find jobs in the private sector – one in an advertising firm; the other in a media consultancy. But, on Lord Feldman's advice, Crosby invited them back. Helpfully, the pair had become good friends (since the 2015 election, they have set up their own consultancy, Edmonds Elder, and work together all the time). 'It was fun,' Elder says.

> You've got to be willing to put the job first for a good few months of your life and certainly for the six-week period at the end. There have got to be people you can have a laugh with. There is a dark sense of humour that everyone shares because, as the saying goes, you're 'all in it together'.[41]

CRD

The Conservative Research Department (CRD) is famous as a training ground for future Tory stars. David Cameron and

George Osborne both worked there decades previously, under the direction of Andrew Lansley, who went on to become Health Secretary in Cameron's first Cabinet. The CRD, led by Alex Dawson, now an adviser to Home Secretary Theresa May, was to play its usual pivotal role in the election of 2015. A decision was taken to fuse the CRD with the Tory media operation, led by head of communications Giles Kenningham, into an 'attack unit' ready for electoral combat. Previously, press officers at CCHQ had been working on specific policy briefs, shadowing government departments, but Kenningham realised this had to change in order to focus on the battle ahead.

The pattern was set. Researchers would unearth damaging information about their opposing candidates, scrutinise Labour publications and policy costings from all the other parties, and the details would be handed to the press team for briefing to the media. Two press officers were dedicated to briefing the media on Labour, and one each was in charge of Tory attacks on UKIP, the Liberal Democrats and the Scottish National Party.

As the election drew nearer, a team was assembled to monitor broadcast footage, with a particular focus on output from the SNP, who were uploading dozens of videos onto YouTube each day. In particular, two of David Cameron's most trusted aides were put in charge of attacking Labour over whether Ed Miliband would do a deal with the SNP in a hung parliament: Adam Atashzai and George Bridges. Atashzai, a Downing Street adviser who ran the 'grid' of party announcements, is highly regarded and was given a key role in ensuring MPs and ministers stuck to Crosby's script.[42] Bridges, a veteran of past campaigns, was made a Tory peer after the election and is now a member of the government's team in the Lords.

A team of eighteen media-monitoring people kept up to speed with all developments, across Twitter and broadcasts as well as the press and news websites such as BuzzFeed. As the SNP grew in importance to Crosby's campaign message, eventually becoming the key warning that would be used to win over voters from UKIP and the Liberal Democrats, more resources were devoted to the issue. According to one source, at one point ten people were watching SNP videos on YouTube full-time, every day, in order to find material to be used in the campaign. One such video was an attempt at a joke from Alex Salmond, in which he declared that he would be 'writing the Labour Party's Budget' after the election. David Cameron chose not to see the funny side. On 22 April, he authorised CCHQ to post a link to the shaky mobile phone footage from his personal Twitter account, which was maintained by the party press office and had more than a million followers. In his message, Cameron stepped up his attack on the dangers of the SNP wielding power over a weak minority Labour administration with the message: 'This footage will shock you: Alex Salmond laughs & boasts he'll write Labour's budget. Vote Conservative to stop it.'

Apart from the remarkable fact of Cameron using his own Twitter feed (or allowing his press officers to do so in his name) to spread what in the trade is known as 'dirt' about other parties, the episode demonstrates the Tories' total focus on stoking English fears about the influence of the SNP. From the most junior members of the research department, trawling the internet for grainy footage of Alex Salmond on a stage, to the Prime Minister, who personally ensured it would have the widest possible audience, one Scotsman's joke justified everything.

Secrets and spies

As well as the standard practice among political parties of monitoring news outlets, social media websites and broadcasts for opponents going off message, the Tories ran a highly organised and far murkier operation, which they used to damage the enemy. In secret, a small special operations team of Tory spies was despatched around the country to events held by rival parties, where they tried to blend in with the crowd and record every word that was said. The focus was on Labour fundraising meetings, think-tank gatherings and union events. Despite denials at the time, the party also sent undercover agents to tape events run by UKIP.

In August 2013, Lynton Crosby brushed aside claims that he wanted a 'below the radar' campaign to be launched to discredit UKIP. He reportedly wanted to monitor all council meetings involving UKIP members, with a view to briefing the press via third parties in order to keep the Conservatives' fingerprints free from the tapes. The reports were seen as evidence that the Tories were shaken by the threat UKIP posed to their hopes of winning a majority. It equally serves to illustrate the kind of measures Crosby's team was willing to consider in order to win power. A Tory source was quoted as saying: 'The claims about Lynton are not true. We don't plan to engage third parties or get [Tory Eurosceptic MP] Bill Cash or anyone fronting a campaign. It's nonsense. We're not denying there was a meeting but the report is wrong about... what was supposedly said.' Crosby himself confirmed he had discussed 'a number of issues' with a public affairs firm but added: 'Somebody is being deliberately mischievous.'[43]

In the end, the Conservatives found a large number of stories about UKIP's dubious and sometimes clearly prejudiced candidates, which they supplied to the papers. These stories were especially damaging in the run-up to the 2014 European Parliament and council elections. However, the Tory spies' most notable 'product', to borrow a phrase from the novels of John le Carré, was sourced from Labour events.

On 29 June 2014, the *Sunday Times* ran a story quoting from a secret recording of comments made by Jon Cruddas, the man Ed Miliband had appointed to chair Labour's policy review. Cruddas, an intellectual, academic and independent thinker, was fed up. He lamented, to a meeting of the Compass pressure group, that 'a profoundly dead hand at the centre' of his party was killing off bold policy ideas. He complained that radical reforms had been 'parked' and replaced with 'cynical nuggets of policy to chime with our focus groups and press strategy'.

Conservative sources have confirmed that one of their spies made the secret recording, which was then handed to the *Sunday Times*. The report appeared on page 1 and embarrassed Ed Balls when he was interviewed on television later that day. The row also overshadowed a major Labour policy announcement by Ed Miliband, due the same day.[44]

'Certainly, in the eighteen months of the run-up to the election, the taping of events and monitoring of Labour events helped set the agenda,' according to one campaign insider. 'Labour had the "opportunity cost" of having to deal with these issues – things like the Cruddas recordings. It put them on the back foot in a way that they did not put us on the back foot.' Many of the events that caused Labour embarrassment were 'in the public domain'. But the Tory operation was 'ruthless' about taping not just national events in London but regional meetings and fundraisers around the country. 'These events were for Labour members to go along to, but there was nothing stopping you from registering and turning up,' the Tory says.[45]

Some Conservative staff may even have registered as members of the Labour Party – using doctored identities – in order to get into these events. 'No one broke the law or anything. There are always ways of walking into these places,' one campaign figure says. 'They probably assumed a false identity but they may have walked in. It may have been the case that some people didn't have a digital footprint, and therefore they could go in and no one would know who they were. Shit happens.'[46]

There is arguably some precedent for this sort of activity. At the party conferences, for example, what is known as a 'prisoner swap' takes place each year. One member of Labour staff – usually from the press office – attends the Tory conference and is free to watch any fringe meeting or other event open to the media. A reciprocal arrangement is then made for a Tory representative to attend the Labour Party annual conference. However, there is, at the very least, no obvious reason to think that any of the Labour or UKIP event organisers knew that Tory spies could be in their audiences.

Whether or not it is illegal – and it's unclear which laws would have been broken – it will be seen by some as evidence that the Tories engaged in 'dirty tricks' in order to win. Those involved are likely to respond that their activities were not substantially different from the work done by undercover journalists, who use false identities to conduct 'sting' operations in order to expose corruption by powerful individuals. Even after the election, the Tory spying operation continued, with Jeremy Corbyn as the new target. Four days before Corbyn was elected Labour leader, Mike Watkinson, a Conservative press officer, fled a Corbyn rally after the

Channel 4 News reporter Michael Crick unmasked him as a Tory. CCHQ said Watkinson had merely been attending a 'public event'. Covert recording techniques have been used in the media for years – with, in recent times, the *Daily Telegraph*'s exposé of gender selection abortions in 2013, and the former MPs Jack Straw and Sir Malcolm Rifkind over 'cash for access' allegations in 2015. The *News of the World* used undercover journalism for its sting on spot-fixing by the Pakistan cricket team in 2010, which led to international sports stars being banned for life and jailed. Countless editions of the BBC's *Panorama* have relied on similar techniques of secret recordings.

However, the Conservatives' critics would equally argue that there is a difference between investigative journalists pursuing the truth to expose corruption, and a political party using subterfuge to wound its opponents and win an election.

PART 2

THE
STRATEGY

CHAPTER 4

THE AIR WAR

'Without discipline, you don't have a message. And message is everything in politics.'[47]

Lynton Crosby's mantra was branded into the minds of everyone who worked on the Conservative campaign. His reputation for ruthlessly enforcing discipline made it almost needless to repeat the point. That did not stop Crosby.

In 2010, Conservative figures, including David Cameron and George Osborne, discovered to their cost how a lack of focus in their communications through the media had ruined their chances of winning the election. They flailed around, talking about the ill-defined concept of the 'Big Society' and becoming drawn into a messy discussion about how much they wanted to cut public spending. There was no clear message that they could use to convince voters to back them in sufficient numbers to win a majority.

But what exactly is a 'message', and how did the Conservatives come up with the right one? At its simplest, the 'message' is the story you want voters to hear. This is expressed in individual slogans, such as 'securing a better future' (Conservatives), or 'a better plan, a better future' (Labour). But the key point is to boil down your party's offer to the electorate into a few simple ideas that will stick in voters' minds and help to persuade them that your party is competent, trustworthy and, ultimately, the right choice on polling day. The discipline element refers to the ceaseless repetition of individual slogans that is required to reinforce the headline messages and – crucially – to exclude other subjects on which you are weak. In the case of the Conservatives in 2015, this involved almost ignoring the issue of immigration – on which the government had dramatically failed – even though it was a key concern among the electorate.

If there were a handbook for election strategists, it would say on page 1: make sure the battle to persuade voters through the national media – the so-called 'air war' – is a discussion about your strongest issues; force your opponents to fight you on the policy battlefield on which you can win. For Labour, this meant focusing on the future of the NHS and saving it from privatisation and 'Tory cuts'. For the Conservatives, home turf was the economy, which was a huge advantage, because everything can be brought back to the money. Cameron himself has summarised Crosby's core lesson as being the need to apply 'common sense'. Another senior Conservative described it as the 'boring is good' strategy. As Crosby himself is fond of pointing out, 'an election is not entertainment'.

One Downing Street figure says:

> Lynton's big thing is common sense. What do the voters want? What are they saying? Not 'What does the Westminster village say?' And also, have you got a clear, clean, crisp message that resonates? Another way of putting it is: what are the questions you're asking? We were very good at defining the questions for voters

as being: Who is best to run the economy? Who is the best leader? What would happen if there is a Labour–SNP government? Those are all very simple questions. They may be dull. But they are actually fundamental. The Labour and the Lib Dem campaigns – and to an extent the UKIP campaign – failed to pose the right questions and to have the answers.[48]

The so-called 'air war' was the battle between Labour and the Tories for supremacy in the media. This meant attempting to dominate the debate in the newspapers and, more importantly, coverage on television and radio. To most of the country, which is made up of relatively solid seats that do not change hands frequently, this national media debate was the beginning and the end of their experience of the election. The first thing the Conservatives had to do – and, ultimately, it became the last and most important message of all – was to frame the election as a straight choice: voters had to decide whether they wanted the Tories and David Cameron, or Labour and Ed Miliband, in power. It is a basic point, but there were only two realistic candidates to be Prime Minister and only two major parties who could lead the next government. Voters had to be encouraged to turn their attention to this choice, above all.

The subjects that the Tories chose to fight on were critical to their success and chosen because they highlighted the party's strengths over Labour: the economy, the personalities of the leaders, and the question of whether Labour would do a deal with the SNP. Equally critical, however, was the need to be ruthlessly focused, to stick to the point and not become distracted. The techniques that Crosby and his team of spin doctors used to enforce discipline on the party and impose their messages on the national media were also key. Then there was the role of the media itself. In its desire to report a thrilling story, the media was instrumental in shaping the nature of the election battle. With almost every media-commissioned poll pointing towards the certainty of a hung parliament, the context of 'the closest election in generations' defined the kind of messages that would and would not work.

The economy

After amassing a large amount of research data, involving gleaning evidence from polls, testing various slogans and concepts in focus groups, and subjecting the results to his detailed analysis, Crosby identified one single issue that was to define the Conservative brand for the 2015 election: economic trust. The surveys and focus groups showed that even before the recovery began, David Cameron and George Osborne held a solid lead over Labour on public trust to manage the economy effectively. The decision to focus relentlessly on the economic message, at its most basic, is the dominant reason that the Tories won. Every other salvo in the Tories' 'air war' was a variation on this theme: they were the party of economic competence, of the 'long-term economic plan', and all their opponents were emissaries of 'chaos'.

The Tories' positive message about their own economic credentials was twofold. First, to stress the party's record in government of rescuing the economy from near collapse under Labour. This, they said, could have seen Britain end up 'like Greece' but instead, thanks to their steady hand, saw 1,000 jobs created each day and modest but sustained growth achieved. The second element was to emphasise that the Conservatives had a plan for the future, 'the long-term economic plan', which would ultimately deliver 'the good life' for everyone in the country 'who works hard and wants to get on'. This meant the promise of tax cuts, and pay rises, in the years to come. In October 2014, Jim Messina drove home the central importance of this economic message at an away day for Conservative MPs near Cameron's constituency in Oxfordshire. He ridiculed the Labour leader, saying: 'I've never, ever lost an election in my life. And I'm not going to start with Ed Miliband.' But he warned: 'Every day not spent campaigning on the economy is a day wasted.' Messina told Tory MPs to be 'relentlessly positive' in comparing the state of the economy in 2010 to its performance since.[49]

The third element of the Conservatives' economic message was a remorseless assault on Labour. This, as much as anything, explains to a large degree Ed Miliband's defeat. While the Labour Party was licking its wounds in 2010 after being ejected from office in the middle of a global crisis, Osborne and Cameron sowed the seed that would grow into a truism which eventually choked the life out of Miliband's struggle to win back power. The Tories propagated the argument – at its simplest – that Britain was brought to the brink of ruin because Gordon Brown spent more than the country could afford. Labour's profligacy with taxpayers' cash was the critical cause of the deepest recession for 100 years, the Tories claimed. Labour was too caught up in what one shadow minister called the 'family psychodrama' of Ed Miliband fighting David Miliband for the party leadership to challenge the Tory line, and it stuck. Never mind the fact that the global crisis began thousands of miles away in New York, when the investment bank Lehman Brothers collapsed – or that every major economy in the West suffered as a consequence,

with several European countries requiring international aid
– Labour spent too much and Britain nearly went bust.

From this starting point, it should have been almost
impossible for Cameron and Osborne to lose. Even a modest
recovery – and to Cameron's dismay, even this was a long time
coming – would show that the Tories were more competent
and more trustworthy than Labour. But such a recovery was a
bonus rather than a prerequisite, as the electorate had already
accepted the argument that Labour could not be trusted. For
a variety of reasons, Ed Miliband and Ed Balls never nailed
this 'myth', as they saw it. The moment when Miliband told
an audience member on the BBC's *Question Time* he did not
believe Labour spent too much was the moment the more
astute members of his team knew that they were doomed.

During the same programme, in the final week of the
election, David Cameron used a battered old stage prop that
had first entered the public consciousness five years earlier.
Reaching into his pocket, he pulled out the note from Liam
Byrne, Labour's outgoing Chief Secretary to the Treasury,
to his successor (a Liberal Democrat, David Laws), which
said, 'Dear Chief Secretary, I'm afraid there is no money.
Kind regards – and good luck! Liam.' The note was written
in the gentlemanly and light-hearted tradition in which a
departing minister welcomes his successor to his desk. It
was supposed to be a human and private gesture from one
politician grappling with a crisis to whoever had to face the
perils of public office next. But, not for the first or the last
time in the campaign, Cameron did not see the joke. His spin
on Byrne's note (which was first made public by Laws in
2010) resonated with voters and was devastating to Miliband.
Labour, Cameron said, spent all the money, and left Britain
broke. You can't trust them again.

One Downing Street figure explains:

> What we were looking for was things to grab hold of that
> will punch home. A lot of people push politics aside and
> think, 'God it's boring, it's going on for a long time.' You
> need to grab things that are really going to cut through
> that. One of those things that cut through was The Note
> – and Labour's refusal to say that they spent too much.
> They may have felt that it was unfair but the reality is
> they had lost that battle. Instead of recognising they had
> lost that battle and moving on, they kept fighting it. That
> resulted in the PM standing in front of the *Question
> Time* audience, waving Liam Byrne's note.

The Conservatives' strategic obsession with the economy drove
some Tories mad with frustration. It meant that if you were an
ambitious Cabinet minister in a 'non-economic department', like
Jeremy Hunt at the Department of Health, or Chris Grayling
at the Ministry of Justice, or even Theresa May in the Home
Office, you could expect to be silenced. It also had its comic
moments – although the amusement waned with repetition
– when every Wednesday at Prime Minister's Questions in
the Commons, a succession of Tory MPs would stand up to
ask David Cameron how brilliantly his 'long-term economic
plan' was working. The House came to resemble a bingo hall,
with uproarious cheers breaking out every time an honourable
member uttered the magic phrase. Even Cameron smiled.

However, in the year before the election, the Prime Minister
was aware that simply repeating the words 'long-term economic
plan', which he did almost as frequently as his obsequious
backbenchers, would not set the electorate on fire. Instead, he

knew he had to find ways to personalise the economic message, making voters see and feel how his party's steady hand was helping them in their daily lives – and why the Tories should be allowed to 'finish the job' of securing the recovery.

Labour, meanwhile, was in disarray on the economy and had been for some time. Ed Miliband's senior team was riven by disagreements over how to attack the Tories on the economy and how far to embrace the need for cuts. David Axelrod, a former adviser to Barack Obama who was hired as Labour's prize foreign consultant for the election, famously dismissed the party's policy offer as 'Vote Labour and win a microwave'. There remains a suspicion that Miliband himself simply did not accept the need for significantly reduced public spending, and so – however politically essential a nod towards restraint was for his credibility – he never really meant it. When he forgot the entire section on the deficit during his final party conference speech before the election, Miliband's opponents had a field day. Their point had been made for them.

One senior Labour figure who worked closely with Miliband throughout the last parliament says:

> From 2013 onwards we did adopt a much more viable position on the economy, but it was never done with conviction and consistency. The day before Ed's 2014 conference speech, Ed Balls spent the whole day saying there wouldn't be any money to spend. Then Ed totally missed out the deficit from his speech. It should have been a bigger section of the speech, obviously. The reason why he was able to forget it was that it wasn't running through the speech like a stick of rock, which arguably it should have been.[50]

There were two major attempts by Labour to overhaul the party's reputation for economic incompetence. Neither of these attempts worked.

The first, on 8 June 2014, came after Labour's mediocre European and local election results, at a meeting of the 'quarterly look ahead' – or QLA – group of senior strategists, held at Miliband's house in Dartmouth Park Road, north London. The group included Stewart Wood, his close aide; Greg Beales, the head of polling and strategy; and Marc Stears, his speechwriter and university friend; as well as his senior adviser Tom Baldwin; Douglas Alexander, the shadow Foreign Secretary and Labour's election chief; and Spencer Livermore, director of the party's election campaign.

They had a blunt warning for the Labour leader: he must change his image and embrace head-on the need to tackle the deficit, or face defeat. According to several accounts, Miliband was furious. One of those present recalls that the party wanted to adopt big new reform ideas on schools, welfare and devolution to the regions. Some of these had been outlined in major reports from the IPPR think tank and Lord Adonis, a former minister whom Miliband had tasked with reviewing industrial policy.

The source recalls:

> We thought there was a disconnect between the strategy we were making in that group and the strategy that was being implemented by Ed himself. So we drew up an agenda for that meeting which involved using the reports of Adonis and the IPPR as big moments to look like we were tackling fundamental questions in a radical, new and interesting way. We particularly wanted to develop solutions that involved big reform rather than big spending. We all agreed we needed to

tackle the spending issue – the suggestion that we were not seen as serious on the deficit – head-on, in a way that we hadn't properly in the previous three or four years. There was agreement among us all that we needed to do more about the leadership brand and Ed himself, which was another obvious problem that we faced throughout the parliament.

But Miliband felt betrayed.

The meeting didn't go well. Ed got wind of the agenda before and was in an oppositional state of mind when we turned up. He felt quite angry particularly with Marc and Stewart, who he couldn't believe had agreed to all this. He thought it was an attempt to push him away from an authentic version of himself into a more centrist, austerity position.[51]

The tension in the room was 'horrible' and everyone just 'wanted to get out', according to those present. Warnings about loyalty followed and Miliband did not speak to Livermore for two weeks.[52]

The second attempt to address the issue came on 14 April 2015, a fortnight into the full-time general election campaign. Ed Miliband launched his party's election manifesto. On the opening page of the document was something new: 'Labour's Manifesto Budget Responsibility Lock'. This was a commitment, inserted into the manifesto at the last moment before it went to the printers, to cut the deficit every year, to audit all party spending commitments independently, and to get the national debt falling and run a surplus 'as soon as possible in the next parliament'.

'Our manifesto begins with the Budget Responsibility Lock we offer the British people. It is the basis for all our plans in this manifesto because it is by securing our national finances that we are able to secure the family finances of the working people of Britain,' the document said. 'The Budget Responsibility Lock guarantees that every policy in this manifesto is paid for. Not one commitment requires additional borrowing.' But with less than a month to go, such a dramatic attempt to reassure voters about Labour's intentions with the economy was too much, too late.

To the Conservatives, Labour's failure to grip the issue of economic trust was as baffling as it was bountiful. Grant Shapps, the Tory co-chairman during the campaign, says:

> Miliband did not have a consistent message. After four or five years of denying they were anything to do with the mess they created, they stick on the front of their manifesto a fiscal responsibility lock. Our programme was clear, concise and we talked endlessly to the point where we were ridiculed about the 'long-term economic plan'. But you know what? People voted for it. Why? Because it was consistent. What Miliband did was on the day he launched his manifesto, he did something new: 'We're going to do fiscal responsibility.' You can't just do that.

Many Labour figures agree with Shapps. One shadow Cabinet minister says the fact that the 'budget responsibility lock' was put onto the front page of Labour's manifesto in an apparently last-minute spasm of panic (and after the document had been cleared by the shadow Cabinet and the party's ruling National Executive Committee) shows that Labour had lost the argument. 'It was a sign of weakness, not of strength,' the source says. 'It was a sign that we hadn't won the argument and we were desperately trying to make up for it. But you're never going to win an argument like that so late.'[53]

What did the Tories do? Week after week, and month after month, they kept rigidly to Crosby's message that only the Conservatives could be trusted with the economy. As for the economic plan itself, the friendliest elements – including inheritance tax cuts, income tax cuts and help to buy homes – were well and widely publicised by an effective Conservative media operation. The nastier bits were kept well hidden.

On a practical level, the Tories also found doors opened to them in the business world in a way that never happened for Labour. Cameron and Osborne would regularly visit businesses, large and small, up and down the land, for photo opportunities and TV clips, to burnish their pro-enterprise credentials. Ed Miliband had great difficulty finding businesses to host his media visits during the 'short' six-week campaign.[54] He had previously attacked 'predator' capitalists and was increasingly a hate figure both in the City and among individual entrepreneurs who had backed the party of Tony Blair at previous elections. Instead of posing for photographs or giving speeches surrounded by factory machinery or shiny new cars, Miliband was reduced to taking his lectern into fields and, on at least one occasion, somebody's back garden.

Leadership

The other subject on which the Conservatives held a long-standing advantage over Labour was the question of who would make the best Prime Minister. Ed Miliband knew he had a problem with his own leadership credentials. Lynton Crosby knew it too. In a speech at the end of March, just after MPs left Westminster for the election, David Cameron accused the Labour leader of presiding over a group of 'hypocritical, holier-than-thou, hopeless, sneering socialists' who had betrayed their values. 'Some might say: "Don't make this personal", but when it comes to who's Prime Minister, the personal is national.' Cameron went on:

> The guy who forgot to mention the deficit could be the one in charge of our whole economy. The man who is too weak to stand up to the trade unions at home could be the one facing down our enemies abroad. The leader who thinks leadership is climbing aboard the latest bandwagon – he could be the one taking the make-or-break calls in the middle of the night.

In this antagonistic intervention, Cameron was not only attacking the Labour leader's personality, he was also emphasising his own statesmanlike demeanour as PM. Lynton Crosby's focus groups had shown voters regarded Miliband as odd and weak. Successive opinion polls showed that he persistently trailed the Tory leader in the public's estimation of who would make the better Prime Minister. Later in the campaign, Cameron would come under pressure over the weaknesses in his public image. The Tory leader, while preferred to Miliband, was not loved by the electorate. His natural diffidence would lead to accusations that he did not care enough and lacked passion for the job. He would be forced to shed the statesman's uniform of jacket and tie, roll up his sleeves and issue a cry from the heart to the public to save the country from the forces of 'chaos'.

Crosby's polling and research told him that, overall, Cameron's leadership when compared to Miliband was a significant plus for the Tories. His focus groups had also identified the fact that many voters still thought of Miliband as the man who 'stabbed his brother in the back' to become Labour leader. The bitter sibling contest between David Miliband – the former Foreign Secretary who was the favourite to succeed Gordon Brown – and his upstart brother Ed caused a rift that has still not fully healed. Intriguingly, another background factor that Tory focus groups identified as having 'cut through' among voters was the fact that Miliband was not named on his children's birth certificates for some time. The Conservatives decided that this was too sensitive a subject to exploit, but quietly noted its enduring interest nonetheless.[55]

They had no such qualms about fuelling public distaste at Miliband's alleged disloyalty to his brother. Defence Secretary Michael Fallon used a speech on Thursday 9 April 2015 to warn that Labour would be ready to 'barter' away Britain's national security in a post-election deal with the SNP because Miliband was so 'desperate' for power. The SNP were opposed to housing Trident nuclear weapons in Scotland, and Miliband would not think twice before ditching the missiles in order to get into No. 10, Fallon said. This was strong stuff, briefed in advance to sympathetic newspapers. But it was nothing compared to the row that accompanied an article in *The Times*, under Fallon's name, printed the same day. In it, the Defence Secretary declared: 'Ed Miliband stabbed his own brother in the back to become Labour leader. Now he is willing to stab the United Kingdom in the back to become Prime Minister.' Miliband reacted with fury, accusing Cameron of getting his 'minions' like Fallon to 'engage in desperate smears'. The Defence Secretary, he said, had 'demeaned himself'.

A senior member of the Tory team explains the origins of the attack:

> Miliband never had a good answer to the question of stabbing David in the back. Our focus groups had shown it was still a massive issue. People didn't see it as a sign of strength, they saw it as a sign of duplicity, and that was a problem for him. Labour never managed to confront that.

Everything about Fallon's intervention was drawn from the Lynton Crosby campaign manual. Revealingly, the startlingly personal attack came in a week when Labour was dominating the air war, especially the breakfast and evening news bulletins. Miliband was delighted that his flagship bashing-the-rich policy of abolishing non-domicile tax status had gone down so well. It set the agenda for the entire day of Wednesday 8 April. Miliband and Stewart Wood, who accompanied him on the launch trip to Warwick University, were delighted. The Tories were not happy. The attack on 'non-doms' was seen as damaging for the Conservatives, but, worse, it was an issue that meant the public debate was moving away from their preferred ground of economic security to Labour's territory of inequality, and the sense that society operates with one rule for the rich and another for the rest.

Something had to be done. It was time, in the Crosby lexicon, to 'throw a dead cat on the table'. At least then everyone would be talking about what you had done, however unpleasant and offensive it was. Fallon, to his own private distaste, was cast in the role of cat (deceased). The Defence Secretary had always been due to make a speech warning about the threat that a deal between Labour and the SNP could pose to British national security. The SNP had already expressed their determination to scrap the nuclear deterrent, which was clearly a legitimate subject for political debate. But Crosby decided that Fallon's speech should be brought forward by a day, and accompanied by the article in *The Times*. One source close to the process says: 'Fallon was always going to do a speech. It got spiced up. Lynton oversaw the whole thing and the "stab in the back" line came out of a conversation between him, Cameron and Osborne.'[56]

Fallon spent much of the day on broadcasts defending the newspaper article, despite his private misgivings. He was backed up by Cameron, Osborne and Iain Duncan Smith, the Work and Pensions Secretary. Miliband and a succession of Labour figures condemned Fallon's smears. Nick Clegg criticised his 'really nasty language' and Vince Cable said the Defence Secretary's intervention was an 'appalling way to conduct the debate'. For good measure, Nicola Sturgeon, the SNP leader, said any formal deal between her party and Labour would require a promise not to renew Trident. Crosby's cat had done its work.

In his only party election broadcast, Ed Miliband appeared to acknowledge the public's queasiness about how he had treated his brother in the leadership contest five years previously. 'I ran for the leadership because I believed I was the best person to move us on from New Labour,' Miliband said. The fact that it was still an issue, even for him, on the eve of the election, tells its own story, as does the broadcast itself. It was made by Paul Greengrass, the director of two of the Jason Bourne action thriller films, and was entitled *Ed Miliband: A Portrait*. Another attempt was being made, at a perilously late stage, to put the case for why Miliband was the best man to be Prime Minister. 'I feel that the last

four and a half years have been leading up to this moment,'
Miliband said in his own voiceover. His aides now concede
that those four and a half years should have been spent trying
far harder to define his image.

It is no accident that Labour's official party election
broadcasts were made and presented by celebrities. The
'portrait' by Greengrass – who had worked with Miliband
for some years – was the only Labour TV election broadcast
to feature the party leader during the short campaign. The
others were fronted by the *Hobbit* star Martin Freeman and
two comedians – Steve Coogan of *Alan Partridge* fame
and Jo Brand.

While Miliband's movie was aired less than a week before
polling day, Cameron made his first appearance in a Tory
election broadcast at the very beginning of the campaign,
on 30 March. He was shown on the touchline at a children's
football match, cheering on his son, as he said, 'like any
parent'. Later, the camera moved in slow motion over a soft-
focus tableau of the PM and his smiling wife Samantha, her
hair slightly awry, as they ate a family meal with their children
around an ordinary-looking table.

The contrasting broadcasts reveal the weaknesses that
Labour and the Conservatives saw in their own candidates
for Prime Minister. Miliband's 'portrait' showed him in his
suit and tie, striding purposefully towards his destiny, through
the corridors of power and into the House of Commons.
The struggle was to show a man with authority, a nation's
leader in waiting. For Cameron, however, all the effort was
focused on showing him as an ordinary dad watching his son
play football; 'in touch' on the touchline. It is, of course, far
easier to portray yourself as Prime Minister material if you
are already Prime Minister. Grant Shapps says Cameron's

personal lead over Miliband became more important as the campaign drew to its close and voters had to make their decisions: 'The leadership issue crystallised the choice.'[57]

Yet, one week before the full-time election campaign began, David Cameron did more than Labour ever achieved to undermine his own chances of winning a second term as Prime Minister. In an unguarded moment during an interview with the BBC's James Landale, a fellow Old Etonian, he confessed to having no desire to fight another election in 2020. 'Terms are like Shredded Wheat,' the Prime Minister said, while chopping vegetables in his kitchen with Landale. 'Two are wonderful but three might just be too many.'

The election after next may seem like a distant prospect to many voters, but it is a highly dangerous thing for any political leader to put a shelf life on his or her career. What made it potentially fatal for Cameron was the fact that the Tories were fighting as the party with the 'long-term' plan for the economy and the country. Cameron's admission that he would be gone before the end of the next parliament (so a new Tory leader could be chosen) comprehensively undermined the message of stability and continuity that formed the basis of his offer to the electorate. How could there be a long-term plan when, for the Prime Minister, there was no 'long term'?

Craig Oliver, the Downing Street communications director, was beside himself after the PM's gaffe. He knew how badly it would play out in the media and left his boss in no doubt about how he felt. Lynton Crosby was also dismayed. He feared that Labour would seize on Cameron's lapse and that it would become the key question of the entire election. And all because the PM was not disciplined enough to dodge a journalist's question over his own future during a friendly television interview at home in his kitchen. A 'sheepish'

Cameron knew how dangerous his mistake could prove. One senior source says: 'It could have been huge. It could have been defining in the campaign. But Labour completely failed to grab it.'[58]

SNP

As the campaign entered its final weeks, the Conservatives stepped up their drive to frame the election as a choice between their economic 'competence' and the 'chaos' of their opponents. The message crystallised into the question that would ultimately frame the 2015 election and shape its outcome: would Ed Miliband do a deal with the SNP to get into No. 10?

With every opinion poll pointing towards a hung parliament, pundits and media organisations were unanimous in predicting that no party would win an outright majority. The endlessly fascinating diversion in the media then became to war-game different outcomes, playing with the idea of a Tory–Lib Dem–DUP alliance, to keep Cameron in power, or a Labour–Lib Dem–SNP collaboration, to propel Ed Miliband into Downing Street. For Crosby and Cameron's campaign, the surge in support for the SNP in Scotland was as helpful as it was disastrous for Miliband. It allowed the Conservatives to state, every day in subtly new ways, that Miliband was planning to enter No. 10 by clinging onto Alex Salmond's coat-tails or squeezing into Nicola Sturgeon's top pocket. Posters, designed by M&C Saatchi, depicted a miniature Miliband peering out from the top pocket of the SNP leader's (and, often, the former leader's) suit jacket. The image proved far more effective than the Tories had reason to hope. It was reproduced repeatedly in national papers as part of their coverage of the SNP–Labour story.

This was the sharp end of the campaign. In Iain Duncan Smith's words, it was the one 'rough-edged' question in the entire election debate, and a significant proportion of the English public genuinely cared. But why? Was there a whiff of English nationalism about it? Did it stem from an atavistic fear of some kind of Pictish invasion, or the sense that grew in England in the aftermath of the Scottish independence referendum that the Scots were still, and always would be, deep down, the enemy? It is for others to investigate the answers to these questions. What cannot be in doubt is the impact that the north–south division – exploited by both the SNP and Conservative campaigns – made on the political map of Britain.

For the Tories, the preparations for the denouement to their 'air war' had begun months earlier. In the weeks immediately following the Scottish independence referendum of September 2014, Lynton Crosby began to explore the attitudes of the English to their Scottish neighbours. His research was startling. Participants in focus groups consistently showed that the one thing English voters who were tempted by UKIP or the Lib Dems hated more than any other was the prospect of a Labour government propped up by the SNP. Nicola Sturgeon was regarded with suspicion south of the border (though on the left, at least, many Labour supporters developed a rueful, long-distance affection for her). But Alex Salmond, the former First Minister, became a figure of hate, a wild Scottish bandit who should not be trusted. In apparently unguarded and spontaneous, off-the-cuff moments during the campaign, David Cameron seemed to encourage the demonisation of Salmond as a smiling villain, hell-bent on having his evil way with the weak and defenceless Miliband.

On 22 April, Cameron appeared on ITV's *This Morning* to answer questions from daytime TV viewers in a phone-in session. When the session concluded, the host, Phillip Schofield, moved on to the next item, about a pickpocket, saying: 'Up next, a man who can pinch your wallet, your watch and even your tie without you noticing.' Cameron, who was off camera, and apparently wrongly believed he was also off microphone, could then be heard asking: 'Who is that? Alex Salmond?' On other occasions, Cameron would claim that whenever he left a meeting with Salmond, he would always have to check he still had all his fingers and toes.

The Tories took considerable care to calibrate their attacks on Labour over the SNP so that they could keep Miliband under pressure. They did not want to push the question too hard, too soon, and prompt Labour to make a promise never to enter any kind of deal with the SNP. Their interest was in keeping the story alive for as long as possible. 'It was the monkey on their back, they couldn't get it off,' one senior Tory who was involved in the process says. 'Our key aim was to keep this going, to get somebody on the broadcasts, because that's what you need to keep the story going.'

One Cameron aide says the Tories were mystified by 'Labour's complete inability to close it down'. The source adds: 'We were worried that if we pushed too hard, Miliband would come out and promise the English people, "We will never do a deal with the SNP."' Instead, Labour ruled out a coalition. So the Tories asked about a 'confidence and supply' arrangement, under which the SNP would agree to support a Labour Budget and Queen's Speech, as part of a deal. Labour then 'fudged that for a couple of weeks' before eventually ruling it out. 'So we asked about a vote-by-vote deal,' the Tory aide recalls. 'They were trying to keep their options open. They should have just killed it off. If they had killed it off early on, it would have been very difficult for us to deploy.'[59]

The message that had first emerged in focus groups in October was working on the doorstep in April. Each morning, Stephen Gilbert, the head of campaigning, would give a summary of feedback from the field team working in the 100 target seats. To begin with, candidates were raising the question of the SNP's influence over a weak Miliband government with voters they met. 'People were saying, "I don't like the sound of that,"' one Tory in the war room recalls. 'Within a week or two, people were spontaneously raising it with candidates, saying, "I'm worried about Labour and the SNP."'[60]

As Boris Johnson says:

> What was brilliant about the campaign was spotting this phenomenon of the SNP surge and then turning that into the story and creating this incredible narrative, which was so powerful. What it did was it totally legitimated people's hesitations about Miliband. People felt selfishly that they didn't want to vote for Miliband and the Labour Party because they were uncertain about their economic policies and the rest of it. But a lot of people felt, 'How can I vote Tory?' If you're a Labour waverer, how can I justify voting Tory when I think it would just be being selfish? Suddenly, with the whole Scottish thing, there was a public service reason for doing it. You were actually voting for stable government for the country.

That validated the decision of lots of Labour switchers and lots of Lib Dem switchers. They thought, 'God, not only can I vote Tory and have a more prosperous future, but I can vote Tory in the knowledge that that is the right thing for the country and it is perfectly obvious that a Labour–Scottish Nationalist coalition would be a fiasco and we have got to have stability.' It was a brilliant tactic. Absolutely brilliant.[61]

The silences

The essential corollary of settling on a handful of key messages was to decide which policy areas and other subjects for debate were potentially harmful and to be avoided. This was every bit as important as drumming home the Tories' advantage on the economy and Cameron's stature as a leader.

As Labour's greatest advantage, the NHS was largely off limits, although the Conservatives attempted with some success to lay the blame for the Mid Staffs hospital scandal and cover-up at the door of Andy Burnham, whom Miliband kept on as shadow Health Secretary. The task for Jeremy Hunt, the Tory Health Secretary, was to 'neutralise' the potency of the NHS as a threat to the Tories, rather than to promote bolder health policies on which the party would win votes, one senior figure says.[62]

In the eyes of one No. 10 insider, Labour let the Conservatives off the hook by failing to maintain the focus on the future of the health service. 'By September 2014, they had landed on the strategy to bang on about health and were doing the right thing,' the Downing Street source recalls.

It was the only subject they had a lead on and it was a big lead. It was in the news. But shortly afterwards, Labour stopped going on about the health service. They have just not got a Lynton in there saying, 'How are we going to screw the government on health today? How are we going to do it tomorrow? How are we going to do it next month?' It is easier to keep it going with something like the economy than the health service because everything comes back to the economy. Health was their best chance.

Similarly, the Tories did not want to talk about the detail of their plan to cut £12 billion from state welfare. At least in part, this may have been because they did not believe they would ever have to implement such a dramatic reduction in funding. There is a suspicion that the Conservatives gave the figure of £12 billion for future welfare cuts simply so that it could be bargained away in coalition talks with the Liberal Democrats, who opposed cutting welfare spending in coalition. Either way, the details of the reductions were never going to be unveiled before polling day.

Immigration was another issue that caused difficulty for the Conservatives. Back-bench MPs had launched successive rebellions over Europe and immigration in the 2010–15 parliament. Despite imposing new quotas on migrants from outside the EU, the party had failed dramatically to meet its target to reduce 'net migration' to the tens of thousands. In fact, it was running at around 300,000 a year. MPs in marginal seats, such as Richard Fuller in Bedford, and Nicky Morgan, the Education Secretary, in Loughborough, reported that immigration was also a major concern among voters on the doorstep. Yet, during the short campaign, the Conservatives had very little to say on the subject.[63]

Nigel Farage, the UK Independence Party leader, did his best to hijack the national debate and insert immigration into the election. During the only televised leaders' debate involving all seven party leaders, on 2 April, Farage warned that health tourists with HIV were coming to Britain for expensive retroviral treatments, saying 60 per cent of those diagnosed each year by the NHS were not UK nationals. His intervention provoked a storm of outrage from other leaders, generating significant media coverage. It also deeply irritated senior Tories, including George Osborne, who complained privately that Farage had only made his controversial remark so that people would talk about it. Somewhere, the ghost of an Australian cat was stirring.

Arguably the most irritating issues that Crosby wanted to avoid discussing in the media were not to do with particular policies at all. What he loathed more than anything, according to those who worked on the Tory campaign, were 'process stories'. In plain English, this meant any article or broadcast feature that focused on behind-the-scenes details of how the Conservatives were fighting the election. It could be an article about Crosby himself, or an investigation into the tactics the Tories were preparing, or who they were hiring to produce advertisements for the election. To Crosby, all such pieces of coverage were wasted opportunities to talk about what the Tories were doing to help Britain (or how Labour and the SNP would damage the country).

One Cameron adviser says:

> Lynton hated any process stories about campaigns. He was completely allergic to commentary about how we have got a great ground campaign, or we have spoken to 100,000 people, we have surveyed all these people.

It is a sign of a bad campaign that you have to go on
about your campaign because it is time wasted, as he
would see it, from talking about how you're actually
going to help people. Who cares if it is on the *Today*
programme and the lead story? Literally, who cares?
Remember what you're trying to do. You're trying to
get messages through to people. The thing that Lynton
is so good at is developing the strategy and then just the
simplicity of sticking to it and not getting side-tracked.

In other words, discipline.

The discipline

As the Conservatives discovered in their shambolic 2010
campaign, having a plan is one thing, but sticking to it is
quite another. Not only did Lynton Crosby make the rules
on which messages to deploy, but to a large degree it fell to
him to enforce them. A succession of witnesses have described
how he possessed a natural authority, which may in part have
come from his status as an Australian outsider who was not
particularly interested in the internecine struggles of rival
factions within the party. His job as a paid consultant was to
get the Tories back into power. This made him automatically a
more compelling boss. His role was clear and his responsibility
was also plain to see. Should he fail, there would be nowhere
to hide. It was for this reason that he insisted on having total
control over the Tory campaign before agreeing to take on
the job in November 2012.

According to Lord Feldman, the Tory co-chairman, maintaining message discipline was 'the hardest' part of the Tories'

strategy. Crosby 'defined our messages and stuck to them', even though some disagreed with the plan, he says.[64] Sometimes, Cameron had no one to blame but himself when unhelpful stories appeared in the press. On one occasion, Crosby and his campaigns team were dismayed to read in a newspaper details of how many Lib Dem seats they were targeting. No. 10 launched a major leak inquiry. One Tory insider recalls:

> Everyone kicked off and said, 'Who the fuck briefed this? We should not be briefing process stories. We should be talking about things that matter to voters.' There was this big row, and in the end it turned out the PM had said it at some reception. We got that quite a lot. The PM, because of who he is and his personality, whenever there were leak enquiries in No. 10, they would almost always find that the culprit was him.[65]

On another occasion, details of one of the Prime Minister's tours to Cornwall leaked out to the Cornish newspapers before any of the plans had been announced.

> This sent the internal team into meltdown, saying, 'Who has briefed this? Why are we briefing it? The police are on the phone asking why they haven't been told.' It turned out that there had been a reception for activists in No. 10 and the PM had said, 'Oh, I will be coming down to Cornwall to see you' to some of them. He was very often the source of that sort of thing.[66]

Crosby made it his business to talk to ministers, backbenchers and new parliamentary candidates and to get to know them. He wanted to make sure they had his voice in their heads whenever they opened their mouths to speak in public. When candidates in key seats made potentially damaging mistakes, he would be on the phone to demand that they pull back into line. 'You have got this chance; you won't get this chance again. If you screw it up, that's it,' he would say.[67]

Discipline among the Tory strategy directors who sat with Crosby at the central 'pod' in the war room, was, by most accounts, impeccable. 'There were times when Lynton would say, "No, I think that's shit." Normally it was done in a much nicer way than that. But occasionally it was just, "No. It doesn't work." That's what you want so you don't waste your energy.'

Occasionally, he had to stand up to Downing Street to block 'ludicrous' ideas from the Prime Minister's closest advisers. One PR stunt was proposed which would have involved sending 1,000 activists to Ed Balls's constituency of Morley and Outwood, where they would all form the shape of the word 'jobs'. An aeroplane would be hired to fly overhead and take a picture. 'This was somehow supposed to demonstrate that we had created 1,000 jobs a day,' one Conservative campaigner recalls. 'Lynton and Stephen Gilbert just said, "No fucking way."' Party spending on campaigns within constituencies is strictly limited in an election and a stunt like this would have blown the budget in a single day.[68]

Adam Atashzai, a youthful aide drafted in from No. 10, helped Crosby enforce discipline within the government. Atashzai was responsible for the 'grid', a detailed timetable of all government (or party) announcements, events, consultations and sets of statistics that were due to be published in the days ahead. Any minister clashing with the approved plan – by making an unauthorised speech or similar public utterance that was at odds with 'the message' – would be likely to receive a phone call from Atashzai. The duo of Crosby and Atashzai was described by insiders as having a 'master and apprentice' relationship. The intention was to stop any ambitious minister indulging in a 'fancy display of skills'.[69]

The Tories' media team was led by Giles Kenningham, the party's head of communications at CCHQ, while, in Downing Street, Craig Oliver took charge of the Prime Minister's overall media strategy and focused on portraying him in the best light on television. The newspapers were handled by the former *Sun* journalist Graeme Wilson, who was made Cameron's press secretary eighteen months before the election, and Alan Sendorek, a former party press officer who had been a special adviser in Downing Street since 2010. A pool of the most accomplished ministers was drawn up to be made available for broadcast interviews. MPs who were regarded as less effective communicators were kept off the air during the campaign. In addition to Cameron and Osborne, those rated highly for their broadcast skills included Priti Patel, who was a Treasury minister at the time; Nicky Morgan, the Education Secretary (who came across as 'normal' in the eyes of the spin doctors); Michael Gove, the Chief Whip, who could argue his way out of any difficult situation; and Sajid Javid, then the Culture Secretary, who has a background in the business world and an aptitude for making the party's case on the economy.

The airwaves

On his first day at work as David Cameron's new £140,000-a-year communications director, Craig Oliver committed a professional crime that all backroom spin doctors seek to avoid: he became a story himself. To some extent it was inevitable. Oliver, a top BBC executive, was replacing Andy Coulson, the former *News of the World* editor, who had recently quit No. 10 over the phone-hacking scandal. Yet, even without such a fraught context, Oliver would have drawn the media's attention. He struck a curious figure as he walked up Downing Street for the first time in the early spring of 2011. He was mocked for wearing a £170 pair of 'Beats' headphones, designed by the rapper Dr Dre for 'on the street' music, while carrying a (then cutting edge) iPad, bike helmet and 'man bag' and wearing a scarf over his suit and a pink shirt with no cufflinks. His timekeeping was also called into question: he had left himself just three minutes to spare before his first 8 a.m. meeting with the Prime Minister was due to begin. The following week, it was alleged that Oliver had been too late and missed his lift in Cameron's official convoy, forcing him to hail a cab on Whitehall instead.

Despite Oliver's shaky start, he developed into a member of the Prime Minister's most trusted inner circle of advisers and friends, many of whom have worked with him since his 2005 leadership campaign. This is in no small part due to Oliver's assured handling of the broadcasters, especially in the months leading up to the 2015 election. As a former BBC man, his inside knowledge of the country's biggest and most powerful media organisation proved invaluable to the Conservatives' efforts to secure air time for their messages, as well as cooperation from news programme editors more generally.

Nowhere was this more important than in negotiations over the televised leaders' election debates. In 2010, Cameron had been well placed in the polls until the first debate, in which he fell flat and Nick Clegg burst from the shadows to take the country by storm. The Liberal Democrats even came top in some opinion polls that followed, as 'Cleggmania' swept the nation. One of Cameron's closest Cabinet allies described the impact of the 2010 debates on the Conservative campaign as 'like hitting a brick wall'. They were desperate to avoid a repeat in 2015.[70]

Before Lynton Crosby arrived at CCHQ in 2012, Cameron believed that the next round of television debates should exclude Clegg and focus purely on 'potential candidates for Prime Minister'. Superficially, it might seem a good way to contrast Cameron's superior leadership ratings with Miliband. But the Labour leader's team would have leapt at the chance of a 'head to Ed' debate. In autumn 2013, well before negotiations got underway in earnest, one of Miliband's closest advisers said: 'Every challenger in US presidential elections always goes up 3 per cent after the first debate.'

Crosby immediately saw the risk. He vetoed the idea of a two-way debate, which Cameron had been considering. Instead, in the weeks before parliament was dissolved, the Tories, led by Oliver, pushed harder than seemed wise for a deal that would keep their man out of trouble. Eventually an agreement was reached in which Cameron would take part in only one direct debate. He would be part of a panel with the leaders of six other parties – Miliband, Clegg, the SNP's Nicola Sturgeon, UKIP's Nigel Farage, Leanne Wood from Plaid Cymru and the Green Party leader Natalie Bennett. The resulting programme was televisual chaos, horrible to watch, and ultimately a stalemate from which no one individual could claim a clear victory (at times, no one individual could even make themselves heard). By luck, in the drawing of lots to determine where the leaders would stand, Cameron found himself at the end of the row. From this position he could stand apart while the other leaders talked over each other, and claim that the cacophony echoed the political 'chaos' that his rivals all represented, while he, apart and a little aloof, remained the picture of calm, detached competence.

When it came to preparing for the TV debates themselves, Craig Oliver and Crosby coached Cameron intensively. With his particular expertise as a former TV man, Oliver repeatedly pushed the PM to work pithy 'soundbites' into his opening statement or early answers. These key messages delivered early in the show would be 'clipped' by the editorial teams producing the 10 p.m. TV news on BBC One and ITV. Oliver knew from experience that the TV newsrooms would be working against the clock to put their reports together in time for the late evening bulletins. His value to the Tory project at this point was beyond doubt. One figure who saw him directing the rehearsals in the days before the debates says Oliver's command of the format was 'brilliant'.[71]

By law, the BBC, ITV and other broadcasters are required to be politically neutral – in an election, they must give equal weight and prominence to covering all the major parties. During the campaign, both Labour and the Conservatives complained daily to BBC executives across radio and television, alleging that the national broadcaster was failing to report the real story and giving too much credence to their opponents' spin on events. Clearly, this goes with the territory. For Ed Miliband, Tom Baldwin, his senior adviser, Bob Roberts, the party communications director, and Lucy Powell, a trusted MP, led the battle with the BBC. But BBC executives found that Oliver's superior knowledge of how the corporation worked, gained from years spent on the receiving end of politicians' complaints, gave him an advantage. Baldwin, who spent his journalistic career working in newspapers, would normally complain to the BBC's Millbank operation, which produces political programmes and bulletins from an office across the road from Parliament. His chief gripe was that the BBC was functioning as 'an echo chamber to the right-wing press'. Oliver, however, would send his text messages of complaint to the head of output, and at the same time to the programme maker, and to James Harding, the BBC's director of news. In his message, Oliver would demand to know 'why the lead political news item was some Labour story and not the Tories endlessly repeating their long-term economic plan'. A source at the broadcaster says: 'We just thought the news should have something new in it. The Tories weren't saying much that was new, while Labour were announcing policies and new statements. But Craig also knew everybody involved.'[72]

For Labour, the battle was to try to 'toxify' the Conservatives by persuading the BBC (and others) to consider the idea that Cameron could win a majority, and to reflect on what this would mean for public services, like the NHS. But, like every other media organisation and virtually every pollster, the BBC was convinced that there would be a hung parliament.

Bob Roberts, Miliband's communications director, recalls:

> The polls were justifying the media, and the media were reinforcing the polls. You accept when you're running a campaign there are some hostile media and they are going to campaign against you. But specifically the BBC did act very much as an echo chamber to some of their views. I think the BBC was focused too much on their interest in polls and minority government, which was politically interesting to them but not a proper

examination of the issues. We tried very hard to say to
the BBC they should do a proper examination of what
a Labour majority government would mean, what a
Tory majority government would mean, but frankly
they were fixated on the influence of the SNP.[73]

In the aftermath of the election result, the BBC began 'a lot of
soul searching' about how it had treated a hung parliament
as a foregone conclusion.[74]

The BBC's failure to examine the possibility of a Tory
majority, along with that of every other serious media outlet
in the final weeks of the campaign, was grave. It was also
hugely to the advantage of the Conservatives. Whatever
the Tories now say, the fact that virtually the entire country
was swept up in the notion that a hung parliament would
follow polling day meant the 'risk' of the SNP doing a deal
with Labour seemed real. Perhaps a hung parliament was
simply an irresistible story for many journalists covering
the election. Certainly, a majority result left no room for the
dramatic headlines about chaos and constitutional turmoil
that would drive newspaper sales and boost TV audiences.
Perhaps, too, it was the result that some politicians were
hoping for. Nick Clegg, for example, declared repeatedly
that everybody knew it was 'impossible' for either Labour
or the Tories to win a majority. And Cameron told Clegg
shortly before parliament was dissolved that he believed he
would not win a majority and coalition government might
be necessary again.[75]

But the Prime Minister's belief that he would need to do
another deal with Clegg did not stop him pursuing every
possible means of ejecting Liberal Democrat MPs from their
heartland in the south-west. The battle to run Britain was

ultimately decided below the level of the air war, on the ground, where Tories fought Lib Dems, UKIP activists and the Labour Party street by street.

CHAPTER 5

THE GROUND WAR

On 7 May 2015, the Conservatives won the general election, forming their first majority government of the UK for twenty years. But they did so by largely ignoring 85 per cent of the country.

If you lived in any of the other 550 constituencies choosing Members of Parliament, you may have received the odd leaflet but would not have heard much more from David Cameron and his team. If you were living in one of the Tories' 100 key target seats, however, it would have felt like there was no escape. The party spent millions of pounds targeting these key constituencies with leaflets and direct mail, mounted an unprecedented operation to persuade the electorate via email and Facebook, spending millions more, and relentlessly banged on doors and worked the phone lines until the computer database at Conservative HQ knew exactly where its potential voters lived, and had a very good idea what they were thinking.

All the while, the party pursued its plan in near secrecy. The scale of the 'ground war' – the fight for voters on the doorstep, through the post, over the phone and via their personal computers and mobile devices – was so little discussed as to amount to a stealth operation that caught the Conservatives' opponents unawares. The importance of the secrecy cannot be overstated. As discussed earlier, Lynton Crosby hated so-called 'process stories' appearing in the media, and by refusing to allow any details of the Tory campaign mechanics to enter the public domain, he kept Labour and the Lib Dems in the dark until it was too late. 'The biggest lie that Labour believed themselves was that they were out-campaigning us on the ground,' a senior CCHQ figure says. 'For ever people would lazily say that the Tories have the air war but Labour was stronger on the ground.'

The seats

The decision to focus on 100 seats was taken early in the autumn of 2012. In fact, it became known as the 40/40 strategy, the story goes, because the original plan was to target forty seats that the party wanted to win from the Liberal Democrats and Labour, and a further forty marginals that it needed to defend. One senior source insists that it was always more than eighty seats, and nearer 100. However, the idea of calling the party's three-year plan to win the election 'the 50/50 strategy', while possibly more accurate, would certainly have invited mockery.

The man at the centre of the network of target seats was Stephen Gilbert. One of the Tories' most experienced strategists, Gilbert had led the effort in 2010 to win marginal constituencies as part of Lord Ashcroft's target seats campaign. The wealthy peer financed the target seats operation in 2010, while Gilbert ran the teams in the field. Hard-working and loyal, Gilbert sat in the war room alongside Crosby, with whom he got on well. A former election agent, who also worked as Cameron's political secretary in Downing Street, Gilbert is popular among the campaign teams across the country and knows everyone. 'He has been with the party for twenty years – or more. He knows his stuff back to front. He is quite quiet but a nice guy who just gets on with it,' says a senior colleague.[76]

In a private room at the Tory Party conference in Birmingham in 2012, three years before the election, Gilbert outlined his strategy to a gathering of senior party officials. It would be necessary, he told them, to concentrate more intensively than ever on a relatively small number of marginal seats in order to try to win a majority. Half of the 'attack' seats were held by Labour MPs, and the other half by Liberal Democrats. As the campaign was refined in the months before polling day, more Lib Dem seats came into play and were added to the list of targets.[77]

Here, too, stealth was essential, and a defining difference between Ed Miliband's and David Cameron's campaigns. Tom Watson, the Labour Party election coordinator, announced his list of 106 target seats (all of which were attack seats, i.e. Labour was focusing on winning new constituencies, not defending those it held). The Tories, by contrast, never published their full list of eighty to a hundred key seats. Nor was it easy to guess where they were. The Conservatives did not base their choice of targets merely on the seats with the smallest majorities, although this was a factor. Gilbert's private meeting at the Tory conference was also told that the party would be hiring campaign managers in each of the target seats.

When choosing which seats held by other parties to attack, the Tories set about analysing in great detail the demographic characteristics of potential target constituencies: how old the resident voters were, whether they had families, or had recently moved into the area, as well as their past voting patterns. A separate task was to establish the key concerns of these voters, which required extensive research into each seat, asking, for example, whether potential swing voters owned their homes or wanted to do so. By analysing a combination of all these factors, the Conservatives whittled down the list of seats to those forty or fifty targets that seemed to contain the kinds of voters who would be open to persuasion by the party's election offer.

In November 2012, the party announced the first ten attack seats of the forty. In the end, the Conservatives gained four of these ten from their opponents – Morley & Outwood, which Ed Balls lost; Vale of Clwyd from Labour; Sutton & Cheam and Cheadle from the Lib Dems.[78]

The survey

As one senior Tory figure puts it, it doesn't matter whether you are talking to a voter online, on the phone, or on their doorstep, 'the quality of the script is what matters'. It was through mass canvassing, repeatedly questioning voters about their views and intentions, that the Tories built up their knowledge of the electorates in their target seats. These surveys fulfil multiple purposes: to identify solid Tory voters, to find potential swing voters who can be persuaded, to establish what these voters' key concerns are, and to locate which households will never vote Tory and should not be bothered with again. In addition, if you are a candidate, any conversation with a voter is an opportunity to win them over.

Both Labour and the Conservatives designed standard canvassing surveys in their parties' central London HQs and sent them out to constituency campaigns across the country. Since the election, Labour figures have criticised their party's script for being too general in its questions. One Labour MP ignored it entirely and drew up new questions. The MP won. 'If you ask the right questions, you can find out that people are just not going to vote Labour, and knock them off the list. None of the right questions were on our script,' the Labour MP says.

The Tory script was radical and new. Unlike Labour's survey, it reflected the fact the election would be one involving a choice between multiple parties. Stephen Gilbert designed a survey script that was 'totally different from anything we had ever used before', one senior insider says. At previous elections, Tory canvassers had used letters to identify different types of voter. For example, a C would be used to designate a voter as solidly Conservative; Labour backers were coded with an S (for socialist), with L used for Liberal Democrat. If they were wavering, a P would be used to register a 'possible' Tory, a T for a wavering Labour voter and an M for a wavering Lib Dem. But at an election featuring UKIP, the Green Party, tactical voting, people who would never vote Tory because they are Labour but hate UKIP more, 'these letters just don't hack it', a senior campaign figure says.[79]

Instead, the Conservatives switched to a 1–10 scale and asked individual voters to say how likely they were to vote in a particular way. This enabled the party to build up a far more detailed picture of individual voters' states of mind about the election. Someone might be a 7 out of 10 Tory voter, a 9 out of 10 UKIP voter, but a 1 out of 10 Labour voter. This person would be regarded as a UKIP supporter who could potentially be persuaded to vote Tory because they hated the idea of a Labour government above anything else. The Tories would then bombard this individual with leaflets and messages warning that Ed Miliband would walk into No. 10 if they did not vote Conservative. This is known, in Tory circles, as a 'squeeze message'. During the campaign, David Cameron spoke privately of the need to 'squeeze' these UKIP voters, and Lib Dem voters, using messages that would appeal to individuals in different areas. 'What we were able to do was take this much more sophisticated data collection and send squeeze messages to the people who wouldn't normally vote for us,' one senior figure says.

All the data collected by the surveys, over a period of years, was fed back into the Conservatives' central election canvassing database, a system built for the party called VoteSource.

> We ran algorithms that said if someone is a 7 likely to vote Tory, but 9 likely to vote UKIP, it looks like they might be a UKIP voter, but if they hate Labour more, then the squeeze message is 'vote UKIP and you'll let Labour in' and we can shape the message like that. The algorithms were produced by VoteSource. It gave us the ability to then do the squeeze messages.

When VoteSource was completed, the technical department gave a demonstration to senior staff inside the Tory campaign to show how accurate its data was. They decided to use Craig Oliver, Cameron's communications director, as a test case. When they entered his details, however, VoteSource revealed that Oliver was not a Conservative Party member, and was not recorded as a solid Tory voter. 'His record came up and it showed that he had been canvassed in the past and we don't really know how he votes. He could be a Lib Dem,' a member of campaign staff recalls.

As well as the development of the new database, Jim Messina's influence was also critically important to help the Tories with their precision targeting. President Obama's campaign manager brought his specialist expertise to the fine-grained analysis of voter types that the Tories undertook. He helped the party to build a model of the voters who could be persuaded to switch from the Lib Dems to the Tories. The field team then contacted these people directly.

Team 2015

The lure of a beer, a curry and the possibility of a romantic liaison in a strange hotel is a curiously powerful thing. In fact, senior Tories believe it may have made the difference between them being the largest party after the 2010 election and winning a majority and the right to rule alone in 2015. Faced with a crisis in membership numbers – which had halved since David Cameron had become leader – the Tories had to dream up new ways to recruit troops to deliver leaflets, knock on voters' doors, ask questions and pound the pavements in the key constituencies the party needed to win.

When Grant Shapps, the energetic co-chairman of the party, was given the job of running CCHQ in 2012, this dearth of foot-soldiers was his biggest worry. The Tories were suffering from the age-old problem of having too many activists willing to walk the streets leafleting in safe Conservative constituencies, and not enough people where they were needed most: the target seats.

With very little to go on, Shapps began designing a way of supplying cheap, enthusiastic activists who could be used to fill the gaps that grassroots members created when they left the party, whether through death or disaffection. In his own constituency of Welwyn Hatfield, he had assembled a team of people who had volunteered for his local campaign in 2010. This was worth replicating more widely, he thought, and Team 2015 was born. The initiative invited people who were not party members, and were not required to pay any membership fees, to sign up as volunteer Tories. Registering their interest through the party's central website, these volunteers would be invited to help campaign, becoming the ground force that would be essential in the election ahead.

Three months later, 1,000 people had signed up to Team 2015. At a meeting of the political Cabinet in late 2012, the co-chairman set out his idea to fellow ministers. David Cameron was apparently thrilled. 'This is the best thing I have seen come out of CCHQ in twenty years,' he told Shapps.[80] The party chairman then set about signing up as many individuals as he could to build the kind of numbers that would make a difference. The Conservatives already had a massive email list of about half a million addresses at the time of the last election, a number that had tripled by 2015, and Shapps began using the list to recruit volunteers for Team 2015. Shapps sent messages and persuaded David Cameron to sign off emails to the list (a message from the Prime Minister asking for help would have a particular impact on those who had signed up to receive Tory emails).

Team 2015 grew, but progress was not rapid. Then Shapps hit on the idea of marketing the activity as a social event, rather than simply a morning of political campaigning. One of those who worked on the programme says: 'There were three things you needed to get people to come back campaigning with Team 2015: food, drink and social interaction. If you provide food and drink, the third happens automatically.'[81] Campaigning sessions – which often happened on Saturdays – were advertised along with the promise of a curry and a beer afterwards. Instead of meeting in a car park or at a station, volunteers were told to meet in a pub in the area to be canvassed so that the keener drinkers among the teens and twenty-somethings who turned up could have a drink beforehand.

In the spring of 2014, the concept of Team 2015 came into its own. By then the project had grown substantially in numbers and the decision was taken to deploy the Tories' ground force for the Newark by-election sparked by the resignation of former Tory Patrick Mercer, following a 'cash for questions' scandal. The party had already used Team 2015 volunteers for the European elections in May but the by-election on 5 June provided a dress rehearsal for the kind of intense saturation tactics that the general election target seats would need.

Around 300 students and other young volunteers descended on the town of Newark, delivering leaflets, canvassing and campaigning on Saturdays. According to reports at the time, the ferocity of the volunteers' fighting spirit left the Labour team somewhat unnerved. Young campaigners were drawn from university campuses nearby and taken by bus to be deployed on the streets of Newark. As a reward for their efforts, the party paid for them all to have a curry and drinks at a hotel in Nottingham in the evening. One of the younger organisers was quoted saying that 'a dozen or so' of his friends had found romance during their day's campaigning. After the meal, those with the energy went out on the town to the Coco Lounge bar, and then a gay club that stayed open until 6.30 a.m.[82]

One senior Conservative suggests the reputation for socialising may have led more volunteers to find love on the campaign trail in the weeks leading up to the general election. 'Loads of young people went on it,' the Tory says. 'They went out afterwards, they used to go out in the evening to the pub. These things have a habit of bringing people together. Whatever went on in the privacy of people's rooms is their business.'

Apart from the promise of a night out, another key feature of Team 2015 was the mechanism for recognising and rewarding participants for their efforts. Shapps met Jim Messina during a trip to Washington in February 2013 and asked for advice on amassing an army of committed activists to do the leg-work required for the election. Messina told Shapps: 'What you want to do is create a competitive environment where people are not only recognised and thanked but can build their status by receiving more goodies.'

Around the same time, Shapps was talking to his Cabinet colleague Jeremy Hunt, who had been in charge of the London 2012 Olympics as Culture Secretary. Hunt recalled how the Games were a success thanks in part to the army of 70,000 volunteers – the so-called 'Games Makers' – who staffed every venue, guiding spectators on where to go, helping families with children, and disabled or elderly people in wheelchairs, and providing first aid for minor ailments such as grazes and headaches. They were not paid and had to give up a minimum of ten days, find their own accommodation and pay their own way. Yet they seemed to love doing it, and without them the London Olympics may not have happened. Hunt told Shapps that rewarding the Games Makers with special pins and badges had been important to help motivate the volunteers. Team 2015 incorporated these elements into its structure and Shapps ended up officially 'recognising' the work of almost 20,000 volunteers who had turned out for the party by polling day.

However, the development of Team 2015 hit a serious obstacle as it grew. Team captains were being sent on training courses throughout 2013 at hotels around the country. The courses would train individuals in how to motivate their teams, how to fulfil the recognition and reward aspects of the structure and how to ensure volunteers returned in future. But Conservative HQ itself was hardly involved. The party's central London office was acting as a kind of 'dating agency', putting volunteers who signed up via the website in touch with local Tory associations in constituencies, who were then expected to make sure the individuals turned up. Frequently, they didn't.

Shapps's office would receive frustrated calls from local Tory association chairmen and campaign managers telling them their shiny new youth army had failed to show up. CCHQ worked out that it took twenty-one individual steps to make sure that a volunteer who said they would turn up actually did turn up to campaign. Local party associations could not be relied upon to undertake the necessary chivvying to make sure that Team 2015 did not become a phantom army.

In the spring of 2014, Paul Abbott, Shapps's chief of staff, completed a thorough review of the scheme and concluded that it needed radically professionalising. He recommended to Shapps that Team 2015 be brought entirely in-house, run, recruited and organised from CCHQ in Matthew Parker Street, Westminster, at a hefty cost of £300,000.[83] Lord Feldman, the co-chairman who held the party's purse strings, was persuaded to stump up.

One senior figure says: 'A year out, we decided to centralise the running of Team 2015. Unlike the rest of the campaigning, this volunteering effort was run from the chairman's office, and was separate from Stephen Gilbert's professional target seats campaign.' The project was also boosted by the arrival of Deborah Feldman, Lord Feldman's sister, who took over as head of Team 2015's ground operations, running it with Abbott. She had the job of coordinating all the weekend's Team 2015 constituency visits – essentially, monitoring where the buses were going to be sent and making sure that they were full. She filled in the numbers of volunteers against target seat names on a huge whiteboard, keeping the tally up to date. The final critical element was the 'chivvying team': more volunteers who had been sent to Tory HQ from the accountancy firm PricewaterhouseCoopers. Their job was to hit the phones on Wednesdays, Thursdays and Fridays, going through the twenty-one steps and making sure volunteers caught their buses or trains to the constituency for the 'Super Saturday' of campaigning, as promised.

'Then the thing exploded. Super Saturdays turned into Super Sundays as well. We also had buses travelling around every region, full of Team 2015 volunteers,' one insider says. 'It became the most enormous force in the end, and was far more than you would normally see at a general election. They would just go out and campaign in each seat as if it were a by-election.'

On a typical campaign day, a bus with fifty-five people would arrive in a constituency to be met with the same number or more local Team 2015 volunteers who made their own way to the rendezvous. The constituency campaign manager and candidate would meet them, with leaflets and paperwork providing information on the canvassing work to be done. Shapps, meanwhile, a keen amateur pilot with his own plane, would usually fly to a nearby airstrip and join his Team 2015 campaigners as they got off the bus. He would give a rallying speech to 100–150 assembled activists before sending them on their way. The Team 2015 'bus brigades' would saturate one constituency in the morning, and then drive to a second constituency to repeat the process after lunch, completing an intensive day of campaigning in two key seats.

The buses were critical to moving party troops from where they lived to where the swing voters could be found. The central party paid for all the buses and trains, as well as hotels and hostels. During the short campaign, the Tories deployed one train of fifty people and five buses – two in the north-west, one in the Midlands, another in the south-west, and a special advisers' bus leaving CCHQ – every day.

Shapps is proud of how his project developed and the role it played in delivering a victory:

> I diligently from scratch built up Team 2015 – 100,000 people had signed up to it and it was delivering, on the average weekend, 100 different locations with Super Saturdays or whatever. Then during the campaign, every single day, hundreds if not thousands of volunteers to every reach of the country in which we were in contention, to the point where we had half a dozen coaches on the road, full-time volunteer staff, out of hotels, living almost as a family together and campaigning in two seats a day. You know what? That is a ground war.

The post

For all the innovations – Facebook campaigning, a new database developed specifically for the Tories, an entirely

new canvass survey and an army of 100,000 volunteers –
perhaps the most effective weapon was arguably the most
old fashioned: direct mail.

Using the vast databank of information on the VoteSource
computer system, gathered from the party's unprecedentedly
detailed surveys, CCHQ sent individually tailored letters
to voters in swing seats, with leaflets and information that
reflected their interests and their voting habits. Stephen Gilbert
masterminded the multi-million-pound operation through his
campaigning team, sending the 'squeeze' messages to wavering
Lib Dem voters in the south-west, or to UKIP supporters in
Kent and elsewhere.

During the course of the campaign, the Tories sent out
millions of pieces of direct mail, and were, in the words of one
leading Conservative, the biggest direct-mailing organisation
in the country. 'For a long time before the campaign, we were
the nation's single biggest user of direct mail, running more
sophisticated direct mail than any other organisation. We had
more bespoke, detailed, specific literature to your individual
concerns than anybody else,' a senior campaign insider says.

The Tories' central campaign directors – and the VoteSource
system – knew the voters' individual foibles in each individual
target seat as well as any local campaign team or candidate
could have done. In the south-west, where the Tories targeted
the Lib Dems, the Conservative ground campaign was
remotely operated and unmanned; in essence, it was a form
of stealth election warfare. Nick Clegg has conceded that his
teams 'could not see' how the Tories were communicating with
voters.[84] As for Labour, Tory insiders believe Ed Miliband's
strategists spent £1 million a day on their own direct-mail
operation towards the end of the campaign. But instead of
tailoring it and targeting it at floating voters who cared, 'They

sent generic leaflets about the NHS, to everyone. It was the most useless waste of money you can imagine.'

Just as in the air war it was important to avoid certain subjects, so the ground campaign required the Tories to stop talking to certain voters – those who, in the words of one senior strategist, 'had told us they would rather fry in a vat of hot oil than vote Conservative'.[85] Critically, the Tories managed to weed out the unconvertible voters early – between one and two years before polling day. This gave the party valuable time to concentrate its fire and the strictly limited spending amounts in the final six months of the campaign on those voters who were potentially open to persuasion. One senior strategist says the last thing the Tories wanted was to spur Labour supporters to go out and vote by sending them a letter or leaflet containing a message from David Cameron in the final weeks before polling day.

Stealth in the ground war, just as with secrecy over the party's private polling, and its processes, was a critically important operating principle. Not only did senior Conservatives have evidence – which they kept strictly to themselves – to suggest that the public polling was badly wrong, but Tory insiders now admit they encouraged Labour to build up the myth that Miliband and his army of activists supplied by the unions had the better street-fighting campaign. The story ran that Labour had thousands more activists, better trained and motivated, saturating target seats with Labour leaflets and election messages.

Grant Shapps says:

> We heard a lot of nonsense and spin from their campaign which was: 'We are better organised on the ground. The Tories have got the money, we have got the ground

war covered and we are going to have four million conversations and knock on all these doors.'

I could find absolutely no evidence whatsoever to support the notion that they had got this big ground machine. And yet I constantly read that they had the great ground machine and that was their advantage and we had to fight the air war. They were moving I guess imaginary troops around or something. I couldn't find any evidence of it at all and we were swamping them.

To some outsiders – including Lord Ashcroft, who ran remarkably detailed polling in individual seats – the fact that the Tories seemed to be contacting fewer voters than Labour in the final weeks of the campaign gave an advantage to Miliband. An Ashcroft survey of ten Conservative-held marginal seats found most voters remembered receiving leaflets, direct mail, phone calls or visits from both main parties but remarked that 'Labour have the edge in these local campaigns on the basis of this evidence', with more than 70 per cent having heard from Labour in half the seats polled.[86]

Commentators on the Tory side regarded these findings about Labour's higher 'contact rates' as a cause for considerable alarm. One post on ConservativeHome.com, the influential Tory website and discussion forum, was titled 'Is there a problem with the Tory ground war in the marginals? And if so, how big is it?' In his piece, Mark Wallace compared Ashcroft's findings in these ten seats with the contact rates seen in 2014.

The comparison clearly showed Labour ahead in the most recent polls. For example, in 2014, 38 per cent of voters reported having heard from the Conservatives in Tory MP James Wharton's precarious Stockton South constituency, compared to 22 per cent from Labour. By April 2015, however, one month from polling day, Labour's contact rate was up to 75 per cent, with the Tories behind on 66 per cent. Wallace declared the figures 'somewhat worrying', and was not alone in his concerns.[87] Some Conservatives defending their seats against Labour were equally alarmed. When the election results were announced in May, however, Wharton increased his majority, from a tiny 332 to a far healthier 5,046.

Of the ten marginal seats profiled, all of which Labour was targeting, the Conservatives lost only Hove. Ashcroft's mid-April poll of Finchley and Golders Green – which had been Margaret Thatcher's seat – put Labour ahead of the Tory incumbent Mike Freer. Freer was among the MPs who were 'spooked' by Ashcroft's findings. Crosby sent more resources into the constituency in response to his concerns, despite believing the poll to be misleading. Freer held his seat with an increased share of the vote.[88]

Tory insiders now claim their lower contact rates in the closing stages showed simply that they were better organised and more focused, concentrating their efforts on undecided voters. Labour, meanwhile, were playing catch-up too late.

Crash

Despite the meticulous organisation, endless canvassing and highly targeted campaign messages, on polling day itself, the Tories were almost undone. Their prized new computer database, VoteSource, crashed. It contained vital details of the canvass returns that activists had built up over the previous months and – critically – told them which doors to knock on in order to 'get the vote out'. On polling day, there is no time to waste knocking on doors of people who have voted already or those who will never vote for you. Canvass returns are therefore essential in allowing local campaign teams to focus on the right addresses.

But for a few hours, in enough seats to cause a major headache at CCHQ, the system broke. Party campaigners staffing local constituency offices panicked. They could not print out the slips they needed to hand to activists who would then knock on the doors of Tory voters. Some local campaigns were paralysed, while others went back to dig out the paper copies of the canvass returns that had been filled in weeks earlier and left in boxes or cupboards. Back in the war room at Matthew Parker Street, Stephen Gilbert, the Tory campaigns director, frantically battled to get through the problem. Lynton Crosby, sitting alongside him, cursed and felt sick with worry.

Tory insiders now admit that VoteSource was a disaster waiting to happen. The system was only developed in the second half of the parliament and was designed as a one-off, to serve the Tories. This meant it had not been tested in the heat of an election battle, and activists were still being trained in how to use it during the final week of the entire campaign.[89] With relieved understatement, one senior party figure says: 'It was not perfect.'

But such was the intensity of the Tories' ground war in the preceding weeks and months – with its precision targeting of individual households – that the computer failure didn't matter. By then, no voter who had shown even the slightest inclination towards the Conservatives in a marginal seat can have been in any doubt about what they were being asked to do.

CHAPTER **6**

THE CYBER WAR

C raig Elder swore he was never going to work in politics
again. The wiry young Scot had been deputy head of
digital during the 2010 election and had seen first-hand
how 'nerdy' computer wizards like him were regarded as
ornamental extras to the main work of the political campaign.
While the grown-ups were busy plotting to decapitate Labour
Cabinet ministers and find a strategy to force Gordon Brown
from No. 10, the techies were expected to produce amusing
gadgets for Westminster insiders to while away their idler
moments on the internet, ideally featuring pictures of cats.⁹⁰

It was spring 2013, three years since the election that saw
David Cameron enter Downing Street at the head of a coalition
government. Elder, a young man with boundless energy and
ideas, had landed on his feet and was working as an associate
director at a major media consultancy, on household name
brands including McDonald's, Sainsbury's and eBay. Settled
in a long-term relationship and learning a lot in a job that he
loved, he was happy with life. In his spare time, Elder would
meet up with his friend Tom Edmonds, who had also worked
on the 2010 campaign, as deputy head of branding, and was

now working for a traditional advertising firm. The pair would reminisce about the past election and think to themselves how differently they would have gone about their work for the Tories if they had had the experience they were gaining in the commercial world now. Elder told his fiancée: 'I'll never do it again because I don't think a political party will take digital as seriously as it needs to be taken.' Then the call came.

Stupid ideas

Lynton Crosby, newly installed as the Tories' election consultant, officially working only one day a week at this stage, was assembling his team for the battle to come. Andrew Feldman, the Tory co-chairman, had worked closely with Elder and Edmonds on the 2010 campaign and he wondered if they would be free to meet to share their reflections on the past and how the party could do better next time. 'We went in to give them some ideas,' Elder recalls. 'That morphed very quickly into them saying, "Guys, how would you feel about coming in and running this?"'[91]

Initially, they were reluctant.

> As much as I love the party and wanted to help the Prime Minister and Andrew, who I have a great relationship with, it felt like a wrench. We were really enjoying our jobs and we knew it would be a massive challenge. The Conservatives were double-digits behind in the polls at that point.

In fact, the ICM poll in *The Guardian* of February 2013 put the Tories on just 29 per cent, far behind the 41 per cent achieved by Labour, which was still enjoying the boost it had received from Osborne's 'Omnishambles' Budget the previous year.

Two critical factors made Elder and Edmonds change their minds. Firstly, Feldman was offering them seats at the top table, two director-level positions within the party at the heart of the election effort. The chairman's second point, however, was key: 'I understand this needs to be financed properly,' Feldman told them. Elder says the promise of resources and a central role was impossible to reject. 'He was giving us the exact thing that we said we wanted. I said, "Let's give it a bash,"' he says. After some negotiations over the details, Elder and Edmonds were back at their desks by July.

When they arrived at Conservative Campaign Headquarters, at that time located in the Millbank Tower complex of offices, Edmonds and Elder set about changing the party's culture. Particularly for Elder, who was the new director of digital, this meant weaning the party off its 'addiction to posters and stunts' and instead embracing more sophisticated, targeted, digital work, which he believed would be better value for money and also easier to evaluate. This, he admits, was 'a leap of faith' for the Tories at that time. Crosby, in particular, believed in the work they were doing, but for him, faith alone was never going to be enough. He wanted to see the evidence.

So, in October 2013, around the time of the Conservative Party conference in Manchester, Elder launched a 'test campaign' to gather the empirical data that Crosby required in order to know how big a role digital campaigning – the new 'cyber war' in the election campaign – would play. 'Instinctively, they got it,' Elder says. 'But they wanted to be shown.' In this testing phase, Elder's team tried every possible digital platform that they could find, to establish which ones worked well and which should be ignored. They tried advertisements on Facebook, Twitter, Google, 'pre-roll' advertising at the start of videos on YouTube, and display advertising on newspaper websites.

They tested their techniques on the public, using slogans and policies from the party conference, including 'for hard-working people' (the neologism that irritated commentators more than most). Their digital ads featured promises to cap welfare, reduce immigration, tackle the deficit and cut taxes. As Crosby's influence began to be felt, what would become the Conservatives' defining message was also emerging at this time: the 'long-term economic plan'.

Yet, at precisely this moment, when Elder and Edmonds needed to be at the top of their game, a throwback to the bad old days of the previous era threatened to derail their progress. Ed Miliband had used his conference speech in Brighton – delivered bravura style with no notes for the second year running – to make a dramatic policy pledge to the electorate. If Labour won the 2015 election, he declared, the party would freeze energy bills for consumers to stop the 'big six' power firms ripping off their customers with inflation-busting price rises each year. It was, at the time, something of a masterstroke. Miliband made his statement at the start of the annual season of energy companies announcing their prices. This had the effect of keeping Labour's radical policy (which smacked of old-style socialism to critics on the right, but was compelling nonetheless) at the top of the public agenda. The Tories seemed to have nothing to say in response, and were worried.

A high-ranking government figure had the idea that the party should create its own website called 'edmilibandseconomic policy.com'. When people went to view the website, all they would see would be a black page. The 'joke' behind the idea was that the page was black because Miliband's retrograde price freeze would damage the energy industry and lead to power cuts. The lights would go out. Elder and Edmonds knew it was a waste of time but did not feel they had the authority to reject a suggestion from such a senior figure. So they asked Lynton Crosby for his view. In a typically pithy email to Edmonds, Crosby said: 'Stupid idea.' And everyone moved on.[92]

Another Tory insider recalls: 'There was pressure from the top because Miliband's price freeze was dominating the media. We didn't know how to react but we had to do something.' Crosby's view was simple: a website that nobody was ever going to view was a pointless Westminster in-joke. Digital was not just 'the fun department' any more. In 2010, and at times in the run-up to the 2015 election, Elder and Edmonds had to contend with demands to produce eye-catching gadgets and gimmicks and to adopt the newest and most exciting innovations in social networking online.[93]

However, Elder had learned from his time working for major companies that his job was to focus on the target audience and find them, wherever they were, rather than to jump on every new digital bandwagon, as the party had done in the past. 'In the 2010 campaign, we wanted to show people we were smart and clever,' he recalls. 'We wanted to show them shiny things. We always started by saying, "What's the shiny thing?"' When YouTube was taking off in 2006–07, the Tories created 'WebCameron', a regularly updated internet video channel for the Tory leader, punning on the word 'webcam'. When Twitter was launched as a 'microblogging' site, the Conservatives were convinced they needed to be the first political party to sign up, and did so. But they didn't really know what to use Twitter for, opting to make announcements of local and European election results in 2009 – hardly an innovative, vote-swaying piece of communication. 'Was it smart? Was it reaching the right audience? No,' says Elder, still clearly peeved.

He also had a battle with the 300 Tory MPs in the parliamentary party, most of whom were similarly clueless about how best to use Facebook or Twitter to communicate with their constituents. 'The temptation is to create fun, matey, super-irreverent content. But that's not what people want. You are pitching to be the government of the United Kingdom,' he says.

> I presented to the entire parliamentary party and said social media is not just for young people. These are our target voters and if you try to use it as the place to speak to the kids, you will fail. Most MPs had the opposite problem and were too dry and formal.

Choosing the tools

By 2015, however, Twitter was central to every MP's, press officer's and Westminster journalist's day. Even CCHQ had worked out what it was for. In fact, the Conservatives made maximum use of Twitter as an extension of the party's 'air war'. A well-timed tweet from the right person could be hugely influential in shaping the news agenda for the mainstream media – principally, the evening TV bulletins and the morning papers. There was no better individual to convey this material than David Cameron, who had an audience of one million Twitter followers at the election, more than double Ed Miliband's reach. Cameron's personal account was managed by a team inside Tory HQ. This was the same David

Cameron who had once declared his aversion to Twitter, telling a radio interviewer that 'too many tweets might make a twat', apparently not understanding either Twitter or elements of English slang that listeners might not appreciate. In fact, the Prime Minister had two Twitter accounts – one managed by the No. 10 press office and another, @David_Cameron, run by Elder and Edmonds at CCHQ. A Tory insider says: 'We had been running his account from CCHQ and built up his following. Craig and Tom managed it and it was a Twitter account which reflected his views.'[94]

As outlined earlier, Cameron even broke one major story using his own Twitter account, to stir up outrage at Alex Salmond's boast that he would write Labour's Budget after the election. Those who saw the Prime Minister earlier that day knew he was personally excited about the video of the former First Minister and was telling reporters who travelled with him that he would be putting it out on Twitter himself later. The story made it onto page 1 of the following day's *Daily Mail*, on 23 April, with the headline 'Swaggering Salmond boasts: I'll be writing Labour's Budget'. This was at least a more helpful headline than the main lead story for the paper, which attacked the Conservatives' failure to bring immigration under control: 'Voters Tell Cameron to Act on Migration' was the *Mail*'s splash headline above an article on a poll showing dissatisfaction with Tory border policies.

The other accounts used by the Tories included the main Conservative Twitter account, which was helpful for arming activists around the country with Lynton Crosby's approved messages. Then there was the 'CCHQ' account, which was intended to be of interest mainly to Westminster natives, lobby journalists, MPs and party hacks. This was used more for 'hard political knock-about' in the Westminster village, such as rebutting negative media stories, circulating statements to the press and stirring up trouble for the party's opponents.

During the TV debates, Twitter became a battlefield of its own. Each party had teams of big names, MPs and supporters, and lowly desk staff, ready to send out instant reactions to the performances of the party leaders during the televised debates. The seven-way debate on Thursday 2 April, which was the only genuine 'debate' that Cameron took part in, was intense in digital terms. Some 9,000 tweets a minute were sent from those watching it on TV at home and in the parties' war rooms. The digital and press teams had prepared Vines – short videos – of David Cameron dismissing his rivals with the words 'debt up, debt up, debt up', while attack tweets focused on Ed Miliband's weakness on the economy. All of it was played out on Twitter.

For the final BBC *Question Time* leader's special programme, a week before polling day, on 30 April, the Conservatives had a room full of MPs, Cabinet ministers and others at the back of Matthew Parker Street ready to tweet their instant reactions in a frenzy of activity throughout the programme. The team included Jeremy Hunt, the Health Secretary, and Matthew Hancock, the Business Minister, while Andrew Feldman, the chairman, was also in the room to watch. One insider says: 'We had loads of Tory MPs tweeting exactly the same thing at exactly the same time.'

The objective was simply to overwhelm the opposition with a greater volume of messages – and consistency – on Twitter. Journalists who weren't frantically tweeting themselves would be monitoring the contributions of others to try to assess who had won the debates and which leaders had failed. 'There was a Twitter war during the debates when you basically have to crowd it out and define it as three key moments. Broadcasters use it as a reference tool, so it was important,' one senior Tory campaign figure explains.

Facebook

While the Conservatives knew the uses of Twitter and their limits, party strategists felt that Labour relied too heavily on the reassurance that the echo chamber of this particular medium provided. It is something of an article of faith among Conservatives that Twitter is fundamentally dominated by the left. Thousands of Labour activists would tweet every Saturday about their canvassing activities using the hashtag #Labourdoorstep. To Craig Elder, Labour's reliance on Twitter became an expression of a wider political truth. 'I have got a pretty good hunch that Labour people shout it "loud and proud" and Tory people don't. They just get on with their jobs, raise their kids and don't waste loads of time on Twitter telling everyone that they're Tory,' he says.

> From our perspective, that's reflected in the way we approached digital. Labour spent an awful lot of time and resources on Twitter. Others have said there was a danger of an institutional obsession with Twitter for Labour. I absolutely concur. It was almost like a comfort blanket; they could almost ignore what was going on in the real world so long as there were thousands of people saying the Labour Party was amazing and wouldn't Ed Miliband be a better Prime Minister.

Elder says Twitter is perfectly suited to political insiders but far less good at reaching the undecided voters in swing seats who would determine the outcome of the election. Fewer than one in five people in the country were signed up to Twitter at the time of the 2015 election. This is actually a large number – but dwarfed by the penetration of Facebook, which is used by 55 per cent of the population.

'This isn't 55 per cent of people who use a computer, it's 55 per cent of people,' Elder says.

> The fastest-growing group of Facebook users in the UK is the over-55s. You find that the people adding me and my friends on Facebook are not your mates any more, it's your mum, dad, gran and granddad – they want to see your kids' pictures. That's really profound for political parties, particularly those who want to reach very specific segments of the population, because they are pretty much all there. Facebook is a phenomenal campaigning platform and we really, really exploited that.

The results of Elder and Edmonds's October 2013 test of digital avenues were clear. The voters they needed to convert were to be found using Facebook and Google, and not primarily on Twitter or other newer, more cutting-edge products. 'It was about looking at the channels where most people were – that was Facebook and Google – and then figuring out how we demonstrate that we were helping them,' Elder says.

This is where the Tory activities in the digital world really counted. As precisely as Stephen Gilbert, Jim Messina and Lynton Crosby had identified the types of voters in the seats that would swing the election result, so Elder and his team had to convince the same floating voters online. But first they had to find them.

In this, they were helped considerably by Facebook itself, as well as by Messina's expertise from America in the potential to use social media to 'micro-target' specific groups of voters. In the UK, Facebook sells advertising to a wide array of different organisations: car-hire firms, supermarket giants, insurers, charities. And also political parties. Facebook users provide enormous amounts of detail about their lives to Facebook – and companies wanting to advertise benefit from the ability to target their messages at Facebook users who – because of their age, social profile and interests – are most likely to respond. The Conservative election effort used exactly the same techniques. Facebook itself offered the ability to target adverts to residents of particular constituencies. This was a breakthrough development. It meant that Elder and Edmonds could send Tory ads to voters in the 100 key marginal seats that Crosby and Gilbert had identified as likely to sway the balance of power.

But, because of the wealth of personal details that Facebook users share, the Conservatives could also be even more targeted. They could choose, for example, to send particular ads to women aged between thirty and forty-five, with children, living in a swing seat, who were interested in buying a house. All this was possible because Facebook held such detailed information about its users. Elder explains:

> This election for us was fought in 100 seats. Your first
> bit of targeting is making sure you're only speaking to
> people in the marginal constituencies. People said to me
> at various points, 'I don't see anything from you guys.

What are you doing? At the last election, I saw your
tweets, your YouTube videos. What are you doing?' This
was like stealth. Basically, if you didn't live in one of
those 100 constituencies, you're going to see very little
from us. Then, within that, it becomes about different
demographics that you want to speak to.

We were able to work with Facebook using
constituency targeting to focus just on the constituencies
that were going to decide the election, and then based
on what we already know about the demographics of
the people who are going to decide this election, we
could do demographic targeting, and interest targeting,
to focus in on people and present different content to a
young mum in Derby North to maybe a slightly older
gentleman living in Rochester.

The degree of precision involved is striking. It may also appear
to be a departure from conventional political interactions –
as well as from traditional advertising. To those unfamiliar
with exactly how their digital preferences can be used by
advertisers, the Conservatives' activities on Facebook could
seem mildly sinister. But Elder points out that the Tories made
use of 'exactly the same data that advertisers use'. Individual
Facebook users choose to put large amounts of information
about themselves online, which any advertisers can use to
target the most relevant material at the most potentially
fertile audiences.

The Conservatives targeted some Facebook users they
believed could be swayed to vote Tory because they had
Facebook friends who were already party supporters. People
who were friends with Tory supporters on Facebook would
see ads from the party in their personal news feeds with 'social

context' – a small message on the ad saying, for example, that their friend 'James Jones likes the Conservatives'.

'On Facebook, people are proactively offering up the brands that they like, the things that they are interested in, the politics that they like, their age, whether they have got kids. Frankly, you can tell whether or not they are friends with existing fans of the Conservatives,' Elder says.

The technology meant the Tories could send out videos and political ads, from Westminster, to groups of perhaps 10,000 voters living in Bath, or Yeovil, who had particular interests and were thought to be open to persuasion with the right kinds of messages. The information available about Facebook users' personal interests and foibles was so sophisticated that Tory messages could be sent to as few as 1,000 people. These were high-tech, precision strikes, and the party's opponents did not see them coming.

The value exchange

Now that the Conservatives had found their swing voters online, they had to begin a conversation that would ultimately result in them turning off their computers and walking to the polling station to vote Tory. Tone was judged to be essential, and traditional ads were seen as less effective than gambits that would entice Facebook users to interact with the party. As every self-confessed internet nerd should, Elder had his own term for this. 'I call it a value exchange.'

Facebook users would see these softer-style ads as they were scrolling through the news feed in their accounts. A 'sponsored post' would appear, saying it was from the Conservative Party, that offered to calculate how much this individual voter had saved in tax cuts as a result of Tory (and Lib Dem) policies. In exchange, the party would ask for the individual's email address and postcode and then seek to communicate with them directly via email as well. This information was critical to helping the Tories find the swing voters who would decide the election. Once someone's name and postcode had been fed into the VoteSource database, it was usually possible to find their address from the electoral roll and knock on their door or deliver a carefully tailored letter or leaflet containing the Conservatives' key messages.

Elder says:

> It's not naked data collection, it's about saying, 'We think you'll want to know about this and we want you to stay in touch.' You'd enter your salary, get the answer and on the 'Thank you' page be asked for your email address. Also, you'd be asked if you wanted to donate. And a lot of people did.

By techniques such as this – and also by asking through similar adverts for voters' views on reforming the benefits system – the Tories managed to increase their centrally held email list to 1.5 million people by the time of the 2015 election. It was officially around 500,000 in 2010, although in reality probably only 300,000 at that time, as many of those addresses were out of date. Needless to say, David Cameron also had his own Facebook account, which had attracted 500,000 'likes' from other users, compared with 80,000 for Miliband's page, by the time the short campaign was under way.

As well as sending ads to promote policies to people likely to benefit from them – including policies like better pensions, extra free childcare and help to buy a house – Crosby's digital team were able to send his 'squeeze' messages to floating voters. These were the warnings, which became starker and stronger as the campaign went on, about the consequences of voting for UKIP, or the Liberal Democrats. Voters so tempted would be reminded that their actions would let Ed Miliband into No. 10 on the 'coat-tails of the SNP', or in Alex Salmond's pocket.

Persuading Facebook users to part with their personal email addresses meant the Tories could contact them directly – via Facebook itself as well as through email. It revolutionised digital communications between CCHQ and supporters across the country, and also helped the party raise money. Critically for the ground war, some 100,000 of the individuals on the email list of 1.5 million agreed to join the Team 2015 street army, whose role it was to deliver leaflets and win votes in target seats.

'We were able to use digital in a very targeted way to reach the people who were going to decide this election,' Elder says.

> But we were also able to use digital to get our supporters fired up, get them to share with their friends the content we wanted to share – so campaign graphics, campaign videos.
>
> And we were able to reach out to our supporters on a regular basis and say, 'This is what we are going to do, this is the kind of Britain we want to create and if you want to help make that happen, donate £20, donate £10.' Finally, for the first time, we were cracking that issue of large numbers of small donations in a way that makes a meaningful contribution to your campaign fighting fund.

As the Tories' fundraiser in chief, the man who had tempted Elder and Edmonds to return, Andrew Feldman could not have been more pleased.

PART 3

THE CAMPAIGN

CHAPTER 7

WOBBLE

Croydon. Saturday morning. Rain. By 25 April 2015, David Cameron had been campaigning all day, every day, for four weeks. He was, in the words of one of his closest colleagues, 'knackered, completely knackered. Absolutely, fundamentally, tired.'

Of course, publicly, the Conservatives rejected any suggestion that the Prime Minister was feeling the effects of a hugely demanding election campaign in which he was required to start work before six each day, give interviews to local and national media, make stump speeches in several constituencies, talk to donors, meet with colleagues and plan strategy for the days ahead before he could go to bed again. When it came to making a significant speech on diversity, in front of the nation's media on a wet Saturday morning in south London, it was perhaps not the moment for him to ad-lib.

During the speech about increasing opportunities for ethnic minority Britons, Cameron said Britain was a country where citizens could successfully have 'multiple identities'. It was, he continued, a country 'where you can be Welsh and Hindu and British, Northern Irish and Jewish and British, where you can wear a kilt and a turban, where you can wear a hijab covered in poppies; where you can support Man United, the Windies and Team GB all at the same time'. Then he joked, off-the-cuff: 'Of course, I'd rather you supported West Ham.'

This would have been fine, if Cameron was not in fact a self-proclaimed lifelong Aston Villa supporter. Instantly, Cameron's advisers wondered what on earth he meant. Journalists in the audience had the opportunity to ask him. 'I had what Natalie Bennett described as a brain fade,' he explained. 'I'm a Villa fan... I must have been overcome by something... this morning. But there we are. These things sometimes happen when you are on the stump.'

The Sunday papers the following day all had fun at the Prime Minister's expense. His political opponents, however, seized on the gaffe as evidence that Cameron was a faker, and claimed he was making up his sporting allegiances in order to appear 'in touch' with normal people. Alastair Campbell, Tony Blair's former spin doctor, who was working closely with Ed Miliband by this point, said the mistake 'says a lot about his character, which impacts upon policy. Out of touch. Phoney. Believes nothing.'

Cameron's colleagues insist this is unfair and say he was genuinely mortified and baffled by his error. 'He knew he had completely fucked up. But I think the reason for it was he was so tired,' says one. Cameron is not a season-ticket holder at Aston Villa but his officials say he does pay attention to the performances and make-up of the team. Alan Sendorek, Cameron's former special adviser, says:

> Believe it or not, and I know people never will, he
> does actually follow football. We were often on tour

on Mondays and he usually would have caught at least some of the Super Sunday game the day before. The main talking points from the Premier League that weekend would often be the topic of conversation on the train up.[95]

But the 'brain fade' moment fuelled the idea that Cameron's interest in football is simply put on. The mistake was repeated in less damaging ways while the PM was out in the country making stump speeches in the final two weeks of the campaign. One of those who travelled with him to the regions says Cameron would frequently substitute random words in his speeches at rallies. In the final days of the campaign he described the election as 'career-defining', when he meant to say 'country-defining', and gave the date of the poll as 9 May, when it was 7 May.

The weekend of the 'West Ham' gaffe was the moment when his own failings were laid bare for him. It was the point in the campaign when, with the polls refusing to move, and exhaustion setting in, Cameron himself began to doubt.

Tory staff who worked closely with him say the fact that the Prime Minister's fatigue came from overwork made him more irritated with claims that he was not trying hard enough or showing enough 'passion' for winning. This impression was partly a result of Cameron's temperament – he has a very British stiff upper lip – but as a narrative it quickly and dangerously came to symbolise a campaign that was dull, uninspiring and showed little sign of success. MPs, party donors, even Cabinet ministers lined up to demand that Cameron show the country how much he cared. Leadership rivals began quietly sounding out their supporters, should the party lose power and a replacement for Cameron be required.

Newspapers that were previously on-side became quarrelsome. Inside CCHQ, morale began to dip. To make matters worse for the Tories, Ed Miliband was apparently discovering the kind of broad public appeal that even his closest allies had thought impossible – an astonishing internet fan base of thousands of teenage girls professing to adore him.

The major 'wobble' in the Conservative campaign would never have happened but for one critical factor of the 2015 election, which arguably had as great an influence on the outcome as the surge in support for the SNP in Scotland: the polls. Throughout the six weeks of the short campaign, and for several months previously, all major public opinion polls had pointed to a hung parliament. 'Neck and neck.' 'Too close to call.' 'On a knife-edge.' These were the stock phrases journalists used to describe the stubborn deadlock between Labour and the Tories. When the exit poll was announced, putting the Tories on 316 seats, Labour lagging a poor second on 239 and the Lib Dems on just ten, Martin Boon, the director of ICM, spoke for many of his colleagues when he gave his reaction on Twitter: 'Oh shit.' The pollsters – all of them – had been completely wrong.

The polling industry has since begun its own inquiry into the spectacular collective failure, the like of which has not been seen since the great 1992 disaster, in which even the exit poll predicted the wrong result. Worryingly for the pollsters – and gallingly for the Conservatives at the time – it was the Tory share of the vote that they underestimated so badly in 2015, just as they had done when John Major won against the forecasts twenty-three years previously. Martin Boon says the average error in the polls was 'shockingly bad' and 'every bit as bad as 1992'.

But it's worse than that. Obviously, we got the story wrong. The whole point about the polls setting the narrative is that it allows everybody to understand what is happening, what needs to be done as the election looms nearer, and we gave a false perspective to everybody, which cannot be a good thing in any sense.

It is impossible to overstate the significance of the pollsters' collective error in 2015. It set the parameters for the entire election – how the parties approached it, how the media reported it and how voters saw the choices they had to make.

During the short campaign, the deadlock in the polls took on a life of its own. Every day, a new poll was published, which showed Labour and the Tories essentially tied on between 33 and 35 per cent each as the two parties swapped their narrow lead from one survey to the next, or, just as frequently, received identical scores. Every day, the broadcasters and newspapers would crawl over the details for signs of which party was fractionally more likely to form a coalition government. Any thought that either side could achieve an outright majority had been abandoned in the media coverage long ago. And every day, Tory MPs, ministers, donors and campaign staff would chew their nails a little closer to the quick.

David Cameron's West Ham gaffe would not have been so damaging if the atmosphere around the Tory campaign had been more confident about its prospects. But when a leader seems to be in trouble, any mistake, however minor, looks like a sign of a deeper malaise.

Who cares?

'Who the fuck are these people?' Lynton Crosby's enquiry was not wholly rhetorical. He wanted to know why powerful but anonymous party supporters – described as FTSE 100 company bosses – were briefing the press that they were unhappy with this campaign. The *Financial Times*, which was itself critical of the Tory reliance on 'fear' in the election, reported on 24 April that twenty company bosses had major reservations about the Tories making personal attacks on Ed Miliband instead of playing to the party's strong record on the economy. The complaints, published the day before the PM's West Ham 'brain fade', were not unique. Rumblings of discontent had already surfaced in newspapers during the preceding two weeks and Cabinet ministers were even beginning to voice their concerns in public interviews.

One senior Tory figure recalls how serious the alarm was, even at the top of the party. 'Everybody thought that these polls were pretty copper-bottomed. They hadn't really been proved wrong in a dramatic way for years. They were thought to be fiendishly accurate and they weren't shifting. Everybody was in a bit of a flap.'[96] Criticism seemed to be coming from all sides. James Forsyth, the political columnist, warned in the *Mail on Sunday* on 12 April that the Tories had seven days to save their campaign from disintegration, so rattled were the party's troops. In the same paper, Brian Binley, a retiring MP, laid into Lynton Crosby's tactics and the decision to deploy Michael Fallon, the Defence Secretary, to cause a diversion with his 'stab in the back' attack on Ed Miliband. Liam Fox, the former Defence Secretary, criticised George Osborne's 'Dickensian' language of austerity.

Even Iain Duncan Smith, the Work and Pensions Secretary and former Tory leader, bluntly suggested that David Cameron looked like just another 'talking head with a suit on'.[97] Duncan Smith said: 'Raw passion matters. If people know that you care about stuff then they are more likely, if they agree with you, to be stirred by that… He cares. I just need that to come across.'

The great cry was that Cameron had to show more passion. One senior aide who saw him a lot on the campaign trail says the Prime Minister was frequently 'frustrated' by allegations that he was workshy, liked 'chillaxing' or did not care whether he won or lost. 'He was travelling all over the country, working his arse off. It's very difficult if you're doing that and someone comes to you and says, "The problem is you just don't care enough."'

Cameron himself was also grumbling in private. He was said to feel 'hemmed in' by the 'narrow' strictures of Crosby's campaign, which saw him kept well away from unregulated encounters with voters on the street. Those who travelled with him on the Tory campaign 'battle bus' doubt whether he ever met an unemployed person. At one point, he confessed that the Conservative campaign could be seen as too bland. 'There is something about me – I always manage to portray a calm smoothness or something,' he lamented to an interviewer. 'Conservatives are calm, clear-headed people. We want to know not just what the passion is, we want to know what the plan is.'[98] But if he had reservations about the strategy, he never queried it directly with Lynton Crosby.

Others were less inhibited. Nicky Morgan, the Education Secretary, said she believed the polls were not shifting in the Conservatives' favour because Crosby's campaign had focused so much on the economy, when this was already 'factored in'. In a brave departure from Crosby's regime of rigid discipline, she warned in an interview that voters wanted the party to say more about education, the NHS and public services, while immigration was mentioned 'a lot' on the doorstep.[99] The *Daily Mail* agreed. On Thursday 23 April, its front-page lead story, reporting an opinion poll, said: 'Voters want the Tories to be far tougher on mass immigration, a major survey revealed last night. Barely one in ten Britons say they are satisfied with David Cameron's border policies.' In an unusual move, the paper inserted an editorial comment box into its article on the front page, making plain its criticism of Lynton Crosby's strategy of silence on the issue of migration. It said: 'Mass immigration, the subject that dare not speak its name, has been all but airbrushed from this election, even by the Tories... The irony is they're the only party who will do something about it.'

The same day, the lead story in *The Times* was arguably even less helpful: 'Boris Johnson admitted that it would be "wonderful" to be seen as a contender for the Conservative leadership yesterday as the Prime Minister was forced to defend his election strategy from accusations that it lacked passion.' The Mayor of London had been keeping a low profile in the national media campaign but had surfaced for a series of events and interviews, including a grilling on Sky News. For a long time, Johnson had been seen as the favourite to succeed Cameron when the time came.

The Prime Minister had only himself to blame. He had ignited speculation about his leadership when he disclosed to the BBC's James Landale on the eve of the election campaign that he would not seek a third term in office. He named Johnson, along with George Osborne and Theresa May, as one of his potential successors. When Kay Burley, the Sky News presenter, asked Johnson repeatedly whether he wanted to be leader of the party one day, he found it impossible to hold the line. He blustered and evaded for several minutes but ultimately could not keep it up. 'In the dim, distant future, obviously it would be a wonderful thing to be thought to be in a position to be considered for such an honour,' he said.

Johnson was not alone. In addition to the Mayor of London, the Chancellor and the Home Secretary, four other senior Tories were rumoured to have been making plans for possible leadership bids in the event of a defeat. The names mentioned included Sajid Javid, then Culture Secretary (who had joked about standing for leader a few months earlier), Andrea Leadsom, a relatively junior Treasury minister, the Education Secretary Nicky Morgan, and Dominic Raab, a backbencher who was made a justice minister after the election. Cameron's Downing Street team saw the stories in the papers and heard the rumours, and those close to the Prime Minister and the Chancellor were not happy. But, after Cameron himself had fired the starting gun for the race to replace him, there was little they could do.

Lynton Crosby's view of all the 'noises off' was typically blunt. They were all wrong and their contributions were 'fucking unhelpful', he fumed in private.[100] To those working around him in the war room, however, he appeared the picture of composure and tried to keep everybody upbeat. But even Cameron had to ask Crosby whether he was sure the polls were so wrong.

1992

In Conservative Campaign Headquarters, staff were watching the daily poll results in the papers and trying to keep faith with their project. Lynton Crosby and Mark Textor never shared their daily 'tracker' polling, conducted in sixty marginal and target seats, with the wider team. But they insisted to anyone who asked that the national polls should be ignored because they were always wrong. Still, it was hard to dismiss the front page of *The Guardian* on Friday 10 April. 'The Day the Polls Turned' was the paper's headline, beneath which three separate opinion surveys gave Labour a lead of three points, four points and six points. The main news story began: 'The strongest, if still tentative, sign that the Conservatives' narrow and negative campaign is misfiring emerged yesterday when three polls showed Labour moving ahead, and in one Ed Miliband's personal approval ratings were more positive than David Cameron's for the first time.'

When senior members of the strategy team arrived for their 5.45 a.m. meeting that morning, the mood in the office was grim. 'That was the worst day, definitely the worst day of the campaign,' one says. 'We knew it was going to be a difficult day. I remember seeing that front page and coming in, it was top of the pile of papers in the morning. There was just an atmosphere. It was horrible.'[101]

Even Crosby himself privately questioned whether his own tracker polls were wrong. When every poll was saying the same thing, it was only rational for him to think, 'Fuck, am I missing something here?'[102] But there was never outright panic. One insider says: 'It was probably the one time when people asked, is this the right approach? The PM, the Chancellor and Lynton were all very clear: yes, this is the right approach, thank you, and we'll carry on.'[103]

Sitting at their desks in the war room, Conservative staff would try to reassure each other by recalling how John Major won in 1992, in defiance of the polls at the time.

They would consult the Liberal Democrat activist Mark Pack's website, where they could find polls dating back to that campaign more than twenty years previously. Every week, they would compare the Tories' standing at a comparable point in the campaign in 1992 to their position in the latest public polls, and found they told a similar story. 'People did believe it was like '92 and looking at these old polls helped us keep our chins up,' one member of campaign staff says.[104] Andrew Feldman would watch a video of the 1992 election victory during difficult moments in the campaign. He then took it a step further and invited Sir John Major himself to come into the war room to give the troops a motivational pep talk.

'I have seen all this before,' Major told the Tory campaigners. 'I know you are disappointed that the polls are not moving. But hold your nerve: you are doing the right thing.' The former Prime Minister drew parallels with his time as a councillor in Brixton, when, he said, Labour tried to launch class warfare against the Conservatives. 'This charge that the Tories are for the few and not for the many just does not work,' he told them. 'What are you going to say to the fourteen million who voted for us in 1992? Are you saying they are all rich? They are not. We are the party of people who want to get on, the party of aspiration.'[105] One staff member in the room recalls: 'Major was quite folksy, it was almost as if he was on his soap box again. He had a big crowd and got a big round of applause afterwards.' Another Conservative campaigner describes it as 'the best pep talk ever'.[106]

During the campaign, Crosby also brought in John Howard, the former Australian Prime Minister, whom he had helped to four election victories, to deliver a similar speech. 'A lot of it was about holding your nerve,' one Tory says.

Paxman

For the first half of the full-time campaign, at least, Ed Miliband's team was delighted with how well their plan was working. They'd scored a hit with the promise to abolish tax breaks for rich 'non-doms' and their leader had become a darling of the celebrity left-winger Russell Brand. More bizarrely, Miliband was now a surprise pin-up for an adoring horde of adolescent schoolgirls. The Twitter craze that became known as 'Milifandom' baffled but boosted Labour – one of Miliband's aides noted at the time: 'We have no idea what the hell is going on with all these teenage girls – but we're liking it.' And it did nothing to ease the anxiety of Conservative supporters who felt their campaign was falling flat while the world discovered a hitherto entirely concealed star quality to Ed Miliband.

As the polls continued to put Miliband in contention for No. 10, influential Conservative bloggers questioned Crosby's campaign, while the centre-left website May2015, run by the *New Statesman* magazine, made a persuasive case for Miliband having the clearer route to power. In this context, the leaders' performances in the televised election programmes were more important than ever. This had been a major source of conflict between No. 10 and the broadcasters who were hosting the debates. Craig Oliver and Lynton Crosby refused to allow Cameron to take part in a head-to-head debate with Miliband.

The closest he got to debating with Miliband alone was when the pair took turns to answer questions in the opening leaders' programme on 26 March, hosted by Sky News and Channel 4 and presented by Sky's Kay Burley and the former BBC *Newsnight* anchor Jeremy Paxman. During one exchange, Paxman forced Cameron to admit he had no idea how many food banks there were in Britain, to explain his friendship with the sacked *Top Gear* presenter Jeremy Clarkson, and to account for his decision to hire the former *News of the World* editor Andy Coulson as his communications director. William Hague had to defend the Prime Minister to reporters gathered in the 'spin room' afterwards. 'The Prime Minister was not grumpy. He does not get grumpy and he showed no sign of being that tonight,' Hague insisted.

The PM claimed publicly the next day to have been 'really happy' with how it had gone, dismissing Paxman's aggressive interrogation: 'Paxo is Paxo.'[107] The snap polls summarising the views of the three million people who watched on Sky and Channel 4 gave a narrow win to Cameron. But even his own team admit Cameron had a 'wobbly' night.

Seven leaders

With this uninspiring start in mind, Lynton Crosby and Craig Oliver set about intensively coaching Cameron for the next debate, involving seven party leaders, set to be shown on ITV on Thursday 2 April. Rehearsals were held to put the PM through his paces. Jeremy Hunt, the Health Secretary, played Nick Clegg 'brilliantly', while Cameron's special adviser, Oliver Dowden, gave an excellent rendition of Nigel Farage, shouting: 'You promised to cut migration and it's gone up.' Rupert Harrison, George Osborne's chief adviser, played Miliband, and Graeme Wilson, Cameron's press secretary, had the job of playing Nicola Sturgeon and attacking 'Tory austerity'.[108] Craig Oliver was directing the rehearsals, while Crosby and Osborne watched and gave notes from the audience, who included Cameron's chief of staff, Ed Llewellyn, his deputy chief of staff, Kate Fall, and his adviser Adam Atashzai. Craig Oliver was intent on ensuring Cameron made key points in pithy soundbites early in the programme, as he knew his former TV news colleagues would have little time to select clips for their bulletins.

While Cameron felt lucky to be standing apart at one end of the panel, where he could gesture with a sweep of his arm towards the other six leaders, his team knew there were dangers in the format too. He was positioned next to the 'formidable' Sturgeon, and his aides feared the SNP leader could use her proximity to attempt a stunt, handing Cameron a letter or some other prop.

One aide recalls: 'The PM appreciated the rehearsals because they got him in the right frame of mind and it showed how messy it could be, with people shouting over each other.' Cameron's team did not hold back, it seems.

> There was the realisation that he was potentially going to get absolutely battered. We thought, this could be really bloody. The rehearsals were probably a lot more brutal than the real event because everyone just went after the PM. In the debate itself, the other leaders all had a go at him but they had a go at each other as well.[109]

Ed Miliband went away to 'debate camp' for weekend residential sessions in Kent. In the end, the seven-way leader's debate was watched by seven million people. Snap polls again suggested no runaway winner. But the Prime Minister appeared the most capable of leading the country, according to one ComRes poll. George Osborne, for one, was privately relieved. He remembered how badly the 2010 debates had knocked the Tory campaign off course as Nick Clegg stole the show unexpectedly. This time, no clear winner was the best outcome they could have hoped for.[110] This performance was not enough, however, to silence the grumbling within the ranks over the party's campaign. And for the next TV debate, Cameron was entirely absent (as was Clegg), a decision that led to fresh attacks on the strategy being pursued by Crosby.

'Labour are no good at running the country but they can run a bloody election campaign better than we can,' one Tory MP complained privately at the time. 'People might respect Cameron but they don't love him. If people voted with their heads we would have a massive majority but more people vote with their hearts,' the MP lamented.[111] The Conservative campaign would have to persuade the public that voting Tory was not just economically sensible, but emotionally compelling.

CHAPTER 8

PASSION

In September 2014, David Cameron was forced to contemplate the end. A frenzy of nationalism north of the border was threatening to tear apart the 307-year-old Union between England and Scotland. He was in danger of becoming the man who lost Scotland – and, with it, his premiership.

Although he insisted he would not resign if Scotland voted to leave, his own MPs would almost certainly have taken the decision for him. Did he ever regret agreeing to the SNP's demand for a referendum on Scottish independence? If he did, it would have been on the night of the count itself, Thursday 18 September. Unable to sleep, he went downstairs to the No. 10 press office to watch the coverage. His two eldest children joined him, one of whom was wearing tartan pyjamas. 'They knew how worried their dad was,' Cameron later recalled. When the result was declared, giving the pro-Union No vote 55 per cent and the pro-independence Yes vote 45 per cent, he said he understood 'the definition of relief'.

The Vow

Yet the respite was short-lived. In order to secure the victory for the No campaign, Cameron had been forced to agree to what became known as 'The Vow', a pledge by all the Westminster party leaders to devolve more powers over raising taxes and spending on welfare to the Scottish government if Scotland rejected independence. Tory back-bench MPs and several ministers were unhappy. While they could accept greater devolution to Scotland, they were not impressed by the pledge to keep the Barnett formula – the funding scheme that allocates Treasury cash to Scotland in the form of grants for public services. Why keep the formula even though the new powers would enable the Scottish government to raise its own revenues, they asked.

Even worse, despite gaining what some were calling 'Home Rule' for Scotland, the MPs for Scottish constituencies would still continue to have a potentially decisive say over laws affecting only England, while English MPs cannot influence decisions on matters that have been devolved. A succession of Conservative voices demanded that this disparity must now be resolved. They called for 'Home Rule' for England and threatened a rebellion to dwarf the past Commons revolts they had inflicted on Cameron over Europe. Owen Paterson, the former Environment Secretary, demanded that Parliament be recalled to debate the constitutional crisis. Boris Johnson said the vow to keep the Barnett formula had been 'reckless'.

So, on the morning of Friday 19 September, Cameron stepped out from behind the famous black door of No. 10 and made a statement in Downing Street, declaring that he would immediately set in motion reforms to give Scotland those promised extra powers, while simultaneously preparing plans to give more autonomy to England, with a new 'English votes for English laws' rule applying to MPs in the Commons. The new pledge for England came out of the blue. On the eve of Labour's conference, it sent Miliband and his senior team into a spiral of panic about how to respond. If they accepted the idea that English MPs should have a decisive say over English laws, a Labour government that drew much of its support from Scottish MPs would be unable to muster a majority to pass a Budget in the Commons. If they rejected the idea, it would look like they were opposing the English – a stance that Miliband eventually took, much to the horror of his own MPs, especially those in working-class northern towns.

More importantly, Cameron's declaration of 'Home Rule' for England had a dramatic impact in Scotland. It gave the 45 per cent of voters who were already bruised by losing the independence referendum a new cause for resenting Westminster. The SNP stoked the sense of betrayal, which snowballed over the following months, giving Nicola Sturgeon's party an unstoppable momentum into the election campaign. When the election came, those who backed the SNP's case for independence stuck with the party, and while 45 per cent is not enough to win a referendum, in a multi-party election it will deliver a landslide. In the end, the SNP won 50 per cent of the vote in Scotland, taking fifty-six out of fifty-nine available seats, destroying Labour and the Lib Dems in the process.

Cameron was too panicked to have foreseen this outcome, according to a senior government colleague who spoke to the Prime Minister shortly before he walked out to face the cameras on the morning after the referendum. He was 'freaking out' about how Tory backbenchers would react to his devolution proposals. The plan for English votes for English laws had not been 'thought through' enough to calculate its full impact on the general election, the source says.

Despite Cameron's anxiety, it did not take long for Lynton Crosby to spot the potential in the British constitutional machinations to extract a political advantage for the Conservatives. As an experienced strategist, he was running regular focus groups to test various messages and policy plans among key sections of the electorate. These were small group sessions in which individuals would be asked to comment on a series of proposals or potential scenarios and their answers would be analysed and fed into the Tories' planning for their manifesto and election strategy. The results were highly confidential. In October 2014, a month after the referendum, Crosby detected a striking new trend. His focus groups were telling him that the idea of Ed Miliband being unable to win a majority on his own and seeking the help of the SNP to form a new government made English voters recoil in horror. He knew instantly that this would have a major impact in the six months to polling day.[112]

Tory focus groups of swing voters in English seats showed Nicola Sturgeon was seen negatively, the SNP were disliked, but Alex Salmond, the former First Minister, was poison. 'We always tried to talk about Labour doing a deal with Sturgeon, Salmond and the SNP. We always tried to crowbar Salmond in,' one senior Conservative adviser says. 'For people in the south-west, the north-west, across England, he is a very toxic figure.'[113]

Secret polls

The focus groups were one critical element of the data that the Tories were amassing about the views of the voters who

would decide the election that lay ahead. After Crosby started
working full-time on the Tory campaign at the end of 2013, he
began to run polls in constituencies that the Liberal Democrats
held. His intention was to see if the Conservatives could
potentially take seats from their coalition partners. As this
work was being done a full year and a half before the coalition
was due to end, secrecy was essential. The consequences of
disclosure for government relations between Cameron's side
and Nick Clegg's team would have been destructive. It would
also have damaged the Tories' chances had the Lib Dems been
tipped off that they were in Crosby's crosshairs.

The Tories ran their first polls in Lib Dem seats in November
2013 and January 2014. The results were encouraging. Even
at that stage, when the Tories were struggling in the national
polls (although not as badly as Nick Clegg's party), voters in
Lib Dem-held constituencies regarded Cameron favourably.[114]
He was seen as the preferred Prime Minister when compared to
Ed Miliband, and the best able to manage the economy, and the
Tories were even seen as the better party for government in these
seats. One campaign figure recalls: 'In every Lib Dem seat we
polled, David Cameron had a significant lead as people's preferred
Prime Minister. Generally, he was preferred to Miliband by a
ratio of two-to-one. In fact, we found that his favourability was
greater in Lib Dem-held seats than Conservative-held seats.'[115]
Participants in the polls were asked: 'Regardless of what you
think will happen, if faced with a choice of either a Conservative
or Labour-led government, which would you prefer?' In every
Lib Dem seat, they overwhelmingly preferred a Conservative
government.

For Miliband, there was no such encouragement. He was,
Crosby's focus groups said, 'weak'. A campaign insider recalls
that participants described Miliband as 'weak because he's too

idealistic; weak because he can't communicate effectively; and also – not weird, but unable to connect with me (because he is a bit weird)'. Ed Miliband could have promised any policy, made any claim and people would just laugh and say: 'He's going to tell Barack Obama *that*? He's going to say *what* to the trade unions?' According to one party strategist, David Cameron's 'measured reasonableness, which was interpreted early on as a sign that he was not really that committed to the job, in the end was reassuring. He was seen as a measured, considered leader who did not get flustered, who you could be comfortable with.'[116]

The private polling continued and the pattern grew stronger in the Tories' favour in these critical seats as the months went by, from 2014 into 2015. From December 2014, Crosby launched the campaign's tracker polls. These were expensive, detailed and intended to measure progress in a sample of sixty seats, including some in Wales, Cornwall and the north, as well as key target constituencies. From the first of these tracker polls, the picture for the Tories suggested a far more positive result was possible than the gloomy national newspaper opinion polling led the public – and most politicians – to believe. Lynton Crosby and a handful of others in the Conservative campaign knew that they were on course to win 298 to 300-plus seats from the New Year of 2015 onwards, well before the 'short' six-week campaign began.

Crucially, and unlike the vast majority of public polls during the run-up to the election, the Tories' private polling in each target seat included local candidates' names. National opinion polls are not detailed enough and most polling conducted for the purposes of monitoring individual swing seats, such as that published by Lord Ashcroft, did not name candidates at all. Crosby and his polling chief, Mark Textor, wanted to replicate the ballot paper as closely as possible. Jim Messina, who was advising the Tories, also made sure the party's polls used a mix of methods – contacting respondents online, by telephone and by mobile phone.[117] They had one sizeable obstacle, however. Crosby's private evidence told him voters in the fifteen Lib Dem-held seats he was targeting in the south-west simply did not believe the Tories could win there. It was hardly surprising. Yeovil, for example, had been Paddy Ashdown's seat, and had been in the party's hands for thirty-two years. David Laws, the incumbent Lib Dem, was a Cabinet minister, a key ally to Nick Clegg, and sat on a majority of 13,036. To outside observers – including the voters – it looked impossible for the Tories to take. 'In Lib Dem seats, people thought, yes, I want David Cameron as Prime Minister and I even prefer a Conservative government and they are best for the economy but my vote can't make a difference,' one senior strategist says. 'Our whole campaign in those seats was to say, "Actually, your vote locally can achieve that outcome."'

With this in mind, the Tories put up billboards across the Lib Dem heartlands of the south-west, telling voters they were living in one of the twenty-three seats the Tories could win to get a Commons majority. 'That is why we used the phrase "only twenty-three seats for a Conservative majority government". They realised suddenly that meant their vote could make a difference. That is the most important thing of all,' the campaign strategist says.

The logical arguments were clear. But Lynton Crosby needed an emotional edge so that his messages could 'cut through' to voters and motivate them to turn out in force for the Conservatives on 7 May. He had known since October that the SNP's influence on a weak Ed Miliband was the arrowhead he required. Cameron had been deploying the image of Miliband crawling into Downing Street on Alex Salmond's coat-tails for several weeks before the campaign began, at Prime Minister's Questions.

Then M&C Saatchi came up with poster advertisements showing Miliband in Salmond's pocket, Miliband in Sturgeon's pocket and – perhaps most controversially – Salmond stealing cash from the pocket of an English voter. This from the party whose leader had promised a few months earlier to maintain Scotland's Barnett formula of Treasury grants. One senior Tory says the threat of being ruled by the SNP from Edinburgh was critical in persuading English swing voters to side with the Conservatives. 'It certainly had an impact, particularly in those Lib Dem areas, and I think it had an impact in some of those marginal seats with Labour as well. It reinforced the core message of the risk of Miliband. The risk of Miliband was accentuated by Sturgeon and Salmond.'

The threat of a weak Ed Miliband being dominated by a powerful Nicola Sturgeon was used to 'trigger' fear among voters over the risk of allowing Labour into government. Others say it stoked an anti-Scottish resentment among the English voters who were already ill-disposed to Alex Salmond after the referendum campaign. Nicola Sturgeon's assured performances in the TV leaders' debates merely highlighted Miliband's weakness. But with Salmond heading back to Westminster as the parliamentary candidate for Gordon, he would be calling the tune in Ed Miliband's Cabinet, the Tory narrative went.

Lynton Crosby says: 'The SNP would have been irrelevant if Ed Miliband wasn't seen as fundamentally weak, with no real policies of his own and therefore would be pushed around. It was Miliband's weakness that was fundamentally important. Adverts are only effective at reinforcing a prejudice. They don't make a campaign.' A senior Lib Dem, however, says: 'The Tories saw their chance with the SNP and they went for it. They absolutely leathered it. They were just brilliantly opportunistic.'

The passion

Armed with the message, thanks to the focus groups, and with the map, courtesy of intensive polling in target seats, David Cameron went into battle. He toured the country, repeatedly making visits to the south-west, often with other Cabinet ministers, invariably supported by troops from Grant Shapps's Team 2015. Famously, he took the sleeper train from London and held a rally in a cowshed in north Cornwall.

But because Crosby refused to allow any media briefing about the 'process' of the campaign, and because the public opinion polls were so at odds with the detailed (and secret) seat-by-seat surveys he was producing, many Tory supporters felt deflated. Ministers and MPs demanded that Cameron up his game, donors called for more passion and a greater sense of a positive vision, critics said the endless focus on the economic plan was boring and not working.

Lynton Crosby realised Cameron's diffident demeanour had become a problem. He knew that in fact the Prime Minister cared deeply and was putting in the hours. But rather than try to deny that there was an issue, he told Cameron to accept the demands for more passion and use the 'oxygen' the story was giving the Tories in the media to make their case to voters again. Crosby was not alone in his view. Andrew Feldman told his old college friend to 'do a Rocky' and show his passion.[118] The two men led a delegation of the most senior strategists and aides, who went to see Cameron at what was his darkest moment of the campaign. According to one version of events, Crosby told the Prime Minister: 'For God's sake, show some guts and passion or you are going to lose.' The delegation told him: 'You need to demonstrate that you care.' One figure closely involved in the campaign recalls: 'Andrew, Lynton and a few others went to see the PM and really picked him up. They got him back focused again.'

The message itself, however, did not change. In speeches and interviews that the Prime Minister gave from 26 April onwards, the election was still a choice between the Conservatives' economic competence and the chaos of a government led by Miliband in combination with the SNP and any number of others. But this time, with feeling. 'I'm feeling bloody lively,' Cameron declared.

Of course, Cameron's new passionate style was tested in focus groups and found to have gone down well with voters. One senior Tory says: 'We stepped it up and showed the passion. The polling we did after that showed people liked it because they could see, "Well, Cameron really cares," and they thought, "It must be important."'[119] Crosby's team also performed detailed analysis of publicly available polls. They found that swing voters tempted by UKIP were particularly susceptible to warnings that voting for Nigel Farage's 'people's army' would allow Miliband to do a deal with the SNP in the event of a hung parliament.

Iain Duncan Smith, the Work and Pensions Secretary, had been among the senior figures to report back to Crosby that the campaign message about the risks of the SNP dictating terms to a weak Miliband administration was cutting through on the doorstep. Duncan Smith described this issue as the only genuinely 'rough-edged' question of the entire campaign. He was also clear, however, that he wanted Cameron to use the final leaders' TV programme as a chance to show some passion.[120]

One week from polling day, Cameron was due on a special edition of the BBC's *Question Time*, in which first he, then Miliband and Nick Clegg, would take questions from the audience. It was an occasion that senior Tories felt could go badly wrong. They were especially anxious about the BBC's *Question Time* audience, which was usually a highly knowledgeable, spiky group of politically engaged individuals. Duncan Smith warned the BBC they must be 'careful about their audience' and ensure they represent a proper cross-section of society, and told David Dimbleby not to 'over-interrupt'.[121]

But, as with the previous leaders' TV shows, the most important thing was for Cameron to be prepared. 'We worked unbelievably hard with him on that debate,' says one senior figure who was closely involved in making sure the PM focused on the key messages and how they would be communicated: 'Competence versus chaos, they spent too much money, having The [Liam Byrne] Note out there, the influence of the SNP on Labour.' Navigating hostile members of the BBC audience effectively and politely, without being thrown off course, was also essential. 'You had to be able to take on and argue reasonably with people who didn't share your view.'

In the days before the programme, Cameron's team assembled another rehearsal room to put the Prime Minister through his paces. A group of senior staff from CCHQ joined members of Cameron's No. 10 team to form the mock audience for the rehearsal. In all, about twelve people were sitting in seats in front of Cameron, throwing awkward questions at him, and the occasional angry heckle. One of those present says: 'We tried to come up with some difficult questions. People took on roles, saying, "I'm Dave, I'm forty-two, I'm a truck driver"... Then someone shouted at him, "Answer the question!"'

Question Time

Just after 8 p.m. on Thursday 30 April, 4.3 million people turned on their televisions to watch David Cameron skip up the steps onto the *Question Time* stage in Leeds Town Hall, give a brisk nod and a smile to the host, David Dimbleby, and take his seat. The ninety-minute programme gave Cameron, Miliband and Clegg half an hour each to make their cases. It was the final and most dramatic of the televised leaders' programmes.

As the applause died down, Cameron was immediately put on the spot about his plans to cut benefits. Jenny Johnson, the first person to ask a question, challenged him to put to bed the notion that he wanted to cut child benefit and child tax credits if re-elected. 'Thank you, Jenny, for that question – no, I don't want to do that,' Cameron began. Taken literally, his answer was a refusal to deny that he wanted to cut family support. Dimbleby picked up on it, eventually forcing the Tory leader to promise these benefits would not fall. It was a misstep from which Cameron quickly recovered, with the aid of what Ed Miliband called his 'regular prop'.

Six minutes into the show, the left-handed PM reached inside his right jacket pocket and took out the infamous letter from Liam Byrne. 'I bring this with me everywhere,' he told the audience as he unfolded The Note. 'Look. There it is. "Dear Chief Secretary, I'm afraid there is no money." That is the situation I inherited.' Throughout his half-hour session, Cameron was crisp in his answers, focused on the key messages – and apparently passionate about the choice facing Britain between a competent Tory plan for the future and the chaos of Labour propped up by the SNP. Using all the reserves of charm that he could summon, he chose to disagree respectfully and good-humouredly with the more hostile of his interrogators. It was an assured performance, easily the best of Cameron's campaign.

Why did voters not trust him with the NHS? He said he could only tell them what he believed, and recalled how his disabled son Ivan – who died in 2009 – had received 'the most fantastic care, support and I would say love from those people in the NHS' during the days and nights the family spent in hospitals.

Inside the green room backstage at Leeds Town Hall, George Osborne, Craig Oliver and Alan Sendorek, the No. 10 head of political press, were among those who had been watching the live feed. Lynton Crosby watched from his room at the nearby Malmaison hotel. He was keen to be close at hand but did not want to attract the inevitable attentions of the political journalists covering the event by turning up at the studio. 'Everyone was a little bit nervous. You're never sure what the questions are going to be,' a member of the Tory team recalls. Throughout the half-hour, Oliver, who had directed Cameron's rehearsals and prepared him to put on the show of his life, knew it was working and that the PM was scoring heavily. In the spin room, journalists sent to cover the event watched Cameron in near silence, surrounded by spin doctors and senior MPs from all three parties (who would all give their interpretations of how their side had 'won' afterwards).

The final subject was the one that had obsessed reporters and party hacks at Westminster for the entire campaign: what will Cameron do when – and to the political classes it was 'when', rather than 'if' – voters deliver another hung parliament? Which of his policies would he trade away in talks with Nick Clegg? Cameron laughed off the question, saying:

> We have got seven days to go and I'm going to fight, everything I've got, those next seven days to get an overall majority. The trouble with coalition – you have got a great manifesto, you don't quite win the election, you go into a dark room with Nick Clegg or someone else and you start giving away some of the things that were in your programme. I don't want to do that.

He said coalition was the right decision in 2010 but that he did not want to 'barter away' his promises this time and believed that the Tories could 'go one better' and win outright.

It was clear, however, that a coalition was still on his horizon.

> People know with me, if we fall short, I will do the right thing for the country. I did last time. I would again. But I would plead with people, with seven days to go – particularly when you're faced with the alternative of a Labour government backed by the SNP, people who don't even want our country to succeed or even exist – when that is the alternative, put your trust in twenty-three more seats for the Conservatives and we can have a very strong, and very clear, government.

With that, the Conservative leader smiled, waved, buttoned his jacket and strode off the stage.

Cameron marched into the green room to cheering and applause from his team. He punched the air, grinning widely, delighted that after all their hard work, when it counted, he had 'nailed it'.[122]

'He came through the door and I suppose you would describe it as a fist pump. He knew he had done well. He had done very well,' one insider recalls. Cameron was so pleased that he headed out to dinner with Samantha, and did not wait to watch Miliband or Clegg. At the Malmaison hotel, where the team were based, Cameron ordered several bottles of red wine to celebrate with Osborne, Samantha, Crosby and the rest of the team, when they turned up later. 'It was a tough audience but they were pretty representative,' Cameron told them. 'It was just great to see real people getting a say.' The PM was 'buoyed up' by the event and delighted with his success. 'We had a very jolly evening,' one of those present recalls.[123]

For Ed Miliband, however, the wine was left unopened. His first question, from Elizabeth Moody, could have been written by David Cameron. 'Good evening, Mr Miliband,' she began. 'Five years ago, the outgoing Labour Treasury minister left a message: "There's no money left." How can we trust the Labour Party with the UK economy?' The next question was even worse. Catherine Shuttleworth, a 48-year-old marketing company chief executive employing seventy-six people in Leeds, told the Labour leader:

> Going back to the letter, that you called a prop. I run
> a business here in Leeds. The last five years have been

really hard work, but we have got a plan now and the economy is improving. What worries me is you are about to put Ed Balls back in as Chancellor and he called that letter a joke. Now let me tell you, running a business the last few years is anything but a joke, and if that's the way your party wants to treat the economy, how can we trust you?

Miliband said he would cut taxes for businesses like Miss Shuttleworth's. But she said she was not satisfied. 'That wasn't the question I asked you,' she told Miliband. 'Why on earth should I trust a Chancellor who thinks that a letter like that was a joke? If he worked in the corporate world he would have been fired and he would not be allowed back to do that job.'

After a friendly question about abolishing the non-domicile tax status, a man asked Miliband another question on the economy. 'I've just got a really simple question. Do you accept that when Labour was last in power, it overspent?' In the eyes of his own team, Miliband's blunt answer went some way towards sealing his fate. 'No, I don't, and I know you may not agree with that,' the Labour leader said, to gasps from the audience. 'Let me tell you – because there are schools that have been rebuilt in our country; there are hospitals that were rebuilt; there were Sure Start [children's] centres that were rebuilt, which would not have happened; and so, look, I don't agree with that.'

The Labour team had prepared Miliband for such a question. It was an obvious line of attack from Tory supporters in the audience. But unlike the near-perfect performance from Cameron, Miliband failed to deliver the nuanced and carefully phrased answer that he and his team had planned.

It became a defining moment. Under immense pressure, the Labour leader – who had performed better than expected until this point – fluffed his lines. As he stepped off the *Question Time* stage at the end of his half-hour, Miliband stumbled. It was a moment that seemed to symbolise the trajectory of his campaign.

In the final week before polling day, the Conservatives relentlessly hammered home their message in the key marginal seats. A vote for anyone else would let Ed Miliband into No. 10 on the coat-tails of Alex Salmond, while Nicola Sturgeon pulled the strings from Edinburgh. To Lynton Crosby, triggering voters' fears over the risk of a spineless Labour government dominated by the SNP was only ever what one source describes as 'the pinprick that lances the boil'; a poultice must be applied in preparation for the procedure.[124] The real issue, the Tories maintain, was simply that Miliband was a weak leader who could not stand up for Britain's interests.

Lynton Crosby says:

> Miliband's weakness was a fundamental problem for Labour. He was perceived as weak and we needed to frame him in that way and keep framing him in that way. In an uncertain world, both economically and in national and international security, weakness in your leader could be a real threat. We had to make his weakness have consequences.[125]

Yet this is not how it seemed at the time, and it is not how it is seen by many on both the Tory side and in the Labour, Lib Dem and UKIP election teams. To the Tories' opponents, the message contained troubling overtones of English nationalism, and stirred up anti-Scots feelings among voters south of the border.

When it seemed to some anxious Tories to be almost too late, David Cameron had found his passion, or at least a semblance of fire for the cameras. More importantly, thanks to Crosby's meticulous research, the Conservatives had found a question that would stir the passions of their voters.

CHAPTER 9

TWO NATIONS

Scotland

'It was like a cult. There was no appeal to reason. People would physically put their hands up in front of you while you were speaking and say, 'No, no, no, no, no. This is not rational political debate.'[126]

The experience of one shadow Cabinet minister who was deployed to Scotland to campaign for Labour was widely shared. The surge in popularity of the Scottish National Party, and its new leader, Nicola Sturgeon, rendered traditional politics redundant. The methods of persuasion candidates would normally use – new policies, doorstep conversations, rallies and leafleting – were hopelessly inadequate. 'A kind of mass hysteria took hold,' the shadow minister says.[127]

At times, however, the clashes between Scottish Nationalist supporters and candidates campaigning for the other parties – notably Labour and the Liberal Democrats – bordered on violent. 'It was extraordinary. In Glasgow, a few days before the election, it was physically hostile,' the same senior Labour MP recalls. 'At one point I thought the person I was canvassing for was going to get punched – and I was not the only person who had that experience.' According to a Labour aide, who campaigned in Scotland with Miliband, the SNP supporters' behaviour 'had gone way past the stage of rationality and logic'. The aide says: 'It was certainly as nasty as the miners' strike, nastier than fox-hunting demonstrations and as bad as the Poll Tax demonstrations.'[128] The violence in Scotland was not exclusive to pro-independence supporters. In one incident during the referendum campaign, police arrested a group of Unionists after they allegedly attacked campaigners handing out leaflets outside a football ground in Edinburgh. Alex Salmond himself reported that he had been the target of a 'road rage' incident in which a Unionist chased him in his car while waving a 'No' sign. Many of the news reports during the referendum, however, focused on pro-independence campaigners attacking those who supported the Union.

On Thursday 30 October 2014, Ed Miliband travelled to Glasgow for Scottish Labour's gala dinner, held at the Grand Central Hotel near to the city's famous Central Station. Outside the event, 200 pro-independence protesters, some wielding devil's forks and others dressed as the Grim Reaper with scythes, held aloft placards that said 'Taxi for Labour' and 'Labour – the Judas party. Enjoy your last supper.' Miliband successfully evaded the protesters, who were kept in order by a line of police as they shouted 'Red Tories Out'. Inside, however, it was a different story. One Labour figure who attended the event recalls: 'Protesters had gone to the lengths of booking themselves into the hotel. They tried to get into the room where the dinner was taking place to disrupt it. There were scuffles outside.'[129]

In his speech at the dinner, Miliband promised to 'fight with every fibre of my being' to show the people of Scotland that Labour could help them to change their country. 'Over its history we have seen the Scottish Labour Party fight for the values our movement holds dear.' Turning to the election battle ahead, he said: 'We face a tough fight, but no tougher than the fights we have faced in the past.' What must at the time have seemed to be a pragmatic assessment of Labour's chances would prove to be a wishful fantasy.

On 4 May, three days before the polls opened, a rally attended by Scottish Labour leader Jim Murphy and the Labour-supporting comedian Eddie Izzard had to be abandoned after the pair were jostled and verbally abused by protesters. Murphy tried to make himself heard, while protesters played music from a sound system and chanted 'Red Tories Out' through a loudhailer. Murphy condemned what he called 'the ugly face of aggressive nationalism' on display that day. Sturgeon insisted the disruption was nothing to do with her party but later suspended two members of the SNP after what she called the 'disgraceful' incident.

Similar scenes had occurred during the referendum campaign, with Murphy forced to halt his street-by-street rally tour of Scotland on police advice after pro-independence campaigners hurled eggs at him. Murphy said he had been called a 'traitor', 'terrorist', 'quisling' and an apologist for paedophilia as well as being physically intimidated on more than one occasion, adding that he was considering police charges. One Labour source who witnessed the scenes recalls: 'The aggression crossed the line of legality and certainly of acceptability.'[130]

On 7 May, Labour was annihilated in Scotland. This, more than any other single factor, determined the disastrous outcome of the election for Ed Miliband. The tally of forty-one

seats that Gordon Brown had won in Scotland in 2010 fell to just one. The SNP won fifty-six of the fifty-nine seats, with 50 per cent of the vote. Scotland, for decades Labour's heartland, became virtually a one-party state, in terms of how its voters were represented at Westminster, at least. 'Nobody thought Scotland would be as bad as it was for us,' a senior figure says. 'We knew we would lose a lot of seats but we never thought we would lose everything to the SNP.'

Miliband's closest colleagues now insist there was nothing they could have done to avoid the rout. It is certainly true that by the time the short campaign began at the end of March, it was far too late. Sturgeon was enjoying a remarkable honeymoon – she would even win praise and support in England during the TV debates – and the SNP had reached an astonishing high in the polls, at one point rating 54 per cent. Yet it was not the charismatic, fresh face of Sturgeon, who was mobbed wherever she went, that carried the day for the SNP. It was, paradoxically, and in a trend that nobody foresaw, the Yes campaign's clear defeat in the Scottish independence referendum of September 2014. For this, at the very least, Labour was culpable.

Bob Roberts, Miliband's former communications chief, is clear that the rise of the SNP was the 'overwhelming factor' behind the outcome of the general election. 'There was a political and cultural revolution in Scotland, which neither the Labour Party nor Ed Miliband could do anything about,' he says. Roberts recalls hearing of plans to open a nightclub in Glasgow that was named '45' in honour of the share of the vote achieved by the pro-independence Yes campaign. 'When people start going to nightclubs on the basis of their political allegiances, you know there has been a huge cultural shift,' Roberts says. 'That cultural shift was a big, big thing.' As

Sturgeon put it in a TV interview with the BBC's *Panorama* in June 2015: 'Post-referendum, there had been a feeling that Scotland had come alive ... people did not want to let that go.'

The referendum campaign divided Scotland in a way that – again – few at Westminster had anticipated when David Cameron signed a deal with Alex Salmond, then the Scottish First Minister, to hold a 'once-in-a-generation' decisive vote. Nor did Cameron expect that by September 2014 the outcome would be so precarious that he would have to weigh up the very real prospect of going down in history as the Prime Minister who lost Scotland.

In the end, Scotland voted to stay in the United Kingdom by 55 per cent to 45 per cent. But many in Miliband's team are convinced that Labour sacrificed itself for the cause of keeping the UK together. A decision was taken, early in the referendum campaign, for Labour to join forces with Tory and Lib Dem opponents of independence to form a single No group. Better Together, as the No campaign was called, had many detractors and many evident faults, not the least of which was division between the parties, and within Labour, especially, over tactics. Headed by the former Labour Chancellor, Alistair Darling, Better Together's 'No thanks' message needed a last-minute intervention from Gordon Brown to deliver victory.

For Labour, though, the alliance with the pro-Union Tories in particular spelled disaster. 'There was a catastrophic mistake made during the Scottish referendum to campaign alongside the Conservatives,' Roberts says.

> Roughly half of the Labour supporters wanted to vote
> Yes in the referendum. We put ourselves in a position
> where we were seen as their opponents and as allies of
> the Conservatives. That is a tough position to recover

from in the eight months between the referendum and
the general election.

It proved to be not just tough, but impossible. 'Those people
were very angry towards us, for aligning ourselves with the
Conservatives. We gave the impression of being part of
a Westminster elite working alongside the Conservatives
and the Liberal Democrats – because we *were* working
alongside the Conservatives and the Liberal Democrats,'
Roberts says.

The political mistake for Labour was an honest one that
arose because those running the No campaign were focused
on the fight to keep the Union together, rather than on the
election. Nobody in Miliband's team spotted the danger. But
it was clearly 'not wise' to join a single No campaign with
the Tories, Roberts believes. 'There was a lot of emotion,
there was a lot of heat in that referendum campaign,' he says.

> The Labour Party was seen as the representative of
> the established position, and the reason is, there was
> a certain amount of truth in it. We paid a heavy price
> in terms of saving the Union. There was a real risk
> that the referendum campaign could have gone the
> opposite way. I have no doubt we were right to throw
> everything at it in the last three weeks of that campaign
> because there was a genuine danger of the break-up of
> the United Kingdom. In saving the United Kingdom,
> we did a lot of damage to our prospects of forming the
> next government.

Other Labour figures suspect that Cameron always sensed
when he agreed to a referendum that it was largely risk-free

for his party, and that any downside would affect Labour rather than the Tories. If Scotland had voted for independence, the Prime Minister would almost certainly have resigned, despite his protestations to the contrary before the vote, but this seemed a remote prospect until very late in the referendum campaign. One shadow minister says:

> When he agreed to the referendum, Cameron can't have known it would result in this enormous SNP surge that wiped us out. But he probably felt that any downside risk was really going to be ours, not his. He probably instinctively knew we had the most to lose. If Scotland had voted Yes to independence, it would have destroyed us. In the end, Scotland voted No and it destroyed us anyway.[131]

For the SNP, however, the referendum campaign changed Scottish politics and gave the party its historic opportunity at the election. With Labour arm-in-arm with the Tories during the independence referendum, the SNP seemed like the only real counterweight to Cameron at Westminster. A senior figure in the SNP's election campaign says:

> It was the unique circumstances after the referendum which created the potential for the SNP to do well in the election... At previous elections, the SNP never passed the relevance test because the SNP leader could never be UK Prime Minister. But, because there was a view that the election was likely to result in a hung parliament, the SNP could realistically have a significant influence and be a strong voice for Scotland at Westminster.[132]

The senior SNP figure says Scottish voters saw the way Labour politicians literally cuddled up to Tories during the referendum campaign and recoiled.

> It was as if Labour thought the referendum would stop and everything would magically go back to normal. There are so many pictures of Labour people literally with their arms around Tories, hugging them on referendum night, it was politically disastrous. They were not holding their noses and embracing the Tories, they were just embracing. They seemed to be loving it. That led a lot of people in Scotland to say, 'That's not the sort of party I thought Labour were.'

England

Spring on the north Kent coast. Bright afternoon sunshine caught the windscreens of a handful of cars parked outside the Racing Greyhound pub in Ramsgate. Then a sea mist rolled inland, filling the air with a damp, eerie chill, dimming the daylight. Nigel Farage was undeterred. After a customary pint of ale for refreshment, he began another session of knocking on doors, walking the streets of the constituency he hoped would choose to send him to Parliament.

During the course of his sometimes lonely enterprise, Farage found himself the target of vicious personal abuse from his opponents, and from angry locals who objected to his campaign. He was also alone among the party leaders in spending large amounts of time pounding the pavements, trying to win over voters, one by one. He started with those who were not normally voters at all. In Dumpton Park, a run-down district of Ramsgate, residents told him they had never seen a politician before. 'No one wants to know people like us,' one young mother told him, clutching a baby in her arms, litter strewn about the grass. 'Well, I do,' came the UKIP leader's response. 'Oh my God, I'm well voting for you,' she promised. Another local, a man on his way to the off-licence, tried to buy Farage a drink.[133]

David Cameron was worried. In the months leading up to the election, the Conservatives had lost two MPs in defections – followed by costly by-elections – to UKIP. First Douglas Carswell, the MP for Clacton, defected and won the seat for UKIP in October 2014. Then Mark Reckless, the MP for Rochester and Strood, repeated the feat at his by-election a month later. The defections drove the narrative of UKIP's rise at the Tories' expense. At the time of the Rochester by-election in late November, six months before the general election, UKIP was at its high point in the opinion polls, on 18–20 per cent.

As the election approached, the Conservatives' internal polling in South Thanet, where Nigel Farage was standing, painted a grim picture for the Tories. Several public polls put the Tories behind Farage. One poll for UKIP, which was leaked on 22 April, showed him nine points ahead of the Conservative candidate, Craig Mackinlay.

One senior Tory recalls:

> Farage's ratings were off the scale with the voter types that we were having to worry about. We also did a couple of focus groups in Thanet and they were pretty worrying as well. All the Tories in the groups thought it was perfectly safe to vote for Farage because he was clearly going to vote with the Tories and not Labour in the Commons. Therefore, they thought you could have

a Tory government and Farage locally. There was this
feeling that UKIP were making the Tories 'more Tory'.

Lynton Crosby called in Nick Timothy, Theresa May's
special adviser, who had experience of working on successful
by-election campaigns before the 2010 election. He was sent
to take charge of the party's flagging campaign to stop Farage
in Thanet, where Henry Macrory, the party's former press
chief, and Marion Little, from CCHQ's campaign team, were
already on the ground. The CCHQ reinforcements found a
campaign in Thanet devoid of effective messages, with no
strategy for turning the tide. However, the good news was
that the activists in the seat had worked remarkably hard, and
were committed to the cause, while the local party chairman
was also regarded as a key asset.

Crosby threw everything he had at the 'stop Farage'
campaign. A succession of Cabinet ministers, including
William Hague, Liz Truss, George Osborne, Theresa May,
Iain Duncan Smith and others made repeated visits to South
Thanet. A permanent brigade of Grant Shapps's Team 2015
mobile army was stationed in the constituency. And a series
of promises from figures as senior as the Chancellor were
thrown at the voters' most pressing local concerns – including
a new five-point plan to save the local Manston airport,
and the offer of cash for regenerating Ramsgate through a
beefed-up coastal communities fund. The plan helped the
Tories to dominate local newspaper coverage.

'These visits were timed the right way and at the right point
in the week. Every week we won the coverage in the local
papers because we had better visits, from more interesting
people with things to say,' one of those who worked on
the campaign says. The Tories took out vast newspaper

advertisements, including 'wraps' around the front and back covers. 'Our strategy was take ownership of the most important local issues in Thanet, which were Manston airport and then hyper-local issues like traffic in Sandwich and regenerating Ramsgate.'

The Conservatives also concluded it was critical to narrow the choice in voters' minds to a shoot-out between Farage and the Conservative candidate, Craig Mackinlay. Swing voters who were tempted by Farage hated the idea of a Labour government more than anything, according to the Tory campaign's internal evidence. This, the Conservatives realised, would be the key question to raise on the doorstep. They set about trying to toxify Farage as an individual and make him seem dangerous, with warnings that 'if you vote Farage, you could let Labour in'.

One new strand of the Tory campaign targeted Farage in his role as UKIP's leader, which required him to campaign around the country. Their question to the voters of Thanet was 'Where's Nigel?' The message was simply that he was not in the local area working hard for their votes. 'They panicked about the "Where's Nigel?" thing, and brought him back to Thanet much sooner,' one Tory campaigner says.

On a typical day in the campaign, Farage would get up around 6 a.m. and head to a nearby hotel for a breakfast of kippers. His close adviser Raheem Kassam had moved into Farage's flat for the final weeks of the election after the Tories sent reinforcements to South Thanet, and would join him for the meal. After breakfast, the pair would go to UKIP's office and make a plan for the day, which usually involved a lot of street walking and door knocking. 'Then we'd maybe hit a pub for lunch. Then more walkabouts and more canvassing. Then another pint around five o'clock, go out and do more evening canvassing. Then around nine we'd go to The Smugglers [pub] for dinner or we'd go to La Magnolia and have a nice civilised meal.'[134]

Overlooking Ramsgate's Royal Harbour, La Magnolia serves Italian meals of local fish and grilled meats, as well as the staples of pizza and pasta. An added twist of luxury to the ingredients – which include smoked mozzarella and black truffle – and an attractive seafront location made La Magnolia a popular choice for the political classes who were in town for the election. It was a particular favourite haunt for Nigel Farage and his team, and was the place where many a day's campaigning would end and night's carousing begin. Inside, the plain wooden tables are set close enough together to make conversations in the dining area potentially awkward.

On one otherwise unexceptional evening, Farage, his election strategist, Chris Bruni-Lowe, and a number of other UKIP team members were enjoying a meal and relaxing over a few drinks – 'or maybe more than a few, after a long day', one of those present recalls. At a table across the room sat the rival Conservative team, including Henry Macrory and Nick Timothy. Farage spotted the table of Tories and, ever the bon viveur, picked up his glass and wandered over to engage them in conversation.

'So this is what I'm up against, is it?' the UKIP leader joked, in an attempt to break the ice. But there was no sign of a thaw. The table of Conservatives put down their forks and turned to Farage, fixing him with a hard stare. 'We all just kind of looked at him and didn't really say anything. After a while he went away,' one of the Tories recalls. Another source says the Conservatives muttered abuse at Farage and told him he was 'splitting the right' and risked allowing Labour to win. Farage quickly concluded his attempt to socialise with the enemy would be fruitless and so he left. 'Well, if they want to be rude, fuck 'em,' he thought as he returned to his table and sat back down.

The coolness from the Conservatives at La Magnolia is more than a sign of their disdain for the upstart leader of the self-styled 'people's army'. It is a measure of how seriously they were taking their mission to stop Farage, and the kind of focus Crosby required of his team.

The ice queen

The televised leaders' debates were an opportunity for less established parties such as UKIP to gain valuable exposure, showing their wares to a prime-time audience of millions. This is precisely why the Conservatives were determined to keep David Cameron out of as many debates as possible and ensure that the one genuine debate in which he took part was so chaotic as to be almost unwatchable. The so-called 'seven-way' debate on 2 April 2015, featuring the leaders of seven political parties, diluted the impact of all the participants, meaning that none of the underdogs could have their day at the Prime Minister's expense.

Yet Nigel Farage did his best to seize the initiative. In the night's most outrage-provoking remark, he claimed health tourism was costing the NHS up to £25,000 a year per patient for foreign HIV sufferers who travelled to Britain for free treatment. Patients born abroad account for 60 per cent of HIV diagnoses, Farage said. Leanne Wood, Plaid Cymru's leader, and Nicola Sturgeon, the Scottish National Party leader, condemned Farage and said he should be ashamed of himself. It caused a row, created news and inserted Farage into the national debate at a time when UKIP's poll ratings were fading. Senior Tories were infuriated by what they saw as a blatant shock tactic to hijack the news agenda.

Yet Osborne was only too happy to talk up Nicola Sturgeon's performance. 'Ed Miliband as a leader of the left was completely overshadowed by Nicola Sturgeon in that debate,' the Chancellor said. 'That just shows you who would be running the government in a Labour–SNP alliance of some kind. It would be Alex Salmond and Nicola Sturgeon.' On a visit to Nottinghamshire, on the morning after the debate, Osborne said the party was seeing 'a lot of concern locally about the possibility of a Labour–SNP deal. The country is waking up to the danger of this unholy alliance.'[135]

During the debate itself, David Cameron sought to maintain a dignified, prime ministerial distance from the six other leaders, who were squabbling among themselves to his right. However, he used a deliberately provocative soundbite, playing on one of Miliband's key slogans, to unsettle the Labour leader and win private admiration from Nicola Sturgeon in the process. Six days before the debate, Ed Miliband had launched Labour's campaign with the mantra 'Britain can do better than this.' In his opening remarks, in the seven-way debate, Cameron said voters should stick with the economic plan that was working: 'Don't go back to square one – Britain can do so much better than that.' As he uttered the words, Sturgeon, standing beside him, turned to look at Cameron, raised her eyebrows and nodded her appreciation at his mischievous piece of messaging.[136]

Nigel Farage is convinced that David Cameron won his majority through sheer good fortune. 'Cameron got lucky. I have absolutely no doubt in my mind about that,' he says. 'Nobody could have predicted just how great the effect of the SNP was going to be. We started picking it up around 14 or 15 April. We saw it on the doorsteps.'[137]

Lynton Crosby's warnings of the risk that voting UKIP would allow Labour to sneak into power, paving the way for Nicola Sturgeon and Alex Salmond to dominate a weak Ed Miliband in Downing Street, were decisive, Farage says. The message resonated all the more loudly after the televised leaders' debates, in which Sturgeon comprehensively outshone Miliband, he adds. 'In the 'challengers' debate' [which excluded Cameron and Nick Clegg] it was so clear who was going to wear the trousers in that relationship,' Farage recalls. 'Poor old Ed didn't know where to go. He was up against the wall being pummelled and he didn't know what to say. I actually did feel a bit sorry for him.'

Farage says he encountered many voters who felt 'the Scottish tail has wagged the English dog in the most remarkable way' in recent times and were not prepared to allow Sturgeon to continue the pattern. Voters were 'utterly pissed off' with the Scots, saying, 'they're getting our money, they're being horrible about us', he says. 'It's almost your stereotypical London cab driver. There was, yes, some quite vehement anti-Scottish sentiment out there – and fear that with the Ice Queen controlling Mr Miliband, it would get worse not better. There was a sense of indignation.'

Lynton Crosby's private focus groups revealed a similar picture, leading him to believe that warning of the menace of the SNP was the key to convincing UKIP supporters to vote Conservative. The UKIP vote was always 'soft', according to the Tories' internal research, with many people who said they were planning to back Farage actually just disgruntled

Conservatives. Focus groups conducted during the campaign showed high levels of awareness of the threat of the SNP propping up a Labour government among UKIP voters. Participants in the sessions were spontaneously raising their concerns over the idea of Miliband requiring a deal with Sturgeon and Salmond in order to win power. The Tories' focus groups also found that Sturgeon was increasingly being seen as a strong leader, one who would dominate the weak Miliband in a power-sharing deal. UKIP voters in particular were worried that she would hold the country to ransom in order to pursue her agenda for Scotland. They were so concerned at this scenario that they were ready to think again about voting for Nigel Farage's party in order to try to keep the SNP and Ed Miliband out of power.[138]

As well as conducting their own private polling in target seats, and a daily tracker survey for the final month of the campaign, the Conservatives also conducted deep analysis of public opinion polls and surveys from polling firms, commissioned by the media. Public polling by YouGov told Crosby and his team that UKIP voters were the most susceptible to the message on the SNP. Those UKIP voters apparently hated the idea that Britain could end up with a minority Labour government that relied on Nicola Sturgeon's support to keep power. They gave this scenario a negative approval rating of -72 (9 per cent thought it would be a good thing, 81 thought it would be bad). The population as a whole was hardly delighted by the idea either, giving it a net approval rating of -43 per cent.

Further analysis of the YouGov figures suggested that the Tories should focus their fire on just 4 per cent of the electorate. These were people who were planning to vote UKIP but hated the idea of Labour doing a deal with the SNP more than they disliked the prospect of voting Conservative. The analysis found that 8 per cent of all voters in England and Wales thought that a hung parliament was likely, that Labour would do a deal with Sturgeon, and that such a deal was a bad thing. They also thought the Tories would be preferable to Labour in this situation, but were not planning to vote Conservative. Half of this group of 8 per cent said they were planning to vote UKIP.[139] It is hard to tell precisely whether this 'squeeze' message about the dangers of a Labour–SNP deal made the difference in South Thanet and other UKIP target seats. But UKIP's vote share fell from around 16 per cent in the New Year opinion polls to 13 per cent on election day.

Dirty tricks

Nigel Farage has become a target. He is regularly accompanied by personal bodyguards, paid for by the party rather than out of the public purse. His security detail have provided near constant company for the UKIP leader since an ugly incident in Scotland in 2013, followed by another shortly afterwards in Hove, at which he required police help to be escorted from a mob of violent protesters who had invaded a party meeting. In Thanet, a UKIP councillor was targeted with graffiti, while anti-UKIP action groups distributed leaflets and took out newspaper wrap-around advertisements claiming UKIP wanted to privatise the NHS.

Farage says he faced 'hatred' during the election.

> A woman in the high street screamed at me, 'You want to abort my baby.' I think the campaign against me was the most vicious that we've seen since Peter Tatchell all those

years ago in Bermondsey in 1983. It probably didn't
help. The kind of negativity against us wasn't normal
political discourse, it was a whole injection of things
that simply weren't true at all, and quite beastly really.

The UKIP leader did not appear the picture of health during
the campaign. His chief of staff, who resigned amid a vicious
internal party row after the election, disclosed that no one in
Farage's inner team had realised how unwell he was. The pair
regularly went to a steam room in an attempt to condition
Farage for the hot lights of the TV studios so that he would
not sweat so much in front of the cameras.[140] But Farage was
fighting a constant battle against chronic back pain, believed to
be a legacy of the plane crash that nearly killed him during the
2010 election. He went public with his condition on 25 April,
and scaled back his schedule for the rest of the campaign.

In the final week, UKIP's canvassing team believed he
was on course to win South Thanet. Then, they detected a
slight softening in their support, as voters raised their fears
about Ed Miliband doing a deal with Nicola Sturgeon. About
8,000 people in the constituency said they were likely to
vote for Farage or could be persuaded to do so, according
to the party's campaign team. 'In order for Nigel to win
the seat we needed around 40 per cent of those undecided
voters in South Thanet to vote for us,' one UKIP strategist
says. 'At about 3 p.m. on polling day we rang them and we
were on about 18 per cent. We knew we had lost.' Despite
having told canvassers just a few days previously that they
were supporting UKIP, these voters had turned. 'They said
they just couldn't let Miliband and "that Scottish woman"
into Downing Street. At the final moment, people hovered
and thought, "No."' UKIP's campaign ran into the same

phenomenon in the three-way marginal seat of Thurrock, where the party's candidate, Tim Aker, finished third behind Labour. The Tories held the constituency by just 536 votes.

After hoping to finish with more than ten seats, and in fact returning with just one MP, the Tory defector Douglas Carswell (in a surprisingly close fight in Clacton), Farage could have been disappointed. He failed to win South Thanet and duly announced his intention to resign. The party's national executive refused to accept his resignation, however, realising that he represented their most valuable asset, and persuaded him to stay.

After a summer of reflection, Farage insists that he would not have done anything differently in the campaign. UKIP won almost four million votes across the country and finished second in 120 constituencies. If proportional representation had been in operation at the general election, UKIP would have eighty-two seats in the Commons, as many as the SNP and the Lib Dems combined.[141]

Looking back, Farage says,

> If you had said to me on 1 January that there is going to be a dramatic swing towards the Conservatives, that they are going to form a majority government because of the SNP factor, and despite that UKIP would still get four million votes, apart from laughing very loudly, I would have bitten your bloody arm off. From our perspective in the longer term, if we add up all the people who voted for us this year and in 2014, it's about six million people. That's very interesting.

He says he was 'demonised' after warning about the impact of health tourism on the NHS but UKIP is the most trusted party to deal with the immigration crisis, which escalated dramatically after the election as tens of thousands of migrants crossed the Mediterranean from Libya to Europe. This puts UKIP in a strong position for the future, he says.

> Given that we lost half our voters from [the European elections in] 2014, the fact that we still got 13 per cent was remarkable. What it showed was that while we were losing Conservatives to the SNP threat from mid-April, we were replacing that with a lot of people who were either Labour or who had never voted in their lives. Most experts thought we would melt away to about 8 per cent. Very few gave us more than that. There are some disenchanted voters out there. There are voters who voted UKIP who don't see much result from it, so in the short term they are going to be somewhat neutral – sort of 'sod politics'. But the issues on which we did fight are now coming back to the fore in a very big way and as far as the EU referendum is concerned, we think UKIP is the key to the grassroots campaign in the country.

Farage also argues that the rise of the SNP in Scotland is part of a wider pattern in which national identities feature more prominently in people's lives. 'I think naturally devolution has led to a greater sense of identities of all parts of the UK,' he says.

> Certainly, you see a lot more English flags flying now than you did twenty years ago. There are a lot more people who call themselves English first and British second. Whether we regret it or not, it's the way that it is and it ain't going to change in a hurry, I don't think.

I just personally want to see the Scots given far more
fiscal autonomy. I want the Scottish Parliament taxing
the Scots – then attitudes will change quite markedly.

In their battle with UKIP, the Conservatives ran through every
available approach before finally finding one that worked.
They tried insulting them as 'fruitcakes, loonies and closet
racists'. They tried patronising them, telling UKIP voters it was
time to 'come home'. They tried matching UKIP's Eurosceptic
agenda, promising a referendum on EU membership and a
crackdown on immigration. Finally, they turned to the root
motive for many of UKIP's supporters in marginal English
seats: a deeply held sense of national identity and a fear that
it was under threat from a powerful foreigner from the north.
Crosby and Cameron beat Farage by turning UKIP's most
potent weapon on itself.

CHAPTER 10

LABOUR PAINS

Pig's ear

Ed Miliband woke early on the morning of 21 May 2014. It was the final day of campaigning before voters went to the polls to elect hundreds of local councillors and seventy-three members of the European Parliament, representing every region of the UK.

All the main political parties were using the European elections to 'stress test' their campaign machines for the general election due to be held a year later. For Labour strategists, it was a valuable opportunity to put their own leader to the test. A major national set of elections, important in themselves, provided Labour aides with the chance to hold a 'dress rehearsal' to prepare Miliband for his first general election as a candidate for Prime Minister. His opponents – David Cameron, Nick Clegg and Nigel Farage – had all been through the 2010 election as party leaders and knew how gruelling the final run into polling day would be.[142]

With this in mind, Miliband's team devised a marathon for his final twenty-four hours of the European election campaign. It involved ten visits on a last-day tour between London and his constituency of Doncaster, where he was to vote, starting, shortly after dawn, at the New Covent Garden flower market in south London. The market was chosen for the simple reason that it was one of the few photogenic venues open at the ungodly hour of 6.30 a.m.

But Miliband's team had not properly planned the first visit of the day and had to improvise. They decided the Labour leader would visit the market café before buying a bunch of flowers for his wife Justine. 'It hadn't been properly recced,' one of Miliband's close aides recalls. 'Ed was chatting to the owner of the café. He said, "Do you want a bacon sandwich?" So he ordered a bacon sandwich.'[143] The café owner, Tony Foufas, made his star customer a handsome breakfast, with doorstep-sized slices of toasted white bread, lashings of butter and ketchup squirted out from a plastic Heinz bottle. As Miliband clutched his paper plate and grinned for the *Evening Standard*'s photographer, the danger of what was about to unfold gripped the Labour leader's press team.

Miliband's aides attempted to intervene to take the sandwich from him but were unable to persuade him to part with it. One member of the team urged the party leader to take the food to a table and eat it. Everyone who worked closely with him knew Miliband was 'not a morning person'. Getting between a potentially grumpy politician and his breakfast was therefore equally as perilous as allowing him to be photographed eating. 'I think he wanted some food,' one of those present observes.

> It was not a set-up. We didn't say, 'You've got to eat a bacon sandwich on TV now.' He's just not very good in the morning. He goes to bed late, is up late working, reading and calling people. When he wakes up, he's a

bit grumpy. So he got this sandwich. He wanted to eat
it. He ate it. He looked like a fool.[144]

Despite the best efforts of Miliband's press team to keep the
media away from their boss while he ate, some dismally bad
photographs were taken of the Labour leader hunched over
a table, grappling with his chewy breakfast. The pictures
that appeared in that afternoon's edition of the *Standard*
showed precisely why the first rule in every political press
officer's handbook is never to allow their candidate to be
photographed while eating. The *Standard* published a cruel
gallery on its website featuring thirteen photographs of
Miliband's 'battle' with his snack. The images immediately
became a source of mockery on the internet. Other news
websites picked up the theme and displayed the pictures
prominently, while Twitter users had seemingly endless fun
adapting the image of Miliband, mid-bite, with his half-
closed eyes. He was superimposed onto Leonardo da Vinci's
'The Last Supper', and joined Meg Ryan and Billy Crystal
at the table as she faked an orgasm in the film *When Harry
Met Sally*.

   However trivial such a mistake might appear, the Labour
leader's opponents relentlessly returned to the episode and
used it as an example of how hapless he was and how hopeless
he would be if he were put in charge of the country. On
Wednesday 6 May 2015, the day before the general election,
The Sun ran a close-up of the image of Miliband with the
sandwich and the same zombie-like stare in a brutal front
page. The caption said: 'This is the pig's ear Ed made of a
helpless sarnie. In forty-eight hours he could be doing the
same to Britain.' The main front-page headline was: 'SAVE
OUR BACON. Don't swallow his porkies and keep him OUT.'

After his attack on the Murdoch press in 2011 over phone hacking, Miliband was never going to win an endorsement from *The Sun*. But his former advisers and shadow Cabinet colleagues are clear that the bacon episode deepened the doubts that were already forming in the public's mind: here was a man who could not even eat a sandwich properly. Could we really elect him as Prime Minister? 'Voting is at its root a very basic decision: who do I think should be in charge?' one adviser says. 'Ninety-nine per cent of people who vote don't think about politics much at all, so they will take a few small examples that inform their thinking – it could be a bacon sandwich.'

The Conservatives' unexpected majority would not have been possible without a correspondingly disastrous election performance from their main opponents, Labour. It is easy to assume, looking back at the result, and on incidents such as the bacon sandwich fiasco, that Ed Miliband could never have won. But this is not how it seemed to members of his team, to experienced Westminster observers, or even to the Tories themselves. By most commentators' reckoning, Miliband had a good campaign. He improved his personal ratings during the six weeks to polling day and attracted the endorsement of a string of celebrities, as well as inspiring an unlikely following on the internet among teenage girls.

Yet the fatal flaws in Labour's strategy were there to be seen by anyone who cared to look – and the Conservatives were keener observers than most. Under Miliband's leadership, Labour's reputation for economic competence, badly wounded in the financial crisis, was never given the attention it needed to be capable of withstanding the scrutiny of an election contest.

A confused set of messages and policies, which never really registered with the electorate, led the party to take desperate measures late in the campaign, with the disastrous result of the infamous 'pledge stone'. Inside the party, there was a false confidence in Labour's campaign machine – especially its operation on the ground. Allied to this was a misguided desire to boast about the party's campaigning prowess in a way that Lynton Crosby would never have allowed. There were tensions within Miliband's senior team of advisers and a lack of clarity over who exactly was in charge of the party's election campaign. Those who worked most closely with him believe there was confusion, too, within the mind of Ed Miliband, as he struggled to reconcile his own competing priorities. Critically, these tensions within the leader and his team fuelled the public's doubts over Miliband's own leadership credentials. He was seen, as the Labour Party's own internal polling told him, as weak and awkward. His struggle to project himself as a credible Prime Minister through the lenses of the national media was ultimately fatal to his own hopes, and critical to the triumph of the Tories.

Deficit attention disorder

Ed Miliband has another reason to curse the Scottish independence referendum. While propelling the SNP towards its landslide in Scotland, the referendum was also indirectly responsible for another damaging blow to Miliband's hopes of gaining power. The result, declared on the morning of Friday 19 September, came just two days before Labour's party conference opened in Manchester, leaving hardly any time to prepare. The final conference before the election, this was a vital opportunity to build momentum, inspire and energise the party's activists and gain public attention with new policies. It was also the last opportunity for Ed Miliband to deliver a leader's speech and project himself as Britain's next Prime Minister. Instead, it collapsed into a farce that almost ended Miliband's leadership of the Labour Party.

In the last three weeks before the referendum, the pro-Union Better Together campaign was gripped by panic. It seemed, according to a succession of polls, that the vote was on a knife-edge and that the 300-year-old Union was on the point of breaking apart. 'A vast amount of Labour resources – including Ed himself and several key people – were despatched up to Scotland for three weeks,' one insider says. 'But these same people also had to put the key bits of conference planning together.'

There were two big announcements Labour wanted to make at conference. One was on raising the minimum wage to £8 an hour. The other was what insiders described as a 'complex' but 'comprehensive' plan to reinvest in NHS staff. The new 'Time to Care' fund would pay for 3,000 more midwives, 5,000 care workers, 8,000 GPs and 20,000 nurses to create a 'truly world-class 21st-century health and care service'. But the details were intricate, with the funding due to come from a combination of the mansion tax, a tobacco levy and 'very complicated changes to rules governing hedge funds'. In fact, the policy was still being worked out the night before and – by some accounts – had not even been signed off until the morning of the leader's speech itself. This last-minute scramble was 'a direct result of people being sent to Scotland and not having time to sort it out', one adviser recalls.[145]

Miliband had decided that for the third year in a row, he would commit the entire speech to memory and deliver it without a script or notes, to an audience of thousands in the hall, and on live television. The nation's media were all gathered to watch and television news producers were waiting for suitable clips to use for the evening bulletins. A further complicating factor was that overnight, the US had led air strikes on the so-called Islamic State in Iraq and the Levant (Isil). Downing Street had indicated that Parliament was likely to be recalled at the end of the week for a vote on authorising British forces to join the air strikes. A new section had to be inserted at the beginning of Miliband's speech to deal with the sobering development. 'Ed's mind may well have been dwelling on the difficulties of having to remember the details of what had been agreed,' a Labour staffer says. 'He did forget bits of it.'

Disastrously, Miliband's greatest omission was a brief but carefully crafted and politically essential passage on how Labour would cut the deficit. Though none admitted as much in public, everyone in Miliband's inner circle knew voters did not trust Labour on the economy. The Tories had already declared their intention to target this weakness and Labour strategists now agree they 'did not do enough, early enough' to address the issue. When Miliband forgot even to mention the deficit during a speech lasting one hour and five minutes, it was 'a pivotal moment'.

One senior Labour figure who watched the speech unfold says: 'I remember thinking, "We have just given the Tories a massive pre-election boost here because we've done something symbolic: we have forgotten about the economy."'

'Fuck. Fuck. Fuck. Fuck.' Ed Miliband cursed under his breath, spitting expletives through gritted teeth, as he paced up and down his room in Manchester's Midland Hotel. Five minutes earlier, he had been soaking up the applause of the crowd as he stood on stage with his wife, Justine, after delivering what he thought was a completed speech. Only when he stepped off the podium did he realise his mistake.

James Stewart, Miliband's long-serving press aide who travelled almost everywhere with him, recalls: 'I think I was the first person he spoke to when he came off stage. He was utterly furious with himself. He realised before anybody else who worked for us what a problem it was.'

Miliband shut himself in his room. He was due to be calling newspaper editors to answer their questions personally and attempt to secure favourable coverage for his most important speech of the year. But these calls had to wait. Instead, the Labour leader paced the room, swearing and calling his closest colleagues to ask for reassurance. When each of them tried to calm his anxieties and play down the problem, he told them no, it was a disaster, before calling another ally and repeating the conversation. Those close to him say this is a typical reaction from Miliband at moments of crisis, turning to others for assurances and then blaming himself. With him in the room were his wife, Justine Thornton, and Rachel Kinnock, the daughter of former Labour leader Neil Kinnock, who was his 'gatekeeper', while others returned as the scale of the error became clear.

Stewart now argues that attempting to memorise the speech – for the third year in a row – was a strategic misjudgement as well as an unnecessary risk. 'I thought on that occasion it was a waste of time for him to be learning the speech,' he says.

> In general, we weren't very conscious of risk. It's not just memorising the speech. We had just come through the referendum, we were in the middle of this argument

over English votes for English laws. We didn't take a
decision that this was a 'get through, don't screw up,
look prime ministerial' speech. The main political event
had happened already with the referendum. We didn't
think, 'Let's just manage the risk.' The way to do that
is not to put him on stage with no notes and an hour's
speech to deliver that will be analysed to death.

Miliband's mistake was compounded by a second error.
While the Labour leader tore his hair out in his hotel room,
the party's digital team published a version of the speech
as it was meant to have been delivered, complete with the
missing section on the deficit. Inside the Tory campaign
headquarters in Westminster, staff from the Conservative
Research Department scrutinised Miliband's speech, as they
always did on such occasions. Then one member of the Tory
economics team announced: 'I don't think he mentioned the
deficit.' CRD and the press officers went into overdrive. A
staff member in the room at the time recalls: 'There was a
lot of frantic Ctrl+F-ing to search through the document for
the word "deficit". Then we broke up the video of the speech
into ten-minute sections and everybody was given a chunk
to watch.'[146] When Miliband's mistake was confirmed, the
Conservatives seized on the evidence and used it to maximum
symbolic effect.

Labour strategists privately concede that the omission was
genuinely revealing. If fixing the deficit had run all the way
through the speech as a constant theme, it would have been
impossible for Miliband to forget. The Tories could claim that
the economy was not important enough to Labour, and, on
this occasion at least, they were right. Knowing better than
anyone how bad it was, the Labour leader refused to leave

his room and would not be consoled. He missed most of the celebratory party that he had been due to attend along with major donors and visiting celebrities.

One Labour insider says: 'Conferences are key things for political parties, they should lift you up and you go back to Westminster after a great conference and it's all fine for the next few months. Exactly the reverse happened to us at a very crucial time.'

Two weeks later, a plot was drawn up to replace Miliband as leader. The chosen candidate was the popular Blairite former Cabinet minister Alan Johnson. He had been Miliband's first choice as shadow Chancellor before stepping down for personal reasons a few months after taking on the role. Senior aides regard it as 'no coincidence' that the coup rumours began after the disastrous party conference. Up to forty MPs were said to be ready to back Johnson in October 2014.

But despite repeated efforts by senior colleagues, Johnson – a former postman who had written two acclaimed volumes of autobiography – would not be persuaded to stand against the leader. He apparently told supporters that he was enjoying life too much on the book-tour circuit. One shadow Cabinet minister says: 'We are terrible at killing our leaders. It would require a level of organisational skill that the sensible wing of the party does not have.' Another shadow Cabinet minister claims Miliband's leadership was only saved by the fact that Labour was not trailing the Tories significantly in the opinion polls: 'The polls totally misled us. Pretty much everything else follows from that. If the polls had been accurate, Ed would never have survived that long. We would have got rid of him well before the election and put someone else in.'

Messy messages

Hired alongside Tom Baldwin shortly after Miliband became leader in 2010, Bob Roberts was for a long time regarded as the 'good cop' to Baldwin's more aggressive 'bad cop' when it came to the party's public relations. But, although he is rarely lost for a quip or a smile, Roberts's affable demeanour noticeably changed as the full extent of the right-wing press's hostility towards Miliband became clear. In the months and weeks leading up to the election, Labour adopted a bunker mentality towards Miliband's media appearances. Roberts, himself a veteran of the lobby as former political editor of the *Mirror*, was largely held responsible for such a cautious approach.

When the election campaign was just beginning, an astonishing incident occurred that was barely reported at the time. Accounts of it vary, but what seems clear is that Miliband was involved in some form of physical confrontation during a stunt that went wrong. According to a Labour staff member who witnessed the incident, a newspaper reporter 'pretty much assaulted Ed' at an event in Bermondsey, south London. A crowd of Tory supporters and staff wearing Alex Salmond masks and carrying Ed Miliband puppets – sent on Lynton Crosby's orders – had found out about the event and turned up to mob Miliband in the hope of getting a picture of him surrounded by the pranksters. Labour's press team were trying to ensure that the picture did not happen and had a plan to speed Miliband out of the entrance, into the car and away before he could be surrounded by the crowd in their Salmond masks.

'We got our driver to park outside one entrance and drive round so Ed could quickly jump in,' one Labour insider recalls. 'He was driving around, Ed came out and the journalist pushed him into the side of the car, and slammed the door shut so Ed had to go around to the other side. It was quite violent.' Labour complained to the paper's editor, who decided not to use the pictures. Miliband's team also chose not to make a public fuss about the incident as it would have distracted from the evening's televised debate at Sky News, presented by Jeremy Paxman.[147] Another version of this event, from a witness on the Tory side, holds that the clash was with a protester, not a reporter, who shoved Miliband into the side of a car. Afterwards, however, Miliband's police protection detail arrived, a couple of days before they had been due to start protecting the man who could be Prime Minister six weeks later.

Among the most bitterly held frustrations harboured by leading members of Miliband's team was the intense irritation at the way the Conservatives' core message about the danger of a post-election deal between Labour and the SNP was reported by the press and especially the BBC. The Tories also had their issues with the national broadcaster, which, with other television and radio networks, was legally bound to demonstrate fairness, balance and impartiality towards all the parties. But in the final fortnight of the campaign, Miliband felt the BBC was doing too much to amplify the Tory message. It seemed to the Labour leader's team that the focus was entirely on there being a hung parliament in which Labour would have an easier route to form a coalition but would need the support of the left-wing SNP to do so. Nicola Sturgeon was making it impossible to ignore the prospect by alternately offering to help Miliband, setting out her price for doing so and warning that voters would never forgive him if he refused to join her and thereby allowed the Tories back in. Bob Roberts was especially unimpressed. 'I cannot remember one serious piece of coverage about what a Tory majority would mean. It was just not examined as an issue,' he says. 'Certainly, Nicola Sturgeon and David Cameron were a good double act. She kept saying she would have influence, he kept saying they would have influence under a Labour government. They did what they had to do.'

Tom Baldwin and Lucy Powell, the MP who became deputy chair of Labour's election campaign, both complained to the BBC over its coverage of the SNP issue. Baldwin says Cameron and Sturgeon were 'playing tag team' and using the same language to undermine Labour. 'One of the reasons the Tories achieved a majority was because the focus in the short campaign was largely on the risk of a Labour/SNP government,' he says. 'Responsibility for that lies not only with the pollsters and a highly partisan Tory press but also broadcast media, which became obsessed with the story of what would happen if the polls were correct.'

Privately, Labour insiders admit they did not do enough, early enough to neutralise the SNP 'risk' message coming from Lynton Crosby's campaign. One shadow Cabinet minister says:

> Cameron was absolutely ruthless about preying on Ed's weakness so he could portray him as being popped into Sturgeon's pocket. We didn't come out fast enough to say it wasn't true. Even when Ed said there would be no deals with Nicola Sturgeon, nobody believed it because the maths could end up meaning we had to do a deal.

Carved in stone

Ed Miliband and his entourage of assistants and advisers boarded a dawn flight from Glasgow on the morning of

Saturday 2 May. He had been at a rally in Scotland the night before, with the Scottish Labour leader, Jim Murphy, dodging yet more protests from pro-independence demonstrators, who had gathered outside the building. The Labour leader and his aides were increasingly frustrated that their policies were not getting covered properly in the media, because papers and broadcasters were only interested in what kind of deal Miliband would be prepared to cut with the SNP. So the party devised a plan for a stunt on the Saturday before the election, which they hoped would seize the agenda and eclipse the national obsession with the ramifications of another hung parliament.

The plan was to unveil a totemic image that would persuade the public to believe that Miliband was serious about delivering on his promises. His symbol of choice was an 8ft 6in. slab of limestone, engraved with Labour's six key election pledges, signed by the leader, to be installed in the No. 10 garden as a reminder to the incoming Labour government of the promises it had made to the people. First, however, Miliband and his team had a local logistical difficulty to negotiate.

The stone slab was so large and so heavy that it could only be erected with the aid of a scaffolding structure, on a piece of ground stable enough to take its considerable weight. Transporting the stone to Hastings was also not straightforward, as some roads were not strong enough to cope. Labour's event planning unit eventually identified a school car park that could take the strain. Unfortunately for Miliband, the local Green Party candidate, a journalist, film-maker and blacksmith by the name of Jake Bowers, discovered that Labour were planning a media event at the school. He drove his horse and cart into the car park before the Labour team could close the gates. As TV crews, photographers and reporters gathered, awaiting the arrival of Miliband's battle bus, Bowers refused to move. His horse and cart were placed within the camera shot, a sight that would have made the resulting pictures even stranger than they were, and which Labour media officers were determined to avoid. Prolonged negotiations began between a Labour press officer at the school, who pleaded with Bowers to move. Miliband, meanwhile, was in the bus, being driven around Hastings in circles, as he could not afford to arrive and be ambushed by Bowers and his horse.

James Stewart recalls:

> The Green candidate had a horse and trap. He heard this was happening so he wheeled his horse and trap into the school before we could close the gate and say, no, thank you. Then the police got involved. As we were driving to the school, we got a series of phone calls saying, 'There's a horse and trap with the Green candidate in.' We drove round in circles while this negotiation was taking place.

Eventually, Bowers agreed to allow Miliband to enter the school and unveil his pledge stone without being disrupted, on the condition that he could meet the Labour leader afterwards. Stewart explains: 'The deal was, please don't ruin our event. He said, "I'm not moving the horse and cart but I won't disrupt your event if I can chat to Ed at the end of it on your bus." It was a farce.'

Miliband stepped off the bus into the grey morning, met the local Labour candidate and delivered his impassioned plea for voters' trust. 'These six pledges are now carved in stone,' Miliband told the small crowd gathered in the car park.

They're carved in stone because they won't be abandoned after the general election. I want the British people to remember these pledges, to remind us of these pledges, to insist on these pledges. Because I want the British people to be in no doubt: we will deliver them. We will restore faith in politics by delivering what we promise at this general election.

As a ploy to impress floating voters, the 'Ed Stone', as it instantly became known, was not a success. In fact, it became, with the bacon sandwich and forgetting the deficit at conference, an emblem of Miliband's shortcomings. The reaction – on Twitter as well as in the mainstream media – ensured that the public would not forget the image of Miliband in front of a giant 'tombstone', even if voters could not remember the details of the six pledges themselves. Twitter users said Miliband appeared to have developed a 'Moses complex'. Simon Blackwell, co-creator of the BBC's political comedy series *The Thick of It*, suggested the stunt was beyond parody: 'Ed Miliband builds a policy cenotaph. And you wonder why we stopped doing *The Thick of It*.'

Even *The Guardian* was not impressed, its sketch-writer John Crace concluding: 'In one of the tightest elections in fifty years, which looks set to be won by the party leader the public mistrusts the least, Ed Miliband has just raised the stupidity bar still higher. It makes Neil Kinnock's 1992 "We're all right" Sheffield rally moment look almost clever.' Chris Leslie, the shadow Treasury minister, appeared on the BBC's *Sunday Politics* programme within hours of the images being published and was forced to defend the stunt under withering attack from the presenter, Andrew Neil. At one point, Leslie was asked whether Labour would need planning permission before erecting the stone in the Downing Street garden. One shadow Cabinet minister recalls: 'I was horrified by it. What a stupid idea.'[148] Another senior MP says, with heavy sarcasm: 'I remember just thinking, "Whose brilliant idea was this?"'[149]

The answer, according to numerous sources, was Miliband's director of policy, Torsten Bell. Ferociously bright, Bell had the job of providing the bold vision for connecting Miliband with the electorate. His role was to put the manifesto together and to veto ideas from other people in the team that did not fit in with the project. This latter part of his remit seems to have been one of the reasons why he managed to get the pledge stone through up to ten separate planning meetings. Those who thought it was a bad idea didn't really appreciate how bad it was. When concerns were raised, and half-hearted attempts made to stop the project, it was too late: the stone had already been carved.[150]

Internal opponents of the 'Ed Stone' hoped it would simply disappear into a void without attracting much attention. This might have been possible, had the party not been so determined to give it a high profile. On the morning the stone was unveiled, the Duchess of Cambridge went into hospital, where she was to give birth to Princess Charlotte. All the television channels and newspapers were full of the happy news from the Palace. The stone looked like it was about to sink without trace. But Labour decided to embargo the pictures and television footage until the following day, when the royal birth would have faded a little from the news agenda, ensuring it received wide coverage.

On the drizzly morning of Sunday 3 May, David Cameron and the Tory battle bus pulled into a sports club in Nuneaton, ready to campaign in a key battleground seat, a symbolic constituency that would herald the coming Conservative majority when Marcus Jones held it for the Tories on election night. In a dank changing room at the sports centre, with hooks on the walls and team benches to sit on, the Prime Minister and his advisers, including Craig Oliver, his communications director, and Graeme Wilson, his press secretary, gathered around a smartphone. 'They can't actually have done this, can they?' Cameron asked his team, refusing to believe that Labour could have committed such a gaffe. The Prime Minister had to be shown photos on Twitter as proof.

With TV reporters desperate to ask the Conservative leader for a comment on the 'Ed Stone', Cameron and his team had to decide how best to attack their opponents' blunder. In the end, they settled on the line that it was another clear demonstration that Miliband lacked the judgement needed to be Prime Minister. They did not need to overdo the ridicule – Twitter was taking care of that.

When the scale of the mistake became clear, Labour staff inside the party's Brewer's Green HQ christened the slab the 'Torstone'. But one senior figure thinks it is too harsh to lay the blame solely on Torsten Bell. 'It was a collective failure. It was something we as a team should have just strangled at birth. It obviously just became the symbol of a failed campaign.' Another Miliband aide says:

> In a campaign, people put suggestions forward. This obviously wasn't one of the best ones but it certainly wasn't one which rang massive alarm bells. In simple terms, it slipped through the net. It was never really meant to be a big stunt, but it was mishandled on the

media side of things because it all became about the
picture. We didn't release the picture to the Sunday
papers so there became a mystery about the picture,
and the pictures then got a negative reaction on social
media. Was it our finest moment on the campaign? No.
Was it particularly significant? I don't think it shifted
many votes one way or the other.

It could have been worse. To begin with, Labour strategists
had proposed what would surely have been an even grander
folly: to carve the party's pledges – complete with Miliband's
signature – into the side of a rock face. Various locations were
considered, including Cheddar Gorge, for the plan. In the end,
none of the options that were proposed could be made to work.
'It's hard to explain to the outsider how intense and creative an
election campaign has to be,' one Labour official explains. 'The
ideas and brainstorming sessions were essential. Sometimes
you have to be creative just to buy yourself some time, and
we were under a lot of pressure over the SNP thing. There's
any number of barmy ideas going around at any one time.'

On the ground

With a revolt simmering among his troops, Scotland in tumult,
and his personal ratings as a potential Prime Minister lagging
far behind David Cameron's, it might have seemed inevitable
that Miliband was doomed. In fact, Labour MPs clung to
one glimmer of hope: their party had a formidable army
of local members and union activists who would knock on
more doors, deliver more leaflets and, come polling day, get
out more votes than the Conservatives could ever muster.

On Wednesday 8 April, midway through the second week of the campaign, with another month to go, Labour was having a good day. In warm spring sunshine, the party's silver and red battle bus pulled into Warwick University, a favoured venue for Labour leaders (Gordon Brown used it twice), for Miliband to deliver a speech announcing the party's pledge to abolish non-domicile tax status. This had long been a difficulty for the Conservatives and Miliband was determined to seize the initiative by ending the right of a few rich individuals to avoid paying tax in the UK simply because they were not 'domiciled' in Britain.

The policy showed early signs of being a popular and eye-catching idea, in the same way that the Labour leader's 2013 pledge to freeze energy prices had dominated political debate for weeks. Conservatives claimed it unravelled within hours (a video showing Ed Balls questioning the effectiveness of such a crackdown months earlier quickly emerged). But the truth is that George Osborne had been considering a similar crackdown himself. Labour almost announced their move in March 2015, the week before the coalition's final Budget, because they were convinced Osborne was going to make his move then.

The 'non-doms' pledge had led the morning broadcasts and Miliband was clearly enjoying himself. In his closing remarks after his speech, he told supporters in the airy atrium of Warwick's International Digital Lab that they held the fate of the country in their hands. 'The big thing about the next four and a half weeks or so is that you can make the difference,' he said.

> Because this election could come down to a few hundred
> votes in a few dozen constituencies. And, you know, the

Conservative Party is a virtual party. They sort of exist as a sort of Lynton Crosby hologram. I am not sure the hologram is doing so well at the moment. But they don't really exist in reality, because the problem is they can't find people to knock on doors for them. Now, I wouldn't want to knock on doors for the Conservative Party either. But here is the thing. People do want to knock on doors for our party. Not for the sake of our party but for the sake of the kind of country we can be.

Miliband was correct in his analysis of the situation: the election would be decided by swing voters in marginal seats. But the Tories were not, as he would later discover, a hologram.

Labour promised to have 'four million conversations' with voters on the doorstep, with an army of thousands of activists pursuing their prey up and down the land. In Patrick Heneghan, Labour also had the target seats strategist credited with helping Gordon Brown avoid an even worse result – and preventing David Cameron winning a majority – in 2010. But the scale of Miliband's eventual defeat in 2015 led Labour MPs and officials after the election to lament that their leader's boasts about the party's ground game had been hollow.

In the aftermath of defeat, accounts emerged of significant failings in the party's organisation of the street-by-street battle for votes. One shadow Cabinet minister says:

Our field ops were weak in some places and very weak in others. On one or two visits, three weeks before the election, nobody was there. In the Easter holidays, I made a five-hour round trip to this constituency in the Midlands. The candidate wasn't even there. We didn't have anyone to talk to, we didn't have any press there.

It was a real tumbleweed moment. Then I went up three days before the election to one of our must-win seats and, again, the candidate was not there. There was a protest going on outside our office.

Another shadow Cabinet minister agreed that, contrary to the hype, Labour's 'ground war' was poorly organised where it counted most.

The Tories ran a much more sophisticated ground operation than we had any knowledge of. Because we didn't see them out on the streets, knocking on doors very much, we thought we had the most fantastic ground operation. But we were not targeted enough. The Tories knew the areas and the people in those areas who they could push and cajole. We were door-stepping everyone.[151]

Tom Baldwin, who was a senior adviser to Ed Miliband, says: 'There are clearly lessons [for Labour] from the Tories' ground and field operation. We believed, wrongly, ours was better. Jim Messina appears to have identified and targeted voters with a degree of sophistication not seen before in this country.'[152]

The impression that Labour was piling up votes where it didn't count, and working the streets in electorally irrelevant neighbourhoods, appears to be borne out by the results. On 7 May, Labour's share of the vote increased from 29 per cent in 2010 to 30.4 per cent. Despite achieving a higher national share of the vote, however, the party won twenty-six fewer seats in 2015 than in 2010.

Like the Conservatives, Labour candidates and canvassers were given a script, produced at party headquarters in Brewer's

Green. But the questions they asked appear not to have been as sophisticated as the Tory survey – designed by Stephen Gilbert – to gauge the support they had in a particular area. The first question was 'How are you going to vote?' Question two was 'How did you vote last time?' This was followed by 'Would you prefer a Conservative or Labour government?', and finally, 'How are you going to vote in local elections?' By combining the answers, canvassing teams could rate the likelihood of each voter to back Labour in the election. However, even successful candidates report that the questions seemed inadequate at the time. Some even went to the lengths of devising their own canvassing surveys. As one Labour MP concludes:

> We weren't asking the right questions because we weren't weeding out the people who were never going to vote for us and therefore we were not concentrating on the groups of voters who were genuinely undecided. It's all very well having four million conversations, but if you have got a crap message and crap techniques it is not going to do you much good.

Target practice

A conspicuous difference between Labour and the Conservatives in their campaign mechanics was the willingness of Ed Miliband to publicise his party's strategic intentions. In January 2013, more than two years before the election, Tom Watson, who was Labour's campaign coordinator at the time, held a press conference with political editors in Westminster to announce all 106 of Labour's key target seats. They were all, he said, 'offensive' seats, meaning resources would be focused on making gains from other parties rather than defending existing marginal constituencies held by Labour. Four out of five seats on the list had been won by Tories in 2010, while eighty-eight were seats that Labour had lost at that election under Gordon Brown. Fifteen of the seats had not been coloured red since the 2005 election, while three on the list had not been Labour even under Tony Blair.

The decision to focus on attack seats, rather than defending marginals, ultimately proved fatal to Labour's chances of victory. Labour's own election chief, Douglas Alexander, was swept away in the Scottish National Party tidal wave, along with the party's leader in Scotland, Jim Murphy, and shadow Scottish Secretary Margaret Curran. Ed Balls, the shadow Chancellor, meanwhile, was left hopelessly exposed in Morley and Outwood after campaigning in nearby seats, only returning to attempt to salvage his own in the final days of the contest, by which time it was too late. In a result that would have seemed unthinkable to Watson that afternoon in 2013, Balls lost his seat – to a Tory. Labour's pollsters never apparently bothered to survey marginal seats that the party had to defend, such as Ed Balls's. Labour presumed that the swing would be against the Tories and in their favour, and spent minimal resources in protecting English seats that proved vulnerable once the swing went the other way.[153]

At his press conference, Watson declared that Miliband's 'realistic' aim was to achieve a sixty-seat majority in 2015. Miliband appointed one of President Obama's mentors, Arnie Graf, to train 1,000 party workers who would run local campaigns in the target seats by the end of 2013, Watson said. 'We are determined to be a one-term opposition,' he added. 'If we win all of the seats on the list, we will have an eighty-seat majority.' At the time, Labour were ten points

ahead of the Tories in the polls, which might help explain
Watson's optimism. According to Watson's analysis, Labour
needed a national swing of only 1.75 per cent to be the largest
party, while a swing of 5.3 per cent would deliver Miliband
a majority of twenty.

By contrast, the Conservatives were rumoured to have forty
attack seats and forty defensive seats. But the party has never –
even now – published a list of which constituencies these were.
Various attempts were made by journalists and commentators
to guess which seats the Tories were prioritising, but the
party always insisted that nobody got it right. The waters
were muddied further when it emerged that there were in
fact closer to fifty target seats and roughly the same number
of defensive seats.

At this point, in early 2013, the Tories were firmly on the
back foot. By coincidence, on the same day, 8 January, David
Cameron held a meeting with about 100 of his back-bench
MPs, to prepare them for the election. Andrew Cooper, then
the Prime Minister's pollster, gave a presentation in which he
pointed out that no party had come from Labour's position in
the polls to win since 1951. He also showed polling evidence
in a series of slides entitled 'The Road to 2015' that suggested
Labour's ten-point lead was 'soft'. MPs present did their
best to sound enthusiastic, periodically banging on tables
and breaking into applause during the hour-long meeting in
a committee room in Parliament. Cameron had to concede,
however, that voters were 'pissed off' with the Tories. Lord
Ashcroft, the former Tory treasurer and major donor to the
party, who ran a high-profile series of polls of marginal seats
during the months leading up to the election, observed at that
time that the odds favoured Labour, while a Conservative
victory appeared 'comparatively remote'.

It is worth noting that Cameron's briefing on that winter evening was held in private, behind the closed doors of a parliamentary committee room, and attended only by MPs and senior party advisers. Watson's briefing, however, was for reporters to disseminate as far and as widely as their editors and audiences would allow. As a member of Miliband's shadow Cabinet ruefully observes, when it came to the ground war, 'the Tories were doing it under the radar'.

1 Brewer's Green

For much of Ed Miliband's time as Labour leader, it was not clear who exactly was running the party's election campaign. There was Tom Watson, later replaced by Douglas Alexander, as the party's general election coordinator. There was Spencer Livermore, the general election campaign director. Then there was Patrick Heneghan, the party's executive director for elections. Torsten Bell, Ed Miliband's director of policy, was also unofficially running the campaign. The contrast with Lynton Crosby's totalitarian structure at CCHQ was stark. According to one shadow Cabinet minister, the lack of clarity at Labour's headquarters at 1 Brewer's Green, Westminster, was a critical weakness. 'I thought, "Who's in charge?" There was no Lynton. There were a lot of people walking around, looking really important and being really inefficient. We were still writing policy three weeks before the election.'

If the team at Labour's HQ was dysfunctional, it perhaps reflected Ed Miliband's own personal complexity and the fact that, as it appeared to some of his closest aides, he could never finally decide what sort of a Labour leader he wanted to be. Members of his team describe 'strategic tensions' that ran through Miliband's five years in charge. Miliband himself and Stewart Wood were seen as representing a fairly straightforward centre-left position. Greg Beales, Labour's strategy director, was seen as advocating a more populist, antagonistic version of Miliband's vision that focused on taking on the rich and fighting powerful 'vested interests' in society – the media giants, big business. Then there was the approach that has been described as the 'One Nation' agenda, which was led by Marc Stears, Miliband's old friend and speech writer, and Jon Cruddas, the academic MP who was running Labour's policy review. The aim of this strand of Labour thought was to find new ways of expressing the party's values in an era when there was no money to spend, through raising productivity in the economy, improving skills and education, and building resilience into communities. The message was more unifying in tone and sought to work with business rather than fighting predatory capitalists. 'All three of these conversations were going on internally all the time,' one senior source says.

'Similarly, there were three Ed Milibands on stage at any one time.' His natural character was of a 'decent, principled, very polite, slightly otherworldly intellectual' who liked to be a unifier and was friends with many Tory MPs. At other times, however, Miliband saw himself as someone who thought he could be 'a hero of the left, his father's son, a class warrior'. Lastly, there was the Ed Miliband who had been shaped by his experience of working for Gordon Brown for ten years – a calculating tactician. The three competing strategic outlooks and the three versions of Miliband's personality all vying for supremacy at once was a recipe for dysfunction that must have made the battle to produce a clear, concise and coherent message to take to voters almost impossible.[154]

There were also tensions over the party's economic message between Miliband and Ed Balls, the shadow Chancellor. Balls and the party's pollster, James Morris, wanted Miliband to say more about the need to tackle the deficit. They constantly urged the party leader to hammer home the point that there would be no money to spend if Labour won. He seemed a reluctant convert to austerity. Balls was also among those urging the leadership to address immigration and welfare as these were the critical issues that the party's internal polling suggested lay behind voters' unease about the economy. At its crudest, the polling was showing that voters were worried that Labour would favour others who did not deserve government support – like some benefit recipients and foreigners – rather than rewarding those who work hard. Again, Miliband was reluctant to face up to voters' anxieties about these questions.[155]

Brand Ed

'I just utterly hate him.' It is fair to say that Russell Brand, the comedian and self-styled revolutionary, is not universally adored by all Labour aides. But the party's strategists saw that organising an interview with Brand would give Miliband an opportunity to break out of the Westminster village and convert millions of the comedian's internet fans to vote Labour. It was a chance to raise Miliband's media profile and potentially help him to shed the awkward image that had dogged him for years but had become more acute since the bacon sandwich incident. Russell Brand was enlisted to help revive 'Brand Ed'.

The disgruntled aide above (who was not alone in expressing dismay) is scathing:

It just showed we were going for the mythical youth vote. OK, they may have supported us. But the proportion of people aged 18–30 who actually turn out to vote is ridiculously small. The proportion of over-65s who vote is huge. That is the problem with a strategy of going after non-voters. They are non-voters.[156]

Another adviser recalls that Brand's team initially approached Labour offering to endorse Miliband: 'The approach came in. The offer was there to make it a proper "you should vote Labour" endorsement.'[157] Instead, however, Labour decided to give Brand's internet TV channel, The Trewz, an interview, in the comedian's north London house. Rather than accept an immediate endorsement, it was decided that making it seem as if Miliband was working to win over his interviewer would deliver more voters into Labour's hands. Lucy Powell, whom Miliband had recently appointed to the powerful position of vice-chair of the election campaign, was instrumental in 'making it happen', and convinced the Labour leader it would be a good idea, according to her colleagues. A combative new MP who had entered Parliament in the 2012 Manchester Central by-election, Powell had already caused controversy by circulating a briefing document in which she is alleged to have urged Labour candidates not to discuss immigration on the doorstep but to move the conversation on to a more comfortable subject for the party.

Bob Roberts, Miliband's former communications director, was said to be among the voices arguing against giving Brand an interview with the man who wanted to be Prime Minister. But Miliband wanted to do it. Several days after completing the peculiar interview, in which Brand repeatedly swigged from a large water bottle between questions, the

comedian came out with his endorsement. He urged voters
to back Labour wherever they had a chance, apart from in
Brighton Pavilion, the constituency held by the Green Party
MP, Caroline Lucas. When the Conservatives won a majority,
Brand backpedalled. 'I think for a moment I got caught up
in some mad *The Thick of It*, oh wow, Ed Miliband's in
my house,' he said. Brand's influence derives from the huge
fanbase he has on the internet. His interview with Miliband
on his Trewz YouTube channel was viewed online more than
1.3 million times and he has more than nine million Twitter
followers. But he blamed the 'old media', by which he meant
right-wing newspapers, and 'the establishment' for ensuring
that David Cameron was returned to No. 10 'with more seats
than before'. Brand was the highest-profile celebrity to back
Labour, but not the only one, with other comedians including
Steve Coogan and Eddie Izzard also endorsing Miliband for
PM. The Tories, meanwhile, courted business leaders and
sniffily suggested they would rather have endorsements from
the money men than the funny men.

There were signs during the campaign that Ed Miliband's
appeal to the nation's youth was working. One of the oddest
episodes occurred was when a teenage girl, Abby Tomlinson,
unleashed what became an internet craze dedicated to the
total adoration of Ed Miliband. The kind of obsession usually
reserved for pop stars was suddenly being heaped upon the
Labour leader, as the craze grew exponentially on Twitter.
Tomlinson, who was studying for her A levels at the time,
told her 11,000 followers that Miliband now had a 'fandom',
slang for a group of fans who are desperately in love with
their idol. Speaking to the website Buzzfeed, Tomlinson said
she just wanted the world to see a different side of Miliband
because he was a really 'great guy'. A Labour member, she

was, nevertheless, too young to vote. The Twitter trend gained national attention after participants posted messages such as 'i love ed miliband so much it is painful' and 'this all started out as a joke but now i think i legitimately fancy ed miliband'.

A senior Labour staffer says 'Milifandom' was 'a major shock', but 'I don't think Ed ever took it very seriously'. Maybe not, but he certainly encouraged it, sending a message to Tomlinson thanking her for her support. Some Conservatives were momentarily alarmed. Tory teens launched a rival fan club on Twitter called the Cameronettes, which turned out to be nothing like as successful.

Portrait of a leader

It was an open secret. Everyone inside Labour's HQ and the shadow Cabinet was well aware that Ed Miliband hated TV and struggled to deliver the 'soundbites' that the news programmes needed to be able to clip for their bulletins. Anxious shadow Cabinet ministers had been given assurances that there was 'a plan' to deal with the problem by hiring a media specialist who could coach Miliband for his TV appearances.

Yet, the plan remained for a long time just that. Until the final year of the parliament, nobody in Miliband's team had come from a senior position in broadcasting. Bob Roberts, Miliband's trusted communications director, was a former press man, having worked for two decades covering politics in Parliament as a lobby correspondent and latterly as political editor of the Labour-supporting *Mirror*. Tom Baldwin, another of Miliband's senior aides, responsible for set-piece speeches by the leader, was a former political journalist at *The Times*, who seemed to model his abrasive style of media-handling on Alastair Campbell, Tony Blair's former press chief. Later, in 2013, Patrick Hennessy, political editor of the *Sunday Telegraph*, was hired to bolster the press office operation. While the appointment of another senior newspaper journalist improved Labour's day-to-day relations with the political correspondents, the issue of 'the pictures' – Labour insiders' shorthand for Miliband's dismal public image – remained unresolved. 'We failed to put Ed's best side across,' one former adviser recalls. 'The lack of consistently thinking about how Ed appeared on the TV – that was really bad. For a long time we were putting him in situations where he just didn't look like a Prime Minister.'

In the summer of 2014, as the Labour Party searched for a head of broadcasting and pictures to take charge of the leader's media image, they tried to recruit Nick Robinson, the BBC's political editor. Robinson recalls in his *Election Notebook* that a senior individual in the party called him on what was a crackly mobile phone line to ask if he would take charge of addressing Miliband's 'presentational difficulties'. The Labour figure told the BBC man: 'The party knows it has a problem and is determined to fix it. The leader needs advice, and it has to come from someone with sufficient stature to ensure he'll listen to it.' When Robinson realised he was being offered the job, he had to fight back fits of laughter, before politely declining.

The party made a similar approach to the BBC's revered political producer at the time, Paul Lambert. Balding, wide-eyed and with a fanatical zeal for shouting impertinent questions at the Prime Minister outside No. 10, in an attempt to get a reaction on camera, Lambert is universally known at Westminster as 'Gobby'. 'We tried to hire Gobby,' one Miliband aide says. 'We wanted him to do the same job that George Osborne's adviser Thea Rogers had done in transforming his image, for Ed. The timing didn't work.' Later, Lambert did leave the BBC; he went to work as director of communications for UKIP.

Labour eventually appointed Matthew Laza, a former BBC producer, as head of broadcasting, but the appointment was made only in September 2014, by which point it was too late. One aide recalls:

> A lot of the problems were problems pretty much from when Ed was elected leader. It doesn't take long for people to form their impressions of a leader. It's less about policy and more about the style. Cameron was very tight on the imagery, even at the start of his leadership. It is images that stick in people's minds more than stories. We spent a long time papering over the fact that Ed was not that popular – and Cameron contrasted to Ed was quite a significant thing.

Those around Miliband – and he himself – recognised the scale of the problem with his image and the fact that they had failed to deal with it in time. Uncomfortable as it must have been, he could not hide from Labour's internal polling, which consistently showed the public's doubts over Miliband as a leader. With this in mind, he chose to give a bold speech, bordering on the masochistic, in July 2014, in which he declared that if the public wanted a Prime Minister with the slickest image, they should vote for 'the other guy'. Labour sought to turn Miliband's awkward public persona to his advantage – not for the first time. He even openly courted his own caricature, comparing himself (as his opponents frequently did) to Wallace from the *Wallace and Gromit* animations. The speech, championed by Tom Baldwin, was a major risk and a 'very painful' process. Not everyone was convinced that 'taking ownership of awkward Ed' was a good idea. Miliband himself 'took a lot of persuading' but eventually agreed to address his own weakness publicly. He could see the threat and was determined to do what he could to neutralise it.[158]

'David Cameron is a very sophisticated and successful exponent of a politics based purely on image,' Miliband told his audience.

> I am not going to be able to compete with that and I don't intend to. I want to offer something different. I am not from central casting. You can find people who are more square-jawed, more chiselled – look less like Wallace. You could probably even find people who look better eating a bacon sandwich. If you want the politician from central casting, it's just not me: it's the other guy.

Yet the strategy of trying to make a virtue out of his weaknesses was never followed through with other speeches or media events to emphasis Miliband's different style. One Labour figure says the brand should have been developed to emphasise that Miliband was 'serious, principled and decent'. But the leader himself was reluctant. The insider says:

> Like any politician, Ed didn't like to admit that he wasn't good at some things. It's very hard to admit if you're a professional politician that you're not great at photo opportunities, the things that politicians are meant to do. It was quite hard to get him to do the speech and he did it well, but afterwards people who

didn't want him to do it in the first place – including
himself – parked it.[159]

Another personality problem that Miliband faced was the
basic fact that he had stood against his brother, the former
Foreign Secretary, David Miliband, for the party leadership
in 2010. Labour aides believe this remained a drag on
Miliband's chances right up until polling day. 'The seeds of
Labour's defeat go back to Ed Miliband being elected as
leader,' one shadow Cabinet minister says. 'We chose the
wrong brother and we ended up being a sideshow in a family
psychodrama.' One of Miliband's advisers adds: 'The stuff
with David didn't help. It just didn't go away as a bad thing;
it followed him around. The damage had been done and it
lodged in people's minds as one of the things they thought
about Ed.' Another party staffer disclosed that Miliband
found his brother's 'colossal strop' after losing the leadership
election 'hugely frustrating'.

Bob Roberts, Miliband's former head of communications,
says the Labour leader's self-confessed image problem did
not have a 'significant' impact on the party's fortunes, and it
is certainly true that, personally, at least, he performed above
the low expectations that had been set for him during the six
weeks of the short campaign. 'He obviously faced a hostile
media but in the end he came across as a guy of decency,
ideas and principle,' Roberts argues, with some justification.
'There was a huge improvement in the public perception of
him during the campaign so I don't think the stuff about Ed
was a massive factor compared to the other big factors.'[160]

As a former tabloid journalist, Roberts would be well
placed to assess Miliband's popular appeal – or lack of it
– though his view on the impact of Miliband's un-prime

ministerial style is clearly filtered through the lens of loyalty. His analysis is not the majority view among Miliband's former team. One says: 'Ed was always a difficult sell as a potential Prime Minister, whereas Cameron can be seen as an attractive, breezy figure with a bit of natural authority.'

Those who disagree with this fatalistic view have one shining example in mind of how image matters – and how it can be overhauled: George Osborne. The Chancellor has enjoyed a remarkable personal transformation, in part as a result of the work his advisers did to change his media image. After he was booed at the Olympics in the dismal year of the 'Omnishambles' Budget of 2012, the Chancellor was persuaded to stop hiding away in his Treasury bunker and get out into the country. He also lost several stone through a radical diet, got a new haircut, and, at the time of writing, was newly installed as the bookmakers' favourite to succeed David Cameron as Tory leader and Prime Minister. Nicola Sturgeon, too, underwent a dramatic makeover, which left her looking and sounding far more like a powerful and popular political leader.

It is open to question whether better advice and a greater willingness from Miliband to embrace a more radical overhaul of his personal style would have delivered a similar turnaround. Some of his former colleagues believe it would have been too much of a stretch.

'The public never really liked Ed or wanted him as Prime Minister,' one senior Labour figure says. 'He never appealed to people as a potential Prime Minister, I think, ever. That's just too big a mountain to climb.'

Despite the defeat, many of Miliband's former colleagues remain loyal and willing publicly to defend his record. James

Stewart says Miliband deserves credit for recognising the 'fundamental challenge' that Labour faced to find new ways to invest in public services when funding is tight.

> Ed recognised the basic challenge and thought, 'We need to find new ways to raise money from tax.' A lot of the policies he came up with will not be disregarded quickly – you can see that from many of Osborne's post-election policies. The fact is New Labour got lucky by being in there at a time when a lot of tax revenues were coming in easily, the economy was growing. They could spend a lot on more hospitals and schools. That's not going to happen again. There is not going to be a time when people are as free and easy about public spending because they will remember when the whole show went belly up.[161]

Tom Baldwin says it was always 'an uphill struggle' for Labour to win back power after one term in opposition. 'Many mistakes were made, but Ed Miliband's leadership defied historical precedent and expectation by not only holding the party together but also remaining just about competitive for most of the parliament,' he says. 'That was no small achievement.'[162]

CHAPTER 11

THE WILD WEST

D avid Cameron took off his jacket, left his tie behind and rolled up his shirtsleeves. Inside the packed and increasingly hot village hall in deepest Somerset, his task was to show the world that he cared. He was, he insisted, passionate about his mission to keep Britain on the path to prosperity, and ready to take the Tory fight anywhere in the country.

It was an important moment. Barely twenty-four hours earlier, he had suffered his Natalie Bennett 'brain fade' moment, forgetting the name of his own football team. Cameron launched a fight-back that was to become one of the defining episodes of the Conservatives' victory. The public display of passion, a week and a half before polling day, was designed primarily to quieten those voices of dissent on Cameron's own side that had grown louder in recent days.

'If you want political excitement, maybe you could go to Greece,' he said. The audience laughed but the Prime Minister didn't. 'I don't think that's exciting. I think that's terrifying,' he said. Cameron had no script to read from. He knew the key message he had to get across. Behind him, party activists held placards saying 'Keep Our Economy Strong'. Cameron told them: 'This is all about our economy.' Voters in Yeovil, he said, must know the risk of allowing Ed Miliband into No. 10. The only way to be sure of stopping him was to vote Conservative, he warned. Hair a little dishevelled, red-faced and sweating in the packed village hall, his voice straining, Cameron's rough-edged performance succeeded in showing that he was prepared to throw himself into the fight.

There was another reason, however, why making his speech that day was so important to the Conservative leader. His logistics team of campaign planners, led by Liz Sugg, who has worked for Cameron since his 2005 leadership campaign, had chosen to send him into the deep heart of Liberal Democrat country. The village hall at Norton-sub-Hamdon is often hired out for weddings and other events, with enough seating for 150 people, a fully equipped kitchen and a portable stage. In late April 2015, Simon Harris, who manages the venue, had a busy schedule of bookings for children's parties. When the local Conservative association called with a short-notice reservation request, he told them: 'You'll be lucky – we have got a lot of kids' parties on at the moment.' But the Tories were lucky: Sunday 26 April was free and they booked the whole building.

Harris was given no clues at this point about the nature of the event and no one else in the village had been told of the VIP's impending arrival. Only a few hours before the PM appeared did Harris begin to have his suspicions about the customers who had hired his venue. As the local roads became jammed with television camera trucks, police and the Tory battle bus, he wandered up to watch as Cameron stepped out into the sunshine and met some children at the school next door to the hall.

A persistent criticism of the 2015 Labour and Tory campaigns was how tightly stage-managed the visits were. Political leaders were kept well away from unscripted encounters with real voters. Many residents of Norton-sub-Hamdon never knew that Cameron had been in the area until they saw the evening television news. One local, however, paid especially close attention. The village hall where Cameron made his pitch lay just a five-minute walk from the rural home of Paddy Ashdown, the former Liberal Democrat leader. Now Lord Ashdown of Norton-sub-Hamdon, the ex-marine had been appointed in 2012 to run the Lib Dem election campaign. His former seat, held with a majority of 13,036 in 2010 by David Laws, one of the Lib Dem's brightest and best ministers, was regarded as bankable.

The Prime Minister's bizarre incursion into the Lib Dems' Somerset heartland completely mystified Nick Clegg. The Deputy Prime Minister could not understand what his coalition partner was doing. 'That's odd,' Clegg thought to himself. 'Does he really think he's going to win Yeovil?' He asked Ashdown and Laws, two of his closest allies, whether Cameron had a chance at taking this safest of Lib Dem seats. Ashdown and Laws assured Clegg the Tories were not in contention here. They told him: 'It doesn't look like it, no. It seems like they are just trying to pull our leg.'

A Cameron aide recalls: 'It was a deliberately quite pro-vocative, ballsy move. We were trying to show we were stepping the pace up. The PM was really passionate, rolling up the sleeves. He really cared about it.' Over the remaining week and a half before the election, the area was inundated with visits from Conservative Cabinet ministers, including Michael Fallon, the Defence Secretary, Philip Hammond, the Foreign Secretary, and Liz Truss, who, as Secretary of State for Environment, Food and Rural Affairs, had a special relevance for the countryside communities around Yeovil.

In the end, the Lib Dems were utterly routed. Not only did Laws lose his seat, but another fourteen MPs were thrown out by a devastatingly effective Tory operation in the southwest. The area had been the party's heartland, but in 2015, the Lib Dems failed to hold onto a single seat.

The Tories' success against the Lib Dems – especially in the West Country – was the most dramatic and decisive change in the political tide in England at the 2015 election. In short, it gave Cameron his majority. The Conservatives also wreaked havoc in west London, ejecting two Cabinet ministers – Ed Davey and Vince Cable – from their seats. In all, the Lib Dems lost fortynine of the fifty-seven seats they had won in 2010. Reflecting on the scale of the defeat at the hands of his own coalition partners, Nick Clegg says simply: 'They hammered us.'[163]

Coalition

For Nick Clegg, the extent of the devastation must have felt particularly personal. During the 2010 campaign, he was the darling of the media, as his fresh and appealing performances in the televised debates gave rise to 'Cleggmania' and a record share of the vote. Despite losing a few seats, Clegg now had the chance to show that his party could be part of an effective, stable government. If the project of coalition belonged to anybody, it belonged to Clegg. The elation of that famous Downing Street rose garden press conference – during which the Lib Dem leader joked with his Tory counterpart in dappled sunshine at the birth of the first coalition for seventy years – quickly evaporated.

Senior Lib Dems now concede that the devastating result in 2015 was in part the product of this decision to join forces with the Tories. Entering a contract to share power with the party seen by many grassroots Lib Dems as their implacable 'enemy' was ultimately far more damaging than any single policy choice. Almost at a stroke, the Lib Dems' poll share plummeted, falling from twenty-three points at the 2010 election to thirteen points just three months later. One poll in early 2015 put the party on just 6 per cent.

Public dismay at Clegg's decision to hitch himself to the Tories crystallised around the issue of university tuition fees. One of the Lib Dems' most distinctive policies at the 2010 election had been to sign a National Union of Students pledge to abolish tuition fees, which stood at £3,000 per year. Once in government, however, far from scrapping fees as he had promised, Clegg agreed that fees should be allowed to rise threefold over two years. It was a disaster that led to public cries of betrayal from student campaigners, and private grief inside the party. Clegg and Vince Cable, the Business Secretary, whose department was responsible for higher education policy, did their best to mitigate the impact on student finances, insisting that the new deal was the fairest they could reach.

Aware that he had lost a critical base of support – with several Lib Dems occupying seats with large student populations – Clegg tried to atone for his mistake. Two years after the decision was taken, as the new fee rise took effect in the autumn of 2012, Clegg recorded a party political broadcast in which he apologised for having ever promised not to increase fees in the first place. An internet spoof by The Poke turned the video into a song, which became the soundtrack to the rest of Clegg's leadership. 'I'm sorry, I'm sorry, I'm so, so sorry...' went the mashed-up lyrics. At the time of writing, the YouTube video had been viewed more than 3.1 million times.

Again, in early 2014, the Lib Dem leader tried to free his party from this huge policy millstone. David Cameron was privately scornful. 'Why is Clegg talking about higher education again?' he asked his aides, bemused at his coalition partner's tactics. 'It's like the badly bandaged finger returning to the flame.' Cameron also thought Clegg was making a further tactical mistake by trying to 'differentiate' the Lib Dems from the Tories in government so strenuously, telling friends that the Lib Dems were 'overdoing it and starting to look flaky'.[164]

Later that year, Clegg was given a foretaste of the kind of whitewash that the Tories were to hand out to his party. The European Parliament elections saw the Lib Dems lose ten of their eleven seats, including a wipe-out in the south-west. The party came fifth in the national share of the vote, with just 6.87 per cent. The European results were all the more dispiriting for the Lib Dem leader after he chose to put himself at the centre of the campaign, taking on Nigel Farage, the UK Independence Party leader, in two televised debates in the run-up to polling day. The Lib Dems, Clegg insisted, would be passionately pro-European, the 'party of IN'. He was widely seen to have lost to Farage, who came across as more convincing and far more charismatic than the man whose television performances had electrified the general election campaign in 2010.

The result was so bad that a clearly emotional Clegg was on the brink of resigning in the aftermath of defeat. When his closest advisers talked him out of quitting, Clegg's own MPs attempted to take matters into their own hands and mount a coup. Two days after the local election results of 2014 showed the Lib Dems losing more than 250 council seats, and shortly before the European results were announced, two MPs – John Pugh and Adrian Sanders – demanded that their leader stand down. They were supposed to have led the charge to replace Clegg with Vince Cable, the popular, more left-wing Lib Dem minister, in a plot orchestrated by Cable's friend Lord Oakeshott. But the Business Secretary was uncontactable on a trip to China, and, as the momentum for a leadership challenge faltered, the plotters melted away.

Despite surviving the attempted coup, and embracing public jibes on television and weekly LBC radio call-in shows, Clegg's undoubted personal resilience made little difference to the one result that mattered above all. By his own admission, he came to personify the kind of politician who breaks his promises to the electorate and when it came to the 2015 election, his party was 'damaged goods'.[165]

Polls suggested the Lib Dems had lost a third of their vote immediately to Labour when they went into coalition and had little hope of coaxing them back. During the 2015 campaign, Clegg was repeatedly confronted by Labour and Green Party supporters who had given their backing to the Lib Dems tactically in the past, to stop the Tories winning locally. This time they were so 'annoyed about the coalition' they told him they no longer cared who won.[166]

Stealth

David Cameron is fond of describing politics in the terms more usually used for sport. Preparatory work for a particular policy or campaign theme he invariably calls 'pitch rolling', as a groundsman will do to make the wicket ready before the start of a cricket match. Similarly, political parties are reduced to their team colours in Cameron's eyes. When he first focused his attention on the 2015 election, eighteen months before polling day, the Prime Minister was dismissive of the Liberal Democrats. 'I've got a blue–red fight, and a blue–purple fight,' he would say. 'I don't need to worry about the yellows.'[167]

Lynton Crosby, who was working part-time during his first year with the Tories, had not yet formulated in detail the Conservative campaign strategy. When he did, everything changed. He ordered the first polls of individual Lib Dem-held seats in November 2013 and January 2014. The findings were striking. They showed Cameron had a strong lead as preferred Prime Minister compared to Ed Miliband and that the Tories were preferred to Labour. Crosby concluded that there was no reason why the Conservatives should not win in these Lib Dem strongholds. There seemed to be no major differences between the priorities and values of Lib Dem voters and those of people who were solid Conservatives in parts of the country such as Cornwall. 'They look and sound like Tories,' Crosby thought. The Lib Dem dominance of the south-west appeared to be just an accident of geography and a remnant of history.[168] 'If we were going to win a majority, the path through the Lib Dems in the south-west was how we were going to do it,' one senior Conservative says.[169]

It came to be known as the 'black-widow strategy'. In the same way that the female of the world's deadliest spider species finds a partner, mates with him and then eats him, so Cameron was told he must decapitate the very people who had helped him into No. 10 in the first place. Cameron appears to have been entirely at ease with the idea. He was told by his German ally Angela Merkel shortly before the 2010 election that leading a coalition was not to be feared because 'the little party always gets smashed'. A senior Tory source noted that Cameron had 'no qualms at all' about targeting Clegg during the campaign. The Lib Dem leader's friends report that Cameron expressed not a shred of sympathy about Clegg's predicament when the pair spoke hours after the results were known, at a ceremony for the 70th anniversary of VE Day at the Cenotaph.

With hindsight, it is easy to look back at the Prime Minister's wide grin upon entering coalition with Nick Clegg in 2010 as evidence that he knew this political marriage would end with the other guys being eaten. But this would be to endow him with more foresight and optimism than he in fact possessed. During the months leading up to the dissolution of Parliament, Clegg and Cameron had what one well-placed source described as a 'tacit understanding' that they would happily pick up the phone after the election to thrash out a new coalition deal if voters – as widely expected – delivered another hung parliament.

'There would be asides when Cameron and Clegg talked in Downing Street and said, "You know, coalitions might need to be formed again."'[170] Certainly, the Tories were not expecting a majority, even on polling day. They had scrutinised the Lib Dem manifesto in close detail. Shortly before the campaign began in earnest, 'Cameron told Clegg he didn't think they were going to win a majority. It was as stark as that,' one senior source recalls.[171] Inevitably, such matters were broached informally, but the intent behind Cameron's comments was clear: the two men would be ready to do a deal again.

Yet, throughout the coalition – and especially during the election campaign – Cameron and George Osborne were ruthless in how they appropriated Liberal Democrat policies and claimed them for their own political benefit. The Lib Dems are every bit as deserving of credit – or blame – for the coalition's economic record as the Tories. Nick Clegg can claim to have authored one of Cameron's highest-profile manifesto pledges: to extend the tax-free personal income allowance, which had been in the Lib Dem 2010 manifesto before making it into the coalition agreement and becoming a staple of George Osborne's Budgets. Privately, even those closest to the Prime Minister concede the point that this policy was a blatant act of political plagiarism.

Armageddon

Tania Mathias, a local GP whom the Conservatives chose to take on the mighty Vince Cable, could scarcely have been more surprised to win. Yet the Tories threw plenty of resources at the west London seat of Twickenham. Perhaps most significantly, Boris Johnson, the popular Tory Mayor of London, was a regular visitor. Clinging firmly onto his burly arm as they toured the constituency, Mathias apparently saw it as her role to protect Johnson from the hordes of pavement fans who swamped the Mayor at every turn, demanding he pose with them for 'selfies'.

For his part, Cable was eyeing up a promotion in the next coalition government. In an interview published as Cameron travelled to make his speech in Norton-sub-Hamdon village hall, Cable said he was 'up for' a 'substantial role' running a major economic department – like the Treasury. He also used the opportunity to flatter Cameron and Osborne, telling his interviewer, Simon Walters, that the pair were 'highly intelligent guys and I respect their abilities'. He added: 'I have realised it is possible to be businesslike with them. I can envisage a scenario in which I would stomach working with the Tories if the situation required.'[172]

Nick Clegg always believed the national polls did not matter. If the party was stuck on 8 per cent nationally but could dig in locally, it could still hold onto two-thirds of its MPs. The so-called 'incumbency factor' – the popularity of Lib Dem MPs among their local communities – was traditionally a great help to his party, and offered what Clegg saw as 'a lifeline' to continuing political relevance, even an ongoing role in a future coalition. This confidence led Clegg to believe that 'Armageddon', as he put it, the annihilation of the party, would not happen on polling day. He publicly – and unwisely, as it turned out – commented on briefings from unnamed Tories stating that the Prime Minister intended to 'decapitate' Lib Dems across the West Country, dismissing the prospect as 'a fantasy'.

Clegg now admits, however, that this same attitude effectively gave permission to voters to abandon his party: 'Lots of people who voted for the Tories never expected the Tories would win. You have this bizarre thing – there is all this remorse going on after the election – with people saying to me in large numbers, that was not quite what we meant.' The decision to kill off the Liberal Democrats, especially in the south-west, can be attributed to the meticulous research and polling that Crosby had organised eighteen months before the election – reinforced by findings in the final weeks of the campaign.

One senior Tory explained:

> When we looked at the south-west, we had a real opportunity to squeeze the Lib Dems. The Lib Dem national polling had flatlined and the recovery never came … As the campaign progressed the scale of the opportunity became clear. At the start of the campaign were we seriously thinking, your vote is in the bag? No.

Private polling for the Conservative campaign – which was 'very sophisticated in those target areas' – showed the Lib Dem strongholds in the south-west were in play early in the campaign, according to an aide to Cameron's campaign. Then, in the final fortnight, Crosby gave the order to step up the campaign to wipe out the Lib Dems, even in their 'safest' seats, such as Yeovil, or Thornbury and Yate, the constituency of the pensions minister, Steve Webb, which was thought to be impregnable.

> Lib Dem voters were very worried about the economy. That was a message that resonated. We had a definite toehold in terms of making the case that 'the economy was going in the right direction, stick with the path or put it at risk'.
>
> Secondly, we said to them that 'this is not an election where you can vote another way and get a Tory government. There is no clever third way to that destination.' That was underlined by the fact Clegg and Cable and so on had made clear they were just as likely to go into coalition with Labour as the Conservatives. This time around, people could see voting Lib Dem you could just as easily end up with Ed Miliband and in fact maybe were more likely to end up with Ed Miliband. It was that choice. If you want David Cameron to be PM, vote for it.[173]

In these Lib Dem target seats, the Tories put up billboard posters designed to drive home the message that local voters were living in one of the twenty-three key constituencies that could give David Cameron a majority. Strategists on the Conservative campaign regarded convincing these residents that their votes could make a difference as even more important than the warnings over the SNP doing a deal with Labour.

Another senior Tory figure said the most shocking element of the defeat for the Lib Dems was that 'they didn't see it coming'.[174] Clegg concedes he had no idea that the Tories were working so hard to unseat so many of his colleagues in the south-west. 'They did a lot of phoning – a huge amount,' he says.

> We didn't see any canvassers out on the streets. We would send out teams of canvassers, in the old 'shoe-leather' way. And you just wouldn't see [the Tories], which is why in some significant parts it did completely blindside us. We knew they were firing off huge numbers of letters at folk but by definition we couldn't see how the communication with voters was happening.[175]

Scotland

Danny Alexander had realised months earlier that he might fall, but Clegg 'hoped beyond hope' he would survive.[176]

Alexander, a tall, red-headed Scot with a passion for cricket, was one of Clegg's closest allies and one of the most powerful men in the coalition. He was appointed Chief Secretary to the Treasury in the reshuffle just three weeks after the new government was formed in 2010, when David Laws resigned over his expenses. He was Clegg's unofficial deputy, his 'wing man' in meetings of the coalition's decision-making 'quad' – the name given to the group of David Cameron, George Osborne, Clegg and Alexander. All major policies had to be signed off by the quad, and failure to agree would mean Cabinet ministers lower down the government's rankings would have to go back to the drawing board.

Alexander has been blamed for the Lib Dems' decision to abandon opposition to tuition fees – citing the imperative to cut the deficit as a reason why the bill for higher education should be met by students rather than the taxpayer. Left-wingers in the party would regularly complain that Danny was 'going native' in the Treasury, working so closely with Osborne. Certainly, the Chancellor confessed to feeling sorry for his former colleague after the 2015 election. It is a measure of Alexander's central importance to Clegg's political project that the Lib Dem leader put him in charge of the party's 2015 coalition negotiating team, whose membership was announced in the days before the election. Alexander was expected to fulfil this role even if he lost his seat, which it seemed certain he would months before a vote was cast.

In the closing weeks of the campaign, the Lib Dems knew that the same SNP surge that overcame Alexander posed the gravest threat to the party south of the border too. Not only did Nick Clegg lose all but one of his eleven MPs in the SNP landslide in Scotland, but the fear that Nicola Sturgeon and her partner in politics, Alex Salmond, would totally dominate a weak Labour minority government became – in Clegg's eyes – the single defining question of the entire 2015 election. The Tories, he believes, ruthlessly exploited English voters' 'visceral fear' of being ruled by the SNP, a primal anxiety felt most keenly in the shires of the West Country, about as far from Scotland as it's possible to get in the UK. The consequences for the Lib Dems were catastrophic.

'It was just an incredibly powerful emotional message, reinforced by papers and the BBC, and there was very little we could do about it,' Clegg says. Not for the last time, it was a development that pleased both the SNP leader and the Tories. The Lib Dems only realised the seriousness of the SNP threat at a relatively late stage, and never grasped its full potency until after the polls closed on 7 May.

In mid-April, the party undertook a huge postal vote canvassing operation. In past elections, totting up the postal ballots was seen as something of a niche pursuit, because only the absent or infirm would tend to cast their votes in this way. But more recently, the number of voters choosing to vote by post has risen significantly, and the social mix of the postal electorate now mirrors far more closely that of the millions more who still walk to the polling station to vote in person on election day. For the Lib Dems, this made a detailed analysis of postal voter canvassing data a vital tool. Their results showed that the SNP fear message was having an impact even at the relatively early state, with the race tightening between their candidates and Conservatives in the West Country. Nevertheless, two weeks out from polling day, Clegg felt his party could still hang on.

Clegg says:

> We saw it in our own seats in the south-west. There were seats... where our canvassing evidence, and I'm sure the Conservatives' as well, was showing we were at least five, six or seven points ahead a couple of weeks before the election.
>
> And come election day, very large numbers of people who had either not voted before or who would have been floating voters just decided that the one thing they didn't want above and beyond anything else was Miliband screwing the economy up, dancing to the tune

of Alex Salmond. That just became an overriding thing. The reason why it was so powerful, beyond the technical proficiency of a very well-resourced Conservative campaign, was that it was true. People say it was all very clever. It's not. It was just true. People are not stupid. They knew that was the only way Labour were going to get in. And they didn't want Miliband as PM, they feared for the economy and they hated the idea that England would be dictated to by the SNP.

Ed Miliband in my view made this fundamental error equivocating for so long about his attitude to the SNP. The press whacked it day after day after day. The BBC then picked it up, so that you got this echo chamber so that every time Cameron said, 'Vote for me because I can keep Miliband and Salmond out', which was his basic refrain by the end, Nicola Sturgeon popped up and said, 'Why does Ed Miliband want to deny that I am going to keep him on a short leash?' It was like a ping-pong ball ricocheting back and forth, and it just reinforced itself. And there was nothing we could do about it.[177]

By comparison, the Lib Dem message of giving Labour backbone and restraining the Tories was 'too subtle' to make an impact, he says. In the final week, however, it was clear to Clegg that he had to try something to stop the 'wave' of fear about an SNP-led government. MPs across England were being told that while voters liked them personally and generally approved of Lib Dem politics, they just couldn't risk Labour and the SNP messing up the economy again.

Clegg stunned his senior colleagues, a fortnight from polling day, when he told the *Financial Times* that he would not form a coalition with Ed Miliband if Labour cut any kind of deal with the SNP. The move sent Lib Dem aides into 'panic'.[178] But Clegg told his team bluntly that the party was staring at disaster. The only way to stop the rout was to take an even harder line and rule out any deal, of any kind, with Miliband, regardless of whether it involved the SNP or any other party. Though he realised at the time that such a move would be impossible for a Lib Dem leader seeking to be neutral to the prospect of working with either Labour or the Tories, Clegg's senior team believe that such a declaration would have saved the party several seats.

Instead, on 16 April, Clegg launched a counter-attack. He tried to frame an equally dire warning for voters about the consequences of the Tories stitching together a deal with the Europhobic UKIP after the election, a pairing that would, he said, deliver an extreme right-wing government of which the public should be very afraid. His term for this hideous new spectre was 'Blukip'. But the concept came too late.

Clegg's 'Blukip' warning had a more fundamental flaw than timing, however: it just did not ring true in the way that the idea of Sturgeon pulling the strings behind Ed Miliband did. No public polling in the run-up to the election put UKIP on course to hold the balance of power. By contrast, almost every pollster produced results that showed the SNP were on the way to sweeping the board in Scotland and becoming a major force at Westminster.

The polling merely reinforced the Tory argument that Labour could need the support of the SNP. This, Clegg accepts, was critical to the success of the Tory message. 'I have never in my career in politics seen such a myopic obsession in the media with one set of snapshot data after the next, and it framed everything,' he says.

The arms race

For the six weeks of the short campaign, the Liberal Democrats ran their bid for re-election in a way that would not have seemed out of place twenty or thirty years ago. They hired a traditional election battle bus and took it around the country, ferrying national newspaper correspondents, photographers and TV reporters – for a fee of £750 each per day – from one constituency to the next. The Lib Dem coach turned out to be the only traditional battle bus used by any of the major Westminster parties. Labour and the Tories chose to handpick the media passengers to join them each day 'on the road', reserving room largely for broadcasters, who are bound by law to be politically impartial, unlike the press. In their case, the Lib Dems had chosen a vehicle that was usually used to ferry Crystal Palace football team to and from matches, and had painted it bright yellow.

Travelling journalists were fed and watered, with packed lunches of sandwich platters and salad boxes, tea and coffee, and a well-stocked fridge full of soft drinks. Crucially for keeping the hacks happy, it also had a plentiful supply of beer and wine. The first alcohol on the bus would be served at around six each evening, with dinner booked for overnight stays. When he travelled on the bus, Nick Clegg took over the compartment at the back of the vehicle, separated from the travelling journalists by a doorway. Here, the plush cappuccino-brown leather seating stretched around a central table in a long curve. Clegg and his aides used this space as the leader's office, to conduct media briefings and newspaper interviews.

The Lib Dem campaign was always more interesting to the media when Miriam González, Clegg's wife, joined him on the election trail. On one such occasion, the pair

called in at a primary school in Chippenham, as part of the
party's doomed attempt to help Duncan Hames keep his seat.
González drew a larger than usual crowd of photographers
and television crews, adding some Spanish glamour to an
otherwise dreary political campaign. The couple then cooked
crumble on camera with the children in the school kitchen as
the flashbulbs went off all around. Once back on the bus, the
Lib Dem leader plied his media following with Scottish tablet
made by Miriam, who had been in Scotland the previous day
attempting to stem the flow of Lib Dem votes to the SNP.
Clegg, who was on a strict campaign diet, did not eat the
sweet himself.

In the leader's absence, Clegg's young team of travelling
aides would colonise his compartment at the back of the
bus for the purpose of draining the on-board fridge of beer
and wine, playing music and chatting during long, late-
night motorway drives home to London. Journalists who
interviewed Clegg on the bus found him to be largely relaxed
and philosophical about the potential impact that his decision
to enter coalition with the Tories would have on his own
party's fortunes. Yet he did not believe it would be a disaster.
'This is clearly going to be an election where we have got a
number of very close fights on our hands,' he said in the week
before polling day. 'I would slightly argue that us growing
after this election is more likely than less likely because we
have proved that we can govern as well as protest,' he added.

The sense of 'national duty', doing right by the country,
would always 'trump whatever vituperation or vitriol or
decapitation might be aimed at me by my opponents', he
said. 'We put country before party. I was flattered to see John
Major say it would be graceless for the Conservatives not to
acknowledge that the Liberal Democrats put country before

party and did it at considerable cost – much greater than any cost that has been incurred by the Conservative Party.'[179]

Unfortunately for Clegg, Major was no longer Tory leader and was not in charge of the Conservative operation. Intensive – and expensive – private research for the Conservatives in key marginal seats told Lynton Crosby that he should throw everything at the south-west in the final weeks of the campaign. As Crosby knew that defeating the Lib Dems offered the best opportunity for a majority, he designed the Tories' daily tracker poll of sixty key seats to include a disproportionately high number of Lib Dem-held target constituencies. 'It came down to the kind of work that Stephen Gilbert, Lynton and Mark Textor were doing in terms of the very detailed daily analysis of those key battleground seats. This was showing not that we would definitely win – but that there was potential,' a senior Tory recalls.[180]

So CCHQ targeted swing voters in the south-west seats with huge numbers of letters and leaflets, as well as phone calls, and sent down an army of activists, including pro-hunt supporters from the Vote OK group, which contributed campaigners to twenty-five seats. Conservative Cabinet ministers, and sitting MPs from elsewhere, made repeated visits to the West Country. In London, the Tories' biggest star, Boris Johnson, pounded the pavements to help unseat not one, but two Lib Dem giants: Vince Cable and Ed Davey.

Clegg now attributes the Tory success in part to their superior technical campaign. He disapproves of the way the Tories – as he sees it – found a way around the spending limits imposed on local candidates. Under Electoral Commission rules, candidates locally can spend £8,700 – plus up to 9p per voter – in a constituency during the six-week 'short' election campaign. The Tories used central funding to send individually tailored direct marketing mailshots of leaflets, repeatedly, to individual voters in these key seats whom they had identified through their sophisticated canvassing operation as being open to persuasion. In the long campaign, which began in December 2014, the limit is £30,700, plus up to 9p per voter.

Clegg says:

> They [the Conservatives] ran an unbelievably well-resourced campaign in a way that I had not seen in British politics before. That meant parachuting into people's living rooms and onto people's doormats a campaign from the centre, allowing them to completely work around the spending constraints which exist within constituencies. You've got strict spending constraints within constituencies. But the Conservatives went around having amassed this huge war chest and they were able to flatten any opposition in terms of the money they spent by direct mailing on a scale that I have not seen before – huge amounts of campaign literature directly from the centre into constituencies. I'm not saying they were breaking the rules as such but certainly riding roughshod over the limits that are supposed to exist in an election campaign.[181]

Tory campaign strategists deny that Lib Dem seats were flooded with leaflets and direct mail in a way to circumvent the spending limits. The party had identified so precisely the swing voters it needed to persuade that it only sent mail to these individuals, rather than blanket bombing an entire area. Conservative insiders insist that this would mean the cost of the exercise would not be large enough to exceed the local campaign limits. The evidence is not available to reach a conclusive verdict on whether Clegg or the Tories are right about the amounts spent on centrally funded campaign literature in target seats. Parties have to decide for themselves whether a particular letter or leaflet should fall under local or central spending for accounting purposes. If they are in doubt, parties must ask the Electoral Commission, which regulates these matters, for a ruling. At the time of writing, the details of the amounts the political parties spent during the election had not been published.[182]

All parties build up databases of voters they think they can win over, as well as those they believe will definitely support them on polling day and others who are firmly in their opponents' camps. But in the year before the election, the Tories were spending £100,000 a month on Facebook advertising alone, an enterprise that allowed the party to gain unprecedented insight into the electorate in highly targeted areas of the country, and allowed them to communicate in a far more direct way with undecided voters.

'It has got quite a profound implication because it means all parties will start looking at what the Tories did and start emulating it. And it means that you'll get this kind of data arms race now,' says Clegg.

> Also it begs big questions about whether incumbency really does act as the insurance policy for incumbent MPs that it once did. Clearly it didn't at all in our case.
>
> We all use data. What I do feel quite strongly is that what is different is that the Tories have a level of financial resource which they can throw at this, that just no one else does. That is a) not really quite in the spirit of the campaign spending limits that exist, and

b) means that the Conservative Party, as long as they
have this huge amount of money that they are raising,
particularly from the financial sector, are at a huge,
in-built advantage because you either have the resources
to buy that data or you don't.[183]

Paddy Ashdown, who served in the Special Forces, described
his task in leading the Lib Dem campaign as one of 'survival'.[184]
Ashdown thought he could win twenty-five seats, and aimed
for forty as a target that would allow Clegg to retain some
influence in a future coalition. Even before the campaign got
under way, then, the Lib Dems were not trying to defend the
full fifty-seven seats that they won in 2010.

On the morning of Thursday 7 May, Clegg's campaign
team, led by Ashdown, told him they reckoned it was 'on a
knife-edge' in a lot of seats. But if the party had 'a decent day',
he could expect to end election night with thirty-five or thirty-
six MPs. At the time, even this would have been a sickening
loss. But it would have kept the party in the running to be
part of the next government, once again potentially holding
the balance of power in a hung parliament. To Nick Clegg,
this was always the greatest prize: proving that his party can
govern and that coalition works.[185]

PART 4

THE
ELECTION

CHAPTER **12**

SIR JEREMY

One late summer's day in 2001, Jonathan Powell, Tony Blair's chief of staff, was taking advantage of his boss's absence from Downing Street to hold a meeting in the Prime Minister's private office. Then the duty clerk burst in.

'A second plane has hit the Twin Towers,' the official said.

Powell could not believe it and told the clerk he must have seen a 'loop' TV clip of the terrible accident in which an aircraft had crashed into New York's tallest building earlier that day. But when the full horror of the 9/11 terrorist attack on America became clear, Blair's Downing Street was thrown into chaos. The PM was away at the TUC conference in Brighton. The Cabinet Secretary, the government's most senior civil servant, was himself out of the building at lunch.

So Powell turned to Jeremy Heywood, then aged thirty-nine, who was Blair's private secretary in No. 10. With reports of more attacks on the Pentagon and another plane coming down outside Washington, rumours swept the world that more western cities – including London – were under threat. The scale of the atrocity required an immediate response from the British government. Heywood, Powell has recalled, displayed a 'preternatural calm' that afternoon as the pair began coordinating the emergency.

> Jeremy was there in the private office. The two of us immediately got on the phones and started trying to make sure that there would be no repeat attack or copycat attack here in London. He was extraordinary. He just had two phones with him and he got it all done.[186]

Fourteen years later and Heywood was back at the heart of government trying to avert a different kind of crisis, a task that would test his political and diplomatic acumen to the full. Now Cabinet Secretary, he was the man to whom the political classes would turn if voters delivered a hung parliament in the 2015 election. His task was clear: to ensure that the smooth government of Britain continued after another inconclusive election result, while helping politicians from rival parties to hold power-sharing talks. As if this was not difficult enough, perhaps his most sensitive concern was to protect the Queen from being drawn into any kind of grubby political stunt that could tarnish the reputation of the monarchy and undermine the authority of the established system of government, of which he was the chief custodian.

The role of Cabinet Secretary is a story of power behind the throne. Every Tuesday morning, he can be found seated at David Cameron's side during the weekly Cabinet meeting. He acts as the Prime Minister's chief adviser on everything from top-secret intelligence and urgent matters of national security to arrangements for government reshuffles. To those who have worked with him, Heywood seems born to the role. He has been described as 'quite possibly the most important person in the country that nobody has ever heard of'.[187]

He commands the army of 400,000 civil servants and, with his unflappable, bespectacled demeanour, serves as the personification of British officialdom and the guardian of the established order of things. Fittingly for a man at the apex of the government machine, Heywood has one of the grandest offices in Whitehall. His vast, wood-panelled room deep inside the Cabinet Office contains a large and highly polished boardroom table, a corner desk near to a window, two television screens and a bust of Gandhi. From here he also has easy access to a little-known passageway that dates back to Tudor times. If ever there was an original corridor of power, this is it. The red bricks of Cockpit Passage link the towering white stone palace of the Cabinet Office at 70 Whitehall to Downing Street. Through this corridor, the most powerful member of the permanent British establishment can visit the tenant of No. 10, for, to the civil service, all prime ministers are always merely temporary residents next door.

Meticulous, understated and fiercely private (he once bitterly complained when his engagement to another civil servant became public knowledge in the office), Heywood has been seen by successive prime ministers and their aides as an indispensable crutch at moments of difficulty, the perfect man for a crisis. Nick Pearce, former head of Tony Blair's policy unit, who worked with Heywood in No. 10, has said: 'For somebody like me who believes in decentralising and dispersing power... you don't want one person to have so much power and influence, but I'm pleased it's him.'[188]

The cockpit

In the days before the 2015 election campaign began, Heywood took his usual route through the 'cockpit' to No. 10

to meet Cameron. Except this time it was to discuss the delicate matter of the Prime Minister's political mortality. Heywood's working relationship with Cameron is strong. It dates back decades and was forged in the heat of crisis, when they both worked as key advisers to the then Chancellor Norman Lamont at the time of Black Wednesday. Pictures from the period, when Lamont was forced to pull out of the European Exchange Rate Mechanism, show Cameron as a young special adviser in the background. A thirty-year-old Heywood, then private secretary to Lamont, can also be seen stepping out of the ministerial car behind the Chancellor.

In 2015, with almost every poll and political pundit predicting a hung parliament, it fell to Heywood to prepare the ground for the power-sharing negotiations after polling day, out of which would – he hoped – be formed a new, stable and secure government for the United Kingdom. In order to make the necessary arrangements to facilitate these talks, as his predecessor Gus O'Donnell had done after the 2010 election, Sir Jeremy would need the authorisation of the Prime Minister. At their meeting, he told Cameron he would need to ask him to allow government rooms to be made available for his political rivals to hold their private talks about how to evict him from No. 10. Heywood also needed approval from the PM before any civil servants could be released to support the parties in their negotiations, drawing up policy costings and legal notes.

But, ever conscious of the correct protocol, Sir Jeremy, a former head boy, did not want to make a formal request to the Prime Minister to allow preparations for power-sharing talks to begin 'until it was real'. He simply told Cameron that if the polls were right, and voters delivered a hung parliament, he would be back in touch first thing on the morning of 8 May to ask formally for the PM's consent.[189]

Heywood was also clear about another thing: Cameron must stay on as Prime Minister, even if it was evident that he had little chance of leading the next government, until any discussions between other parties had concluded. Cameron, about to leave No. 10 for the six-week national campaign, told Heywood he understood the facts of political life and would of course agree to his request, if it proved necessary. So convinced was Heywood that a new round of coalition talks would be required that he, and others, began making arrangements in anticipation of the Prime Minister giving his order. Rooms were set aside within the Cabinet Office, as well as inside Parliament, for the parties to use for their negotiations. He even put coffee and sandwiches on standby.

Although the Tories publicly denied preparing for a new coalition, the ever powerful George Osborne, along with Oliver Letwin, a Cabinet Office minister who has been used as a trouble-shooter by the PM, were readying themselves to lead the negotiations. They had both been involved in the 2010 talks with the Lib Dems. For Labour, Lord Falconer, Tony Blair's former flatmate and a former Lord Chancellor, had held initial conversations with Heywood's office about the election aftermath. He was expected to lead negotiations for Miliband, while Lord Adonis, who took part in Labour's failed talks with the Lib Dems in 2010 and had been urging his colleagues to prepare better for a deal this time, was another team member.[190] The Lib Dems themselves decided to publish their negotiating team in advance. The most prominent figures in the team were David Laws and Danny Alexander, two Cabinet ministers, and the well-regarded pensions minister Steve Webb, who was popular with his Tory colleagues in the coalition.

Heywood had also made plans – subject to the PM's approval – for civil servants to be on hand to help the politicians work out how much their policies would cost and to answer other queries during the talks. Each party was to be offered one official to act as a go-between, who would then take requests for information from the parties back to a central team of Treasury and departmental experts. Their answers would be restricted to facts: the cost and the legal status of a particular proposal, and whether it would require primary or secondary legislation.

Sir Jeremy was at pains to ensure none of his officials would be sucked into making political judgements about whether one policy was better than another. He was also alive to the threat that came with a potentially large number of negotiations between a variety of parties. In 2010, the talks were chiefly between the Lib Dems and the Conservatives, with abortive and perfunctory discussions taking place between Nick Clegg's allies and Labour as Gordon Brown tried to find a way to stay in power.

This time, however, it was widely assumed that talks would be held between varied combinations of the Tories, the Lib Dems, Labour, the Democratic Unionist Party, the Scottish National Party, Plaid Cymru, the Greens and UKIP. The civil service was clear that minor parties should not use the negotiations as some form of 'fishing' exercise that would allow them to mine the government machine for useful facts and figures and other privileged information if this was not required in good faith for the purposes of reaching an agreement about sharing power.

A final consideration was causing some amusement in Whitehall at this point. Just hours after the election results were due to be announced on 8 May, all the party leaders were expected at the Cenotaph for VE Day anniversary commemorations. The famously awkward pictures of David

Cameron, Gordon Brown and Nick Clegg in 2010 were to be repeated (with Ed Miliband replacing Brown) in 2015.

But before coalition talks could have been held in the Cabinet Office, the negotiators would first have had to negotiate their way through crowds of veterans and others attending the ceremony. On Saturday, as the VE Day weekend continued, the building was to resound to the tune of marching bands practising outside.

The Queen

For all his natural calm, behind the scenes Heywood was battling a potentially serious threat to the reputation of the political system. For some time now, Buckingham Palace had been uneasy about the consequences of the looming election for the Queen. Senior courtiers feared it presented a number of threats to the Queen's political neutrality, which must be maintained at any cost if the integrity of British parliamentary democracy is to remain intact.

Since the coalition passed the Fixed Term Parliaments Act in 2011, the date of the election has been set in law. The Act removed from the Prime Minister the power to choose when he would go to the country to seek re-election. Crucially, from the Palace's point of view, it also meant that there was no need whatever for David Cameron to visit the Queen to ask her to dissolve Parliament. The date of dissolution had been determined in law, under the terms of the new Act, four years previously.

So it was the cause of some consternation that Cameron chose to visit the Queen anyway as the election campaign got underway. Some at Westminster privately believed the PM was trying to 'spin' the Queen for his own political advantage. Pictures of Cameron at the Palace – beamed into living rooms across the country – reinforced the Tory argument that their man had the better claim to be Prime Minister than Ed Miliband just at the moment when the country began to take the choice seriously. Yet all this was nothing compared to the row brewing over what would happen in the event of another hung parliament, and one which seemed likely to be far messier than the 2010 result.

Sir Christopher Geidt, the Queen's private secretary, is not a man to mess around. Beneath his suave and charming exterior lies a shrewd and steely servant of the establishment. His career has seen him face deadly danger in a war zone and handle sensitive state secrets while doing his duty for Queen and country.

A former Scots Guard and military intelligence officer who trained at Sandhurst, Geidt was chosen as the British government's representative to the European monitoring mission in Sarajevo at the height of the Bosnian War in 1994. He has declined to comment in public on suggestions that he previously worked for MI6. Yet, for all his experience, the prospect of weeks of political uncertainty after the election remained an overriding concern.

As private secretary, Geidt acts as the conduit between the Palace and No. 10 and is given access to secret intelligence. He is also a key adviser on the Queen's constitutional role. By the time the Queen gave the order to prorogue Parliament, the Palace was making it known that Her Majesty was anxious to avoid being drawn into politics if voters delivered another inconclusive result. At this stage, their concern was to protect the Queen and stop politicians using her to prop up a weak government. Short of sleep, desperate for power, after weeks of tortured negotiations, Ed Miliband or David Cameron equally could attempt to borrow the Queen's support, courtiers apparently feared, to lend legitimacy to their claims to power.

The mechanism they would use would be the Queen's Speech. With the date of the election set so far in advance, a provisional date had also been agreed for the State Opening of the new parliament: 27 May. The period of almost three weeks after polling day would give the parties a healthy amount of breathing space to conclude their negotiations and for a new government, either a coalition or a minority with a 'confidence and supply' arrangement with other parties, to be formed.

But royal aides were highly agitated at the prospect of a minority government putting Her Majesty through the full pomp and ceremony of a State Opening of Parliament if the government itself could lose the vote in the Commons on the speech and be overthrown a few weeks later. Such a defeat in a Commons vote could be fatal to the authority of the government and lead to its downfall. It could also weaken the standing of the monarchy, and politicise the Queen herself, they said.

On 19 April, a 'source close to the Palace' warned reporters that the Queen 'absolutely wants to avoid' being drawn into talks over how the next government is formed 'at all costs'. The royal source said: 'One of the concerns that might be there is if the Queen's Speech became a mechanism for testing a particular Prime Minister's control of the House [of Commons]. You wouldn't want the Queen to be politicised by giving that speech.'[191]

Instead, plans were being drawn up for a lower-profile ceremony, with the government's Leader of the House of

Lords delivering the speech instead of the Queen. There would
be no carriage procession, marching guardsmen or any of
the usual trappings of the State Opening of Parliament. Her
Majesty would stay away, at Windsor, and would not take
up residence at Buckingham Palace until it was clear that Ed
Miliband or David Cameron could command a majority in
the House of Commons. Such was the delicacy of the question
for the Palace that a room was set aside in the Cabinet Office
for Geidt himself to use. Thus he would be on hand while
the post-election machinations unfolded behind heavy doors
elsewhere in the building.

Inside the Cabinet Office, Heywood and the government's
constitution director, Mark Sweeney, were also studying the
protocols of government formation. After consulting the
history books, they concluded that precedent suggested that
the deep concern that seemed to be emanating from the Palace
was misplaced. The Queen must deliver the speech at the State
Opening, even if the vote that follows in the Commons sees
this same speech defeated a few days later.

The last time a speech vote was 'lost' in the Commons
was in January 1924, when King George V gave a Tory
King's Speech, which was subsequently defeated by seventy-
two votes. Neither of the candidates for Prime Minister this
time – or, so Heywood hoped and believed, any other party
leader – would want to drag the Queen into anything that
became a 'farce' or use her in some kind of 'shabby political
manoeuvre'. At least, there was no way at all that the civil
service were prepared to concede the point in public.[192]

The Cabinet Office's 'lines to take' in response to media
enquiries were clear: none of our esteemed politicians would
want to compromise the neutrality of the Queen; all would be
acting 'in good faith', genuinely trying to make the right decisions

in the national interest. Moreover, as polling day approached, Heywood let it be known that David Cameron would be required to stay in place until the next government was formed, to avoid a power vacuum.

It was a pre-emptive strike on behalf of the civil service, whose core principle is that there must always be a government. After the 2010 election, Gordon Brown was criticised and called a 'squatter' in No. 10 when he remained in office as coalition talks between the Liberal Democrats and Tories continued. But the official view was clear: Brown, as the incumbent PM, had a duty to stay on until a new government was formed in 2010. Similarly, in 2015, Cameron would have 'the whip hand' as the occupier of No. 10. In the event of a hung parliament, it would his prerogative to seek to form a government first, or, in the delicate terminology preferred by Westminster, to 'test the will of the Commons' by putting his Queen's Speech to a vote. If Cameron concluded – before or after a Queen's Speech – that he could not continue, he would then advise the Queen that she should send for Ed Miliband. The Palace was ultimately persuaded to drop its campaign over who should deliver the first Queen's Speech of the new parliament.

The law

Labour's strategy team, meanwhile, had been making its own plans for a hung parliament. Lord Falconer, the former Lord Chancellor under Tony Blair, who had backed David Miliband for the Labour leadership, was given a key role in Labour's negotiating team. Ed Miliband's aides consulted legal experts in the hope of finding, in some dark and overlooked crevice of election law, a way to force David Cameron out of his cosy Downing Street flat if he refused to go voluntarily.

Eager though some around Miliband were to explore the options, a decision to take a disputed election to court would have been a nuclear option for any party. Two documents were uppermost in the minds of the Labour aides – as well as the civil servants – who were trying to chart a way to establishing a new government. The first, and most important, was the Fixed Term Parliaments Act 2011, a new piece of law that had never been put to the test before and was seemingly waiting for just the right circumstances of a finely balanced election result for a juicy test case to be brought.

As news spread that Miliband's aides were contemplating some kind of legal ambush to force Cameron out of the famous black door to No. 10, senior figures in other parties expressed their dismay. Nick Clegg, the Lib Dem leader, said it would be bad for democracy if the election had to be decided in court. 'We are duty-bound as politicians to behave in a grown-up way.' Chris Grayling, the Lord Chancellor and Tory Justice Secretary, demanded that Miliband rule out any such tactic, saying he feared the Labour leader would stop at 'absolutely nothing' to try to 'hustle his way' into No. 10. 'I've no doubt that if he thinks there's some cynical legal manoeuvre to try, he'll not shy away from doing so,' Grayling said.

While the Act was still being debated in Parliament, constitutional experts and senior parliamentary officials warned that codifying the process of government formation in law could see the battle for power end up in court. A clash of this kind between the judiciary and Parliament would be potentially disastrous in the fevered atmosphere of an inconclusive election result. In 2000, the world had watched with horror as a similar fate befell the American presidential election contest between Al Gore and George W. Bush. The latter ultimately won, but only after the question went to the US Supreme Court.

When the prospect of court action was put to senior civil servants in the days leading up to the election, their best response was simply to say that the judges would be 'very reluctant' to get involved in arbitrating on an election, or on procedures within the House of Commons. They could offer no guarantee, however, that the legislation would never be tested in court.

The second document at the top of Labour reading lists in April was the Cabinet Manual. This was the Whitehall 'bible', prepared for the civil service before the 2010 election to guide officials through the sketchily mapped territory of how to form a coalition in the eventuality that Parliament is hung. In 2010, the civil service had no muscle memory for responding to such a scenario, as there had not been a coalition government for seventy years. The Cabinet Manual, which was updated after the Fixed Term Parliaments Act was passed, outlined the circumstances under which a Prime Minister could be ousted after an inconclusive election. It was not an especially speedy process. The crucial mechanism for bringing down a Prime Minister is a vote of no confidence.

The manual said:

> Under the Fixed Term Parliaments Act 2011, if a government is defeated on a motion that 'this House has no confidence in Her Majesty's Government', there is then a fourteen-day period during which an alternative government can be formed from the House of Commons as presently constituted, or the incumbent government can seek to regain the confidence of the House.

But if no new government could be formed and win an affirmative 'confidence motion' in the Commons within two weeks, Parliament would automatically be dissolved and a new election called.

A separate section of the Cabinet Manual spelled out the circumstances under which a Prime Minister would be expected to fall on his sword and advise the Queen to give somebody else a chance. 'The Prime Minister is expected to resign where it is clear that he or she does not have the confidence of the House of Commons and that an alternative government does have the confidence,' it said.

Before the Fixed Term Parliaments Act, life was much simpler. If the Prime Minister could not get his Queen's Speech past a vote in the House of Commons, this would be viewed as a blatant vote of no confidence in his or her government, which would then be expected to resign. However, since the advent of the Act, all this changed. It would theoretically be open to the Prime Minister to lose a Queen's Speech vote, even then to lose a formal vote of no confidence, which would trigger the fourteen-day period, and still to remain in No. 10, trying to cobble together enough votes in the Commons to win an affirmative vote of confidence before the two-week deadline elapses and a new election is held. 'The PM is accountable to public opinion and Parliament. If he chooses to play hardball, that's up to him. It is not a matter of law. It is a matter of politics,' one Whitehall insider said.[193]

A very British rationale began to emerge for how the country's political leaders would resolve a difficult situation. The Tories could not cling onto power for ever. 'There will come a point where certain decisions have to be taken. It does to a large extent depend on everybody behaving reasonably,' one senior figure said.

For centuries, the government of Britain has rested upon a generally accepted standard of what constitutes 'reasonable behaviour'. There is no other way a constitution that has never been fully codified could survive. It is expected that no party will try to force themselves into power by the use of a legal challenge of some kind. So, too, is it expected that no Prime Minister will seek to 'play hardball' after losing three confidence votes in the Commons, forcing another election on the country without giving his opponent the chance to try to form a government first.

But Britain's constitution has been somewhat muddied by the fact that bits of the process of government formation have been written down – most recently the Cabinet Manual and the Fixed Term Parliaments Act. A senior official confided privately shortly before polling day: 'There is no precedent as to what happens if you lose a Queen's Speech vote in a world of the Fixed Term Parliaments Act. We would be breaking new ground.'[194]

CHAPTER 13

ELECTION NIGHT

Exhausted and anxious, David Cameron arrived back at his Oxfordshire home at 11 p.m. on Wednesday 6 May to the news he did not want to hear. A final opinion poll from ICM for *The Guardian* released the night before polling day gave Ed Miliband a boost. Cameron and his team knew that ICM had a reputation for being among the most reliable of market research firms, having come closest to predicting the final result of previous elections. ICM – whose polling for the newspaper was conducted by telephone surveys, which were more expensive but seen as more accurate than online polling, had also been giving the Tories a consistently better showing than other pollsters. On 13 April, a poll from ICM had given the Conservatives their best result: 39 per cent to Labour's 33. But just when it counted most, the firm's final prediction, updated on election day itself, put Labour one point ahead.

It was a pattern repeated among other polling companies and seemed to confirm the Prime Minister's worst fears: on the eve of the election, momentum was shifting towards Miliband. Internal figures generated by Lynton Crosby and his polling partner, Mark Textor, gave senior Tories some cause for comfort, with a lead in key marginal seats, as well as nationally. However, it was 'only human' for Cameron to have his doubts. 'Oh, Christ,' he said, when an aide told him of the *Guardian* result. The Tory leader's wife, Samantha, joined him for the final leg of the closing campaign tour, an arduous 36-hour marathon which took the Prime Minister to twelve constituencies in England, Wales and Scotland. 'She was brilliant at cheering him up about the polls and taking his mind off the campaign a bit, in the way that only your spouse can,' according to a party worker who saw them on polling day.[195]

After a punishing six-week campaign, Cameron voted in his constituency of Witney on the morning of 7 May and then spent the rest of polling day away from the fray. He was joined by his closest political friend and ally, George Osborne, Crosby and a handful of other trusted confidants. Together they ran through the possible scenarios, drawing up options for a hung parliament and how they could neutralise the threat from the SNP while making Nick Clegg another offer to form a coalition. After lunch, Cameron turned to Crosby as the group began to disperse, and thanked him profusely for directing the campaign. 'Whatever happens next, I don't regret a moment of it,' Cameron said.[196]

Osborne flew to Cheshire for his own constituency count in Tatton. Cameron went for a walk to clear his head before the intense drama of election night began to unfold. 'He just wanted some time to himself,' an aide recalls. 'He's good at remaining calm but you could sense that he was nervous. We were all completely knackered. We'd slogged our guts out for six weeks and there was nothing more we could do. It was out of our hands.'[197]

Nick Clegg completed his 'mad' final tour of the election campaign, which took him from Land's End to John O' Groats, late on the evening of Wednesday 6 May. Paddy Ashdown, Clegg's mentor and campaign director, had arranged for one of his friends to fly the Lib Dem leader and his aides back to Clegg's constituency, ready to vote the following day. For Clegg, this was perhaps the most alarming moment of the campaign. They took off from Wick airport in a tiny, four-seater plane that felt to Clegg like it was far too flimsy to withstand the short journey south. James McGrory, Clegg's media adviser, who was among the four passengers on board, felt increasingly ill as the aircraft was thrown about in the wind. While they bounced up and down in the night sky, feeling every little gust of breeze, Clegg asked the pilot as calmly as he could: 'So, tell me about this aeroplane.' Ashdown's friend replied casually: 'Oh, it's only thirty years old.' They landed at Robin Hood airport, outside Doncaster, and drove to Clegg's flat in Sheffield, where his wife Miriam was waiting for him, having arrived from London earlier in the day.

It was a cool evening in Oxfordshire on Thursday 7 May. At Cameron's constituency home, in the picturesque Cotswolds hamlet of Dean, near Chipping Norton, a handful of senior Tories gathered for dinner and the long wait for results. As the daylight faded, guests at the Camerons' cottage went out onto the patio clutching glasses of wine, wrapped in coats against the evening chill. Cameron was gloomy. While he believed the Conservatives were well placed to win the most seats, he and his senior team felt there was little chance of a majority – and every likelihood that the late twist of the polls towards Labour would be replicated when the results came through. Cameron feared the party would not have enough MPs to do another deal with Nick Clegg to keep Labour out. He prepared for the worst, drafted a resignation statement and read it to his guests gathered on the patio.[198] It was an emotional moment for the PM's team – Ed Llewellyn, his chief of staff, Kate Fall, Llewellyn's deputy, Craig Oliver, the No. 10 communications chief, and Liz Sugg, head of operations – and also for Cameron himself. After five years in No. 10, they were all staring bleakly at the prospect of defeat.

One senior figure present recalls:

> There was a sense that descended on the night among a lot of people that we just weren't going to be able to get enough to put a Queen's Speech together. Although people in our team were feeling confident, the majority of opinion was that confidence was misplaced and as you approach the hour of reckoning, that starts making you think, 'Well, maybe we *are* wrong.' There was quite a mood of 'Oh, God, right, maybe this isn't going to be that great.'

When Cameron had finished his rehearsal, the gathering moved inside for one of their host's favourite comfort-food dinners, a hearty beef pie.[199]

One hundred and thirty miles away, Ed Miliband returned to his house in Doncaster at 7 p.m. after knocking on doors during the early evening. The BBC presenter Jon Sopel was waiting outside and the Labour leader chatted briefly to him before retreating inside to prepare for the results. Miliband and his wife Justine Thornton were joined by Stewart Wood, a long-standing friend and adviser, Bob Roberts, the party's communications director, Greg Beales, his head of strategy, Anna Yearley and Rachel Kinnock. As they ate a meal of chilli, served with water and Diet Coke, but no alcohol, Roberts, Wood and Beales chatted and played around with various versions of the different speeches that Miliband could be required to deliver, depending on the result. Although they had prepared material for all four possible outcomes – a hung parliament with either Labour or the Tories the largest party, victory and defeat – the devastating scale of their loss was not on the Labour leader's radar. 'There were four different scenarios; we were preparing for all four different scenarios. We knew as much as anybody else and we were probably at the more cautious end of predictions. We were certainly not sitting there expecting to go into Downing Street,' one source says.[200]

However, a plan was in place to portray Miliband as the winner in the event of a hung parliament. The outcome from an inconclusive result would rest on the question of which leader appeared to have the best claim to legitimacy. With this in mind, Labour laid on the trappings of prime ministerial power to make Miliband look more like the leader he wanted to be. A helicopter was booked to fly him and his senior aides from Doncaster to London in the small hours of Friday morning. In politics, such an ostentatious mode of transport is generally reserved for presidents and premiers on urgent government business.

Back in London at 1 Brewer's Green, however, Lord Falconer began calling the political editors of newspapers at Westminster to brief them on sections of the Cabinet Manual. He wanted to prepare the ground for the argument Miliband's team intended to make in the hours to come that Cameron could not put the numbers together to form a government, lacked democratic legitimacy and must leave No. 10 immediately. When news of these briefings reached Cameron's team, via a call from the BBC political editor Nick Robinson, the gathering in Oxfordshire went into a panic. A frantic exchange of messages followed, with emails sent to and from Craig Oliver, George Osborne, Ed Llewellyn and Cameron's private office, as they tried to establish whether Miliband could force them from Downing Street. They concluded that – as Sir Jeremy Heywood had privately made clear – the incumbent Prime Minister had a duty to remain in office until a new government could be formed, and that in a contested election, Cameron would have the first right to try to muster a majority in the House of Commons.

Falconer, an arch-Blairite, had been given an increasing degree of responsibility in Labour's election planning. A former Lord Chancellor, he was enjoying something of a political renaissance. Miliband had placed him in charge of the negotiating team who would lead talks with the Lib Dems and other parties in the event of a hung parliament. Unlike in 2010, when Gordon Brown was unprepared for trying to strike a deal with Nick Clegg, extensive plans had been made for talks already. Some reports suggested that Vince Cable had been in direct contact with Miliband. 'An enormous amount of work had been done preparing for it,' one source said of the planning for coalition.[201]

Shortly before 10 p.m., Cameron and his team gathered around the television to await the exit poll, which would give the first indication of their fate. In 2010, Craig Oliver had been working as an editor on the BBC's election programme, where he had had the idea of introducing a five-minute countdown clock to build tension until the moment the polls closed and the official exit poll results could be announced. As he sat watching the coverage, now a key member of Cameron's team, he cursed his own invention. With twenty-five seconds to go, Big Ben began to chime the hour, and David Dimbleby, presenting the BBC's coverage for the final time, prepared viewers for the figures that would shock Britain. Then he announced: 'It's ten o'clock and we are saying the Conservatives are the largest party.'

To those watching Cameron's television, the long wait that followed was torture. They might well be the largest party – but how many seats were they forecast to win? Cameron's aides knew that if they fell short of 290, it would probably be over. One source remembers the unbearable tension, watching the BBC's coverage that night. 'It seemed to take forever to move through to the numbers. It probably was about eight to ten seconds but it felt like forever. I remember just saying to myself, "What's the number, what's the number, what's the number?" That's what mattered.'

Eventually, the BBC displayed its graphic showing Cameron with 316 seats, as Dimbleby said: 'And here are the figures which we have – quite remarkable, this exit poll – the Conservatives on 316, that's up nine since 2010.' Labour were forecast to achieve 239, the Lib Dems just ten and the SNP an astonishing fifty-eight seats, with UKIP on two.

> The number 316 came up and there was a half-second of 'Really?' and then the room just exploded. Our phones rang – we were supposed to be having a conference call with everybody discussing our line to take given the exit poll. Actually, all I remember is everybody

cheering excitedly and not really having much of a sensible discussion.

Lord Feldman, one of Cameron's oldest friends and the co-chairman of the party, came on the line. 'Three-sixteen!' he shouted. 'What about the Lib Dems?' Cameron asked. Feldman replied: 'You can't need to care about the Lib Dems, David, you've got 316.' The Tory leader said: 'Oh my God, yes, I don't care about the Lib Dems.'[202]

Martin Boon, the director of research at ICM, was at home, watching television and doing the ironing when the exit poll results were announced. His reaction to the shock summed up what would be the nightmare to come for the polling industry: 'Oh, shit.'

The official exit poll, which was conducted by NOP and Mori for the BBC, ITV News and Sky News, had questioned 20,000 voters across the country and had been analysed by Professor John Curtice, the country's leading elections expert, from Strathclyde University. But a second on-the-day poll of 6,000 voters, by YouGov, put Labour and the Tories neck and neck again, on 34 per cent each. YouGov's election-night forecast was for 284 seats for the Tories and 263 for Labour, a prediction that immediately provoked renewed soul-searching in the Prime Minister's home in Dean.

Cameron asked if the exit poll could be wrong. But Craig Oliver was adamant. 'No, I've worked with John Curtice, he is an academic, he has interviewed 20,000 people, he has done it in 140-odd constituencies,' he told Cameron. 'He knows what he is doing. Last time everybody told him he had got the exit poll wrong and it was absolutely spot-on. I believe it.' Cameron pressed Oliver again on his experience editing the 2010 election programme. 'Are you sure, are you sure?'

the PM asked. 'It's right,' Oliver replied, adding, for good measure: 'If anything it's probably going to be better.' Shortly afterwards, Curtice appeared on the balcony of the studio set and said his initial figures may have underestimated the Conservative results. As the night wore on, and the results came in, Oliver's faith in his former colleague was justified.[203]

At Conservative Campaign HQ, in Matthew Parker Street, Westminster, pizza, beer and soft drinks had been laid out to keep Tory staff fuelled for the long, sleepless night ahead. Some members of the team, including Craig Elder, the director of digital, had taken advantage of the quiet during the day for a tactical nap in the afternoon. As the clock counted down to the exit poll, a silence fell over the room. When the numbers came up on TV screens, 'the place erupted, people were banging on their desks and cheering'. Junior members of the team were watching Lynton Crosby intently, trying to read his mood and gauge how he felt the party was faring. Crosby and Jim Messina 'visibly relaxed' after the forecasts were announced. But Crosby wanted to make sure Cameron and his team did not 'get carried away'. On the conference call that followed, he stressed that the results were 'only a poll' and that the party must 'wait for the real numbers'. He said the Tory result could turn out to be better than 2010, a claim that so astonished George Osborne that the Chancellor promised to kiss Crosby if it came true.[204]

Another senior Tory who was in the war room recalls that the atmosphere 'just got better' as the first declarations were announced. 'In the early seats to declare, the Sunderlands, there was no Labour surge. In Wrexham, John Curtice said there was a swing to the Conservatives.'[205]

In Doncaster, Miliband and his team were monitoring Twitter as the minutes ticked down towards 10 p.m. They saw a tweet from the BBC's political editor, Nick Robinson, which gave them the first indication that the exit poll would contain a surprise. 'Just seen exit poll. Don't you dare switch off. It's interesting,' Robinson said. To Miliband's team, the message was clear enough: the poll showed that voting had been 'strong, one way or the other', and was far from the deadlock that the public polls of recent days and weeks had suggested.

Then the numbers came up. Miliband turned to Beales and Wood and asked: 'Does that seem accurate to you?' The Labour leader's team were all sceptical. The dramatic exit poll, signalling a huge defeat for their side, went against other private polling evidence and against the anecdotal evidence from Labour's field operations team. 'We were not dismissive but we were sceptical,' one source said. 'Then things moved very fast.'[206]

In Labour's war room at 1 Brewer's Green, staff were expecting the exit poll to reflect the opinion polls, putting the two main parties within ten seats of each other. 'We thought, "Maybe it will take a few weeks but there's a 50 per cent chance Ed will end up as PM,"' a party source said.

> It came to 10 p.m. Then came the exit poll. In the room, we all gasped. Because there were several TVs on all around the room on the main floor, on different channels, with a slight delay, you suddenly heard this gasp being repeated when another group saw it. Then there was just utter disbelief. The mood changed from optimism to dreadful sorrow and anger in a split second. A lot of the staff are very young. It was very difficult for

a lot of people to cope with. There were tears, horror, people walking around like zombies.

Falconer tried to raise morale with a speech, telling shocked staff he did not believe the exit poll, as these polls had been wrong before. 'He got a round of applause.'[207]

Ed Balls, the shadow Chancellor, went on television to say he was sceptical about the exit poll. If it was out by even ten seats, it would be very hard for Cameron to put together the numbers he needed to govern with other parties' support. By 11 p.m., there were rumours that Balls himself was in danger of losing his seat in Morley and Outwood. At Labour HQ, anecdotal evidence started filtering through that Balls would need a recount, while other seats with similar characteristics to his were falling to the Tories. Party workers at counts across Scotland and elsewhere reported back that their results were not looking good. A senior figure at Brewer's Green says: 'I just thought, "We've had it. The exit poll is going to be pretty right."'

Inside Nick Clegg's flat in Sheffield, the Lib Dem leader was with his wife, Miriam, when the exit poll was announced. Clegg, too, could not believe it when he was told he would have just ten seats by the end of the night, although the eventual tally would be just eight.[208] Despite having officially given up smoking, he reached for a packet of cigarettes and lit up. He immediately feared for his own seat of Sheffield Hallam. Earlier on polling day, aides had told him he could expect to hold thirty-five seats if the voting went moderately well. This would be enough to keep the Lib Dems in the running to form a new coalition.

Four of Clegg's advisers – James McGrory, Lena Pietsch, Matthew Hanney and Phil Reilly – were watching in a nearby flat that they had taken for the night. When the exit poll hit, there was 'a huge, indescribable sense of disappointment – and certainly for the first thirty to forty-five minutes a sense that it couldn't be right, we wouldn't do that badly', McGrory says.[209] But the four aides gathered around the TV also recalled the exit poll shock of 2010. Then, they had expected 'Cleggmania' to carry the party to a huge number of seats: perhaps eighty, perhaps 100. Instead, the exit poll suggested the Lib Dems would lose seats, and it had proved to be right. They feared that it could be right again.

Paddy Ashdown, Clegg's campaign director and the former party leader, instantly – and foolishly – dismissed the exit poll as nonsense, promising that he would eat his hat if the Lib Dems won as few as ten seats. A series of frantic conference calls followed between Clegg and his advisers, Ryan Coetzee, the Lib Dem election strategist, and Ashdown as the party attempted to get to grips with the scale of its losses. 'Within the hour, we knew it was more or less as bad as the exit poll was suggesting. We were going to get absolutely battered and it would be way worse that we'd been led to expect,' McGrory says. For Clegg, the next hours passed in a blur. He knew that he would be resigning in the morning.[210]

At 10 p.m., at the SNP's headquarters in Edinburgh, party campaign staff watched a wall of television screens, waiting for the broadcasters to reveal their figures. When the exit poll predicted that the SNP would win fifty-eight out of the fifty-nine Scottish constituencies, giving the party an unprecedented landslide across Scotland, staff in the room stood in stunned silence for several seconds, staring at the screens.

After a few moments, Nicola Sturgeon sent a message to her team warning them to be cautious about the poll. Then, as the night wore on, SNP candidates were overhauling five-figure majorities held by Labour MPs with their own five-figure majorities. At 3.10 a.m., Jim Murphy, the Scottish Labour leader, lost his East Renfrewshire seat to Kirsten Oswald, and the 'unthinkable' scale of the SNP's surge became clear. 'We knew then that we were witnessing a political earthquake,' one of Sturgeon's team recalls.

At around midnight, Twitter rumours began spreading that Nigel Farage, the UKIP leader, had failed in his attempt to win the Tory seat of South Thanet, while reports reached Tory HQ that Vince Cable, the Lib Dem Business Secretary, had fallen to a Conservative rival in Twickenham. When Lynton Crosby heard the news about Cable, those around him saw him instantly relax and knew they were in for a good night. The normally super-cautious Crosby turned to a colleague and said: 'If we've got Vince, we've got a majority, mate.'

In Scotland, meanwhile, the SNP were killing giants. Danny Alexander, the Lib Dem Chief Secretary to the Treasury, and Douglas Alexander, Labour's shadow Foreign Secretary – and election coordinator – were both on their way out.

At 12.45 a.m., the announcement came that Justin Tomlinson had held Swindon North for the Tories, with an unexpected swing in his favour. This gave Crosby and his colleagues their first solid indication that the exit poll had underestimated their success. If it had been right, Swindon North would have seen a 1 per cent swing to Labour. Instead, the swing was 4.26 per cent to the Tories. Labour's team were dismayed. Inside the Tory war room, Crosby picked up a prop he had brought with him to keep himself and his troops amused – it was a hunting bugle, and he blew a fanfare to celebrate the first Conservative victory of the night.

Then, at 1.50 a.m., came the seat that all the pollsters, commentators and party strategists agreed was the weathervane to watch for: Nuneaton. It was in a sports centre in this Midlands town, on a damp Sunday morning five long days previously, that David Cameron had first seen the pictures of the giant limestone slab that would become Labour's symbolic tombstone. Marcus Jones held the seat for the Conservatives with a 4 per cent swing in his favour, a result that John Curtice told viewers could herald a majority for the Tories. 'Nuneaton was the moment when we thought, "Right, this really is good,"' one of Cameron's aides says.

For Ed Miliband, Nuneaton meant the end. A senior team member who was with him in his Doncaster home that night says the signs of Labour's defeat were there from the earliest results.

> We knew very quickly from the results in Sunderland that the swings weren't nearly big enough. Then when Nuneaton came through it was quite obvious that the exit poll was right and it could be worse than the exit poll. After that, there was no despair or crying or breaking down in tears. We were a professional campaign and we acted like a professional campaign should. There was no great emotional drama from Ed. He was obviously bitterly disappointed, but calm and busy.

The Labour leader set about writing his acceptance speech for his safe Labour constituency of Doncaster North, but he knew even then that he wanted to resign. A senior Labour adviser recalls: 'There were questions about what Ed's next move should be. It was very clear that once the Conservatives were on course for a majority he should step down. He certainly had no desire to continue, although other people were urging him to do so.' The Labour leader's wife Justine was also adamant that he should be allowed to leave with dignity.

The plan to fly Miliband back to London was cancelled. The helicopter remained on the tarmac. 'A decision was taken that that is the kind of thing you do if you're about to become Prime Minister, not if you're about to be unemployed,' a party insider says. Instead, he was driven back to Westminster in the car and turned his attention to the speech he would shortly have to give to broken Labour staff in Brewer's Green. Then there was his public resignation statement, which was to follow.

Inside his home at Dean, David Cameron watched as a series of stunning results were declared for the Tories: Brecon and Radnor, Twickenham, Yeovil. 'It just kept happening and we thought, "This is real,"' an astonished aide recalled. Then Cameron had to prepare for his own count, which was expected to see him hold the safe Tory seat of Witney comfortably. The declaration was to take place at the Windrush Leisure Centre in the town. Waiting for the Prime Minister in the hall was a surreal sight. 'There were two guys dressed as Sheikhs who were standing in the election, and then one dressed as Elmo, a *Sesame Street* character.' Cameron and the team who accompanied him from his home were then taken upstairs into a gym to wait for the declaration and watch the TV coverage. 'We were watching the screen in the gym. Each result was coming through and it was getting better and better.'

Alan Sendorek, one of Cameron's special advisers, was monitoring Twitter for reports from counts across the country and giving him updates as they appeared. As the results came in, Samantha Cameron took a keen interest in seats that she had visited during the previous six weeks as she waited alongside her husband for his declaration. Despite all the good news, the Prime Minister could not hide his disappointment and sadness for the colleagues who lost – Nick de Bois in Enfield North, Esther McVey in Wirral West, and Angie Bray in Ealing Central and Acton.

When even Labour activists were conceding that Ed Balls had probably lost to Andrea Jenkyns, the Tory candidate, in Morley and Outwood, Cameron leapt up and roared with delight. He never imagined such a prized scalp could be theirs. But, according to those close to him, his euphoria quickly gave way to pathos. 'It's a brutal old game, isn't it?' he remarked. One member of the Witney entourage noticed how the sobering reality of Balls's demise genuinely struck Cameron: 'When you see an election, it is *Game of Thrones*. A whole load of people figuratively get murdered. If you're an aide, your reputation is trashed. If you are a politician, you get humiliated.'[211]

Back at Conservative headquarters, Lynton Crosby allowed himself to open his first beer of the night. At 4 a.m., he received word from west London that Vince Cable was certain to become another prized scalp.

There were various reports in the night that Twickenham might be in play. Then in early hours of the morning, someone said, 'We've got to get a press officer down to Twickenham, we have won it. Tania [Mathias, the Tory candidate] needs a bit of support.' This was half an hour before the result came through. But it looked like it was in the bag. A taxi was called and a press officer sent down to Twickenham. It was a great moment.[212]

At 4.36 a.m. it was announced that Cable had lost his seat, in one of the biggest shocks of the night. The Tory strategy of destroying their coalition partners had wiped out a 12,000 majority. By this point, Lynton Crosby was cracking jokes and relaxing as he watched the good news coming in on his laptop. As Cable looked on forlornly while the results were declared, Crosby let out another blast on his bugle. 'It was a much more relaxed evening than I think any of us expected. It was just a case of sitting back and watching the good news come in,' one campaign staff member says.[213]

At the indoor athletics arena in Sheffield, Nick Clegg waited for his fate, knowing that, whether or not he had won, 'something very big and very awful' was happening to his party.[214] Clegg's local constituency team had been confident from an early stage that he had held his seat of Hallam. But the disastrous results for Lib Dems across Britain ensured that a media circus of sixty reporters awaited his arrival. For Clegg's team, there was work to do. James McGrory had to keep the press in order; Matthew Hanney was fielding distressed calls from candidates and teams in every seat; Lena Pietsch planned the next day's events; Phil Reilly earlier had

gone to join Clegg in his flat to draft his speeches. 'You're
working. It's a weird working day, it might be one o'clock in
the morning, but it's a working day nonetheless,' McGrory
says. 'We knew it had been a bad night; we knew Nick would
have to resign. But I wanted him to come into the building
for his count through the front door. That's the kind of man
he is. He and Miriam were up for that.'

As they waited in an ante-room in the indoor arena, trying
to make each other laugh with some gallows humour, Clegg
and his team heard a huge cheer from the main hall. They
looked through a window to see Labour activists screaming
with delight as they watched Vince Cable losing his seat on
TV. Clegg could not believe the 'bone-headed' and 'ghastly'
celebrations of the Labour Party to the fact that the most
left-wing member of the Cabinet had lost his seat – to a Tory.

At 4.51 a.m., Clegg gave his acceptance speech after holding
Sheffield Hallam with a majority of 3,000. He said:

> It is now painfully clear that this has been a cruel
> and punishing night for the Liberal Democrats. The
> election has profound implications for the country.
> It also obviously has profound implications for the
> Liberal Democrats and I will be seeking to make further
> remarks about the implications of this election both
> for the country and for the party that I lead – and for
> my position in the Liberal Democrats – when I make
> remarks to my colleagues in the Liberal Democrats
> later this morning.

After the declaration, a 'deeply shell-shocked' Clegg returned
to his flat to work on his resignation speech. He wanted to
go out in an 'orderly and dignified' way.[215]

At his count at Doncaster Racecourse, Miliband was frank about the scale of his party's losses. Speaking after his result was declared at 5.25 a.m., he said: 'This has clearly been a very disappointing and difficult night for the Labour Party. We haven't made the gains we wanted in England, and in Scotland we have seen a surge of nationalism overwhelm our party.' He said he was 'deeply sorry' that so many 'dedicated and decent colleagues' had lost their seats north of the border. 'The next government has a huge responsibility in facing the very difficult task of keeping our country together,' he added.

In Witney, as his own declaration neared, the Prime Minister had to prepare to make his first public statement of the next five years. He turned to his advisers and asked, 'What is our speech? What should we say?' On a night when the SNP had swept the board in Scotland, Craig Oliver had a theme in mind: 'Look, we need to say One Nation, that's what we are fighting for, that's who you are,' he told the PM. Cameron agreed. 'Yes, that's right. That is the right thing that we should do,' he said. Cameron then phoned George Osborne to discuss the speech. A source who knows the PM well believes it was the sort of speech he had wanted to give for a long time, a moment of vindication after a campaign that had been criticised by many who claimed to be on his side. 'He was the One Nation leader, he got a majority. He won it on his own terms. He basically said to a lot of people, "You didn't think I was going to do it and I did."'

Osborne, ever the schemer, would have enjoyed the irony in Cameron's new victory slogan. He was reclaiming Disraeli's phrase which Ed Miliband had stolen from the Tories as Labour's daring new mantra back in 2012, when he used it forty-six times in one speech. Now, Cameron had brought it home. But the slogan was also an acknowledgement of how divided Britain had become, and a declaration of intent to bring the country together again. The surge of the SNP in Scotland, while helping Cameron towards victory at Westminster by dealing a fatal double blow to his Labour and Lib Dem opponents, posed a threat to the United Kingdom itself.

With Elmo and a fake Sheikh standing behind him, a victorious Cameron told his audience in the leisure centre and the country watching on TV that he wanted to reclaim the mantle of 'One Nation' for the Conservatives. He promised that devolution packages for Scotland and Wales would be drawn up 'as fast as we can', adding:

> In short, I want my party – and I hope a government I would like to lead – to reclaim a mantle that we should never have lost: the mantle of One Nation, one United Kingdom. That is how I will govern if I am fortunate enough to form a government in the coming days.

As he left Witney's leisure centre and made his way to his car, Cameron put his arms around a beaming Samantha and gave her a huge hug.

With his police escort still in place, the Prime Minister drove into Westminster as the man who had defied the election rulebook. He had increased his haul of seats after years in office, a feat not achieved in peacetime since Anthony Eden in 1955. Inside CCHQ, surrounded by the debris of the night – papers, cups, bottles and pizza crusts – tired but elated campaign staff watched the Prime Minister approach their building on TV screens mounted onto the walls. As he stepped out of his car and walked towards the entrance of No. 4 Matthew Parker Street, they began to cheer, 'Five more years! Five more years!' When he came in through the door, he met a wall of noise.

Samantha Cameron, Lord Feldman, Lynton Crosby, Jim Messina, Grant Shapps and scores of activists looked on. An emotional Cameron told his colleagues gathered in the war room:

> I am not an old man, but I remember casting a vote in '87 and that was a great victory. I remember working just as you've been working in '92 and that was an amazing victory. And I remember 2010, achieving that dream of getting Labour out and getting the Tories back in and that was amazing. But I think this is the sweetest victory of them all.

For Ed Miliband, there were formalities to be completed. He called Cameron in the early morning to offer his congratulations. In a brief but courteous conversation, the two leaders assured each other they were both in public service 'for the right reasons'. However, despite working closely together at the apex of government for the past five years, there was no phone call between Cameron and Nick Clegg. Crushed by his coalition partner, the Lib Dem leader would resign before the end of the morning.

At Brewer's Green, Labour Party workers organised a welcoming party for Ed and Justine. Once inside, Miliband gave a speech, telling staff they should be proud of their efforts, and went around the room thanking everyone individually. 'We were all in quite a state by then,' one member of Labour's war room says. 'People were slumped in chairs, and had been for hours, crying. Some were just ashen-faced. There was this general sense of being like the defeated army. Then a lot of us went to the pub.'

CHAPTER 14

VE DAY

'I've just been to see Her Majesty the Queen, and I will now form a majority Conservative government.' With these words, David Cameron exercised his constitutional right to announce formally for the first time the outcome of the 2015 general election.

Standing at a lectern in the street outside No. 10, the newly re-appointed Prime Minister seemed to show his fatigue for perhaps the first time. He had been up all night. He had made speeches to his constituency, and to a rapturous Tory campaign team in Matthew Parker Street. He had taken phone calls from triumphant colleagues and vanquished opponents, and watched as the political map of the United Kingdom changed beyond recognition in the space of a few hours. His voice straining with tiredness, he could not help but note, in the manner of a statesman marking the passing of a national figure, how his coalition partners had been destroyed by his own hand.

'I've been proud to lead the first coalition government in seventy years, and I want to thank all those who worked so hard to make it a success; and in particular, on this day, Nick Clegg,' he said.

Elections can be bruising clashes of ideas and arguments, and a lot of people who believe profoundly in public service have seen that service cut short. Ed Miliband rang me this morning to wish me luck with the new government; it was a typically generous gesture from someone who is clearly in public service for all the right reasons.

The results were as much of a shock as the exit poll had been less than twenty-four hours earlier. The Conservatives had won a twelve-seat majority, with 331 MPs. It was the first Tory majority government since John Major's equally unexpected victory in 1992. While Cameron's campaign achieved a net gain of twenty-four seats, with 37 per cent of the national vote, Labour suffered a net loss of twenty-six seats, and polled just 30 per cent of the vote, a gap that no pollster had predicted.

Before the final result in St Ives had been declared, Ed Miliband had resigned as Labour leader, Nick Clegg had resigned as leader of the Liberal Democrats, and Nigel Farage had made good his promise to quit as UKIP leader, although his resignation was later reversed. For Clegg, the punishment from the electorate was particularly cruel. After the heady heights of Cleggmania during the 2010 campaign, 2015 wiped out the Lib Dems across the UK. The party lost forty-nine of its fifty-seven seats, including all fifteen to the Conservatives in the south-west, and ten out of eleven to the SNP in Scotland.

For Nicola Sturgeon, the fairy-tale result could hardly be believed. The SNP destroyed all comers, winning fifty-six of the fifty-nine Scottish constituencies, depriving Labour of its shadow Foreign Secretary, Douglas Alexander, Scottish party leader, Jim Murphy, and shadow Scottish Secretary, Margaret Curran, in the process. The political map of Scotland was almost entirely yellow. England was a sea of blue.

Recognising the newly divided nature of the UK as he sought to pick up the pieces in his victory speech, Cameron said his government must 'bring our country together'.

> As I said in the small hours of this morning, we will govern as a party of One Nation, one United Kingdom. That means ensuring this recovery reaches all parts of our country: from north to south, from east to west. And, indeed, it means rebalancing our economy, building that 'Northern Powerhouse'. It means giving everyone in our country a chance, so no matter where you're from you have the opportunity to make the most of your life. It means giving the poorest people the chance of training, a job, and hope for the future. It means that for children who don't get the best start in life, there must be the nursery education and good schooling that can transform their life chances. And, of course, it means bringing together the different nations of our United Kingdom.
>
> I have always believed in governing with respect. That's why in the last parliament, we devolved power to Scotland and Wales, and gave the people of Scotland a referendum on whether to stay inside the United Kingdom. In this parliament I will stay true to my word and implement as fast as I can the devolution that all parties agreed for Wales, Scotland and Northern Ireland.
>
> Governing with respect means recognising that the different nations of our United Kingdom have their

own governments, as well as the United Kingdom government. Both are important, and, indeed, with our plans, the governments of these nations will become more powerful, with wider responsibilities. In Scotland, our plans are to create the strongest devolved government anywhere in the world, with important powers over taxation. And no constitutional settlement will be complete, if it did not offer, also, fairness to England.

Samantha Cameron, wearing a blue dress with a yellow back, applauded as her husband finished his speech and joined him, holding hands in the doorway to No. 10 and smiling for the photographers before turning to walk inside. They were greeted by the traditional round of applause from waiting Downing Street staff.

With tears in their eyes, Nick Clegg's young team of aides and party workers watched as their leader announced his intention to resign. Clegg said he always knew the election would be exceptionally difficult for his party, but the results had proven 'immeasurably more crushing and unkind than I could ever have feared'. He said: 'It's simply heart-breaking to see so many friends and colleagues who have served their constituents over so many years abruptly lose their seats because of forces entirely beyond their control.' He added that 'fear and grievance have won; liberalism has lost', although he insisted that Britain was stronger, fairer, greener and more liberal than it had been before the coalition was formed in 2010.

After the speech, Clegg said goodbye to his wife, Miriam, who had to go into work. He and his friend and chief of staff

Jonny Oates went for lunch at a hotel near Hyde Park. They sat quietly, watching the television coverage and killing time. Then, after a shower and a shave, Clegg put on a suit and tie and left for the Cenotaph, where all the party leaders were expected to mark the 70th anniversary of VE Day.[216]

Addressing Labour Party workers and television cameras at Westminster, Ed Miliband read out a roll call of the defeated from the previous night. Ed Balls, Jim Murphy, Margaret Curran, Douglas Alexander. He said Labour needed new leadership and that he would be resigning later in the day. He thanked his deputy, Harriet Harman, and the British people, who, he said, had shared their stories with him at train stations, in colleges and in workplaces and schools. 'I have learned so much from you. It has been an enormous privilege. Thank you for the selfies, thank you for the support, and thank you for the most unlikely cult of the twenty-first century – Milifandom.' Labour voters will feel 'disappointed, even bleak', he said. But whoever is Labour's next leader, the party will keep making the case for changing Britain's unequal society and creating 'a country that works for working people once again', he said.

Miliband's final act as Labour leader was to attend the VE Day 70th anniversary commemorations at the Cenotaph. Shortly before 3 p.m., Cameron, Clegg, Miliband and Sturgeon lined up at the Cenotaph in Whitehall. To those present, Cameron seemed 'as surprised as anybody' to be standing at the Cenotaph as the new head of a majority government. The party leaders talked, mildly absurdly, about how they were going to walk in line, carrying wreaths to lay at the memorial, and how they would coordinate bowing their heads together. Beyond these practicalities, Cameron said little, either to his former partner in government, or to his defeated opponent.[217]

That evening, Nick Clegg went home to see his children and talk them through the dramatic change in their circumstances. Ed Miliband did the same. For David Cameron, however, it was a chance to take Samantha out for dinner at Mark's Club, a private members' dining club in Mayfair. Their regular 'date nights' had taken a back seat during the campaign. Shortly after they arrived, they were joined by George Osborne, Cameron's closest friend in politics and the godfather to their children.

At their townhouse in Dartmouth Park Road, north London, the Milibands were receiving visitors. Lord Kestenbaum, a Labour peer, arrived with a delivery of soothing chicken soup. He suggested to Miliband that their shared Jewish cultural heritage offered a good ritual for moments of grief, which could be put to service to help comfort the defeated Labour leader. They decided Miliband should 'sit shiva' for his loss. In the Jewish faith, the week of mourning requires family members to gather at the home of the bereaved, who share their sorrow with their visitors, perhaps talking and exchanging memories.

Members of Miliband's close team were invited to 'sit shiva' with him on Saturday 9 May, two days after the election. Those who joined the Miliband family included Stewart Wood, Miliband's friend and adviser, Douglas Alexander, who had lost his seat to the SNP, Rachel Kinnock and Tom Baldwin. The Milibands served their guests glasses of champagne and a classic Jewish menu of bagels topped with cured salmon. The gathering swapped stories from the past six weeks, trying to make sense of the outcome. Later in the afternoon, Miliband and his guests went for a walk on Hampstead Heath. 'I am really glad we did it,' says one of those who sat shiva with the Milibands. 'It meant that people hadn't left on a huge blow and then not seen each other again.'[218]

CHAPTER 15

OUT OF THE BLUE

A week into his second term as Prime Minister, David Cameron needed to speak to Nick Clegg. It was probably a phone call that neither man relished. But there were some business matters between them to be tidied up in the aftermath of the election. The pair, who five years previously had laughed and joked together in the Downing Street garden at the birth of Britain's first coalition for seventy years, barely exchanged pleasantries during their brief phone conversation. For his part, Cameron made no attempt to acknowledge the devastating impact his campaign to decapitate the Liberal Democrats had on his former coalition partner. As for Clegg, in recent times he has insisted that he never regarded Cameron as a friend and did not expect any apology or expression of sympathy to be forthcoming.[219]

The fact is, within days of their victory, the Conservatives had already set their sights on taking the remaining eight Liberal Democrat seats at the 2020 election. According to one Cabinet minister, the only reason Lib Dems such as Norman Lamb in Norfolk, or Tim Farron in Cumbria, had survived the cull was because of their geographical isolation. It was simply not efficient for Lynton Crosby to flood these areas with activists and busloads of MPs and ministers, in the way that clusters of Lib Dem-held seats in the south-west could be targeted together by large numbers of campaigners on the same day. 'We will get them next time,' the minister said.[220] The 'genius' of Lynton Crosby's campaign, according to one Downing Street figure, was that he spotted the opportunity to take those Lib Dem seats as the path to a majority – and then devised the strategy to deliver it. The plan was ruthless and it worked. But why and how was it so effective?

Scotland

David Cameron took a gamble. He agreed to a referendum on Scottish independence. He came closer than he imagined possible to losing his bet against Alex Salmond's formidable independence movement. Ultimately the Union was saved, but for their part in saving it, Labour MPs and Lib Dems north of the border were swept from power as punishment for joining the Tories and opposing the half of the population who wanted to break away from England.

This book has not attempted to unravel in any detail the mysteries of what happened in Scotland. For one thing, the Tories won their majority entirely without making any inroads into Scottish territory. Their victory came from the seats they gained in England and Wales. But the annihilation of the Labour Party in Scotland meant the Conservatives' main opponents were always going to struggle to form the largest party in the Commons. The turmoil north of the border during the campaign also hit Labour with a huge 'opportunity cost'. As the scale of their likely losses became apparent, Labour

MPs who would otherwise have been working on the party's national campaign – notably Douglas Alexander, the general election chairman – fled north to try to save their own skins.

The SNP revolution also provided what would be the defining question of the 2015 election in England, one which made the critical incision into the thoughts of Lib Dem and UKIP voters and persuaded them to switch to the Conservatives. This was the idea that a minority Labour government would need the support of the SNP to pass laws in the Commons, and that the charismatic Nicola Sturgeon would dominate a weak Ed Miliband in any partnership of the two.

Lynton Crosby's message is not explicitly anti-Scottish. To claim otherwise would be to miss a fundamental truth behind why the Tories' warnings about the influence of the SNP on Labour hit home. Voters saw Ed Miliband as weak. They had seen him as weak long before the election campaign began, but his performances – in contrast to the dominance of Sturgeon – in the TV debates, and some clever Tory advertising, reinforced their doubts. If Miliband had been seen as a likely strong partner in a power-sharing deal with the SNP, the Tory warnings about the Scottish nationalists' influence would have rung hollow. Crosby says:

> It was never a campaign against the Scots. It was never saying the Scottish people were bad. People had two choices. They could have a Conservative-led government or some other government in which Labour was the main party but did not have the power, and would be a victim to the whims of others.[221]

But this is not the whole story either, however much Crosby would like it to be. It must equally be true that unless the

SNP had been perceived as a menace, as some potentially malign force afoot in the land, the warnings over Sturgeon and Salmond entering No. 10 would likewise have fallen flat. The fact remains that voters disliked the idea of a Labour–SNP deal intensely. Whether – as the Tory campaign would argue – this is due to a rational assessment of the SNP's public spending proposals appears debatable.

Critics of the Tories – including Nick Clegg and Nigel Farage, as well as the allies of Ed Miliband and Ed Balls – believe Crosby pursued a classic 'dog-whistle' campaign that played on something else: a visceral antipathy towards the Scots among English voters. Lynton Crosby's own analysis, presented to the Cabinet and Conservative MPs after the election, showed that 83 per cent of the voters who switched from other parties to the Conservatives in 2015 were worried that the SNP would hold the balance of power in Parliament. Half of all voters (51 per cent) felt the same. Even more – 93 per cent – of those who converted to the Tories believed Ed Miliband was too weak to be Prime Minister.[222]

Crosby himself is said to regard the warnings over the SNP as the 'pinprick that lanced the boil' at the end of the campaign, although much preparatory work had already been done in highlighting Miliband's perceived weakness. Had the SNP factor not been available to Crosby, the Tories would have preyed on Miliband's vulnerability to the influence of the trade unions, or made more of his inexperience.[223] But the SNP factor was available and it was highly effective.

Stealth

Secrecy was a key tenet of Crosby's campaign philosophy – and the Tories' prospects of success had to be covered up in order to win. Crosby's tracker surveys, which began in December and were conducted on a daily basis in sixty seats for the final month of the campaign, consistently put the Tories on course to be easily the largest party. For most of the final week of the campaign, the Conservatives were forecasting 329 seats, strikingly close to their eventual tally of 331, with Labour on 242, ten more than the 232 they ended up with. If this secret picture – known only to Crosby, Mark Textor and a handful of others – had become public, the debate would have been different. Crosby even kept the details away from Cameron, speaking to him only twice about seat projections. The Conservatives' prospects had to remain secret in order to motivate the party's troops, and to get sympathetic voters to turn out on polling day.

All the public polls and election experts' seat forecasts – as reported by the media – told an entirely different story. Journalists wrote articles and broadcast features based on the assumed certainty of another hung parliament election. The civil service booked rooms and ordered sandwiches for coalition talks. Buckingham Palace worried about the implications for the Queen.

One of the biggest contributory factors to the shock nature of the outcome was the reporting of the polls before the election. In the final days, the opinion polls seemed to converge, with Labour and the Tories neck and neck on about thirty-four points each. ICM's final forecast on the day of the election – after giving the Tories a lead during its previous campaign polls – put Labour one point ahead.

Without misleading polls and exaggerated reporting of them by papers and broadcasters, who were promoting the idea of a hung parliament, the prospect of Miliband entering Downing Street arm-in-arm with anybody would not have seemed real.

Instead, there would have been far more scrutiny of Cameron's policies and the implications of a majority Tory government.

An inquest has already begun in the polling industry about what went wrong. Initial analysis by the British Election Study has found no evidence of a late swing to the Tories, and minimal signs that people were reluctant to say they were voting Conservative – a phenomenon known as the 'Shy Tories'. There were some indications that people who told pollsters they were going to vote Labour were more likely than supporters of other parties to stay at home on polling day. But this only explains a small portion of the error by the pollsters in the run-up to the election. The rest of the failure is, at the time of writing, a mystery.

Martin Boon, the director of research at ICM Unlimited, says he believes the real failure was a systematic bias in the survey samples – the people whom pollsters were able to question. It was just not possible for any research firm to gather a sample of 1,000 or 2,000 potential voters who truly represent the national electorate. For some reason, Tory voters appeared to be not so much shy as entirely invisible. They just would not take part in the polls. This could potentially be disastrous for polling companies in the future. It is not clear why this behaviour should have been so pronounced in 2015, but Boon argues that the polling ahead of general elections has been mediocre for some time. The refusal of members of the public to take part in political surveys is not a problem for pollsters to address alone. It could suggest a wider disengagement from political debate. At some point, the political classes would do well to ask why it is that voters do not want to talk about voting any more.

Whatever happens next in the polling industry, newspapers and broadcasters will certainly have to be more circumspect about reporting survey results, not least because the public will be far more sceptical themselves. 'One of the dangers of this campaign was the extent to which polling became so dominant through its ability to electrify the media,' says Boon. 'People like me became central to it. I don't think that's a good thing. Who can blame journalists for accepting the evidence that pollsters were supplying? It was a domino effect. We fell first and everything else toppled all around us.'[224]

Superior resources

'David Cameron won it,' says Lynton Crosby. 'He grew into the job of Prime Minister very well – in the second half of his term, in particular. He was critical to the success.'[225]

But every winner needs a portion of good fortune. Crosby and Cameron were lucky to be facing a flawed and disorganised opponent, whose failings made Cameron look stronger and more competent by comparison. When leadership was a key strength for the Tories, it was a glaring failure of Labour's not to make more of the fact that the Tory Party was officially going to need a new leader before the next election. Cameron's gaffe on the eve of the campaign – saying he would not fight for a third term – could have been the decisive factor that dominated the entire election. If Lynton Crosby had been running Labour's operation, it would have been. The truth is that voters did not know who they were voting for to be Prime Minister. But Labour failed to grab their opportunity and gave Cameron perhaps the biggest let-off of his career.

The Tories were also lucky to be fighting an election while Scotland was in the throes of upheaval. And the mass failure of the polling industry to discover the true picture of what was happening to public opinion gave Crosby the cover he needed to make the case that the SNP–Labour deal would be a realistic danger in a hung parliament that was widely assumed to be a certainty. All of these factors were out of the Tories' control and all were integral to their success.

But luck is never enough on its own. To a large extent, in politics as in life, you make your own fortune. The fact is that Crosby's campaign was in an entirely different league in terms of organisation, strategic clarity and discipline to that pursued by Ed Miliband and his team. It was more effectively financed and took more seriously the business of digital campaigning and fundraising.[226]

In the campaign itself, Crosby's relentless focus, unstinting work ethic and natural authority were critical. But David Cameron had already taken the biggest decision of all – to hire Crosby and give him the total control over the campaign that he demanded as a condition of taking on the role. This required Cameron – and everyone else – to submit to Crosby's orders. Inside Labour's HQ at 1 Brewer's Green, it was hard to say who was in charge. Spencer Livermore was the campaign manager, Douglas Alexander and Lucy Powell provided campaign leadership, and strategy was set by Greg Beales. Even Ed Balls and his team spent months leading up to the campaign trying to establish who was in charge.[227] There were also apparently three competing versions of Ed Miliband and several rival political agendas all vying with each other in the leader's core team before any one of them could make it out of the door to take on the Tories. Was Miliband a class warrior, a unifier or a tactical pragmatist? Should Labour take on the 'predator' capitalists or work with business to change society? These questions were never finally resolved.

Crosby's war room was remarkably united, a hard but

rewarding place to work. The personal affection in which he is apparently held by those who have worked for and with him speaks volumes for his style of leadership and the personal qualities he brings to the office with him every day. Projectile koalas and outbursts of pop music helped to lighten the atmosphere during the tenser moments of the campaign. But Crosby was also valued because he was feared. Some Tories privately wish he could have a larger, ongoing role running the government.

The ethical dimension

Despite the Conservative campaign's undoubted effectiveness, questions remain over the longer-term implications of its success. There is a large amount of law governing elections – from fundraising for political parties to misinformation during campaigns. There are clear and well-understood differences between what is legal and what is illegal when it comes to election campaigning. But legalities aside, is there also a right way and a wrong way to win? Or is anything fair so long as it is legal? To many journalists and MPs, Crosby's fixation with message discipline has been infuriating. It denied the media stories about internal party rows and tactical plans and clipped the wings of ministers who were not bearers of the key economic message. It resulted in a campaign that many saw as boring and that senior Tories themselves regarded as too monotonous to be effective. But without clarity and consistency in communications, any kind of debate becomes impossible.

Crosby has called for opinion polls to be banned for two or three weeks before polling day in future. Yet the idea that this would end the media's fascination with the 'horse race' of which party is winning is fanciful. Data about vote shares or seat predictions would inevitably leak out – or be briefed by spin doctors – from inside rival parties' own headquarters. None of it would be independent or trustworthy. The onus instead should be on the pollsters to overhaul their methods so as to be able to generate credible figures once again, and on all forms of media to put opinion polls back into a proper perspective. Politicians are clearly right to say the only poll that counts is on polling day, and the media forgot the truth of this long before a single vote had been cast in the 2015 election.

Although the Tories won a majority, with 331 seats in the Commons, they admit that they only cared enough to campaign energetically in 100 constituencies. This raises the question to what extent such a campaign can really be regarded as a national election. The phenomenon of targeted 'key marginal seats' is not new. But the 2015 election – which involved an unprecedented degree of micro-targeting of batches of 1,000 voters via Facebook, and individual households street by street – delivered the most disproportionate result in history. Below-the-radar stealth targeting by the Conservatives, under the cover of deadlocked public polls and a national campaign described as boring and lifeless, delivered the biggest shock in politics for more than twenty years.

Leaving to one side the question of whether the Tories had the right policies for Britain, critics on all sides (including their own) have raised major doubts over the tactic to stoke the electorate's fear of the SNP's influence on Labour. Gordon Brown accused the Tories of fuelling a 'dangerous and insidious' English nationalism by portraying Scots as a 'menace and a danger' during the campaign. The United Kingdom is once again in peril because the Conservative election campaign chose to 'turn on the tap' of English nationalism, he said.

Brown is hardly an impartial observer, but he is not alone. Lord Forsyth of Drumlean, who served as Scottish Secretary in John Major's government, warned during the campaign that his party was pursuing a 'short-term and dangerous view which threatens the integrity of our country'.[228]

Senior Labour and Lib Dem politicians are tempted to see themselves as the innocent victims of Crosby's divisive dog-whistle campaign that pitched the English against the Scots. But Ed Miliband and Nick Clegg were complicit – both men conceded Crosby's point when they separately ruled out entering coalition with the SNP.

Why would Lynton Crosby – or Jim Messina, Mark Textor, or even Labour's David Axelrod – care? None of them is British. The policy of outsourcing the democratic campaign process to external consultants seems likely to become more popular in future elections. But the risk in doing so is that the focus of the hired advisers will always be on delivering a result for their clients, rather than on any ethical consideration of the tactics required. This is not to say that Lynton Crosby or his colleagues and counterparts do not personally care about Britain, or about keeping the Union together. It is simply not their job to care. It is, however, clearly the responsibility of the candidates, the politicians seeking election with the help of external consultants, to make judgements about what is in the best interests of the country they hope to govern.

Nicola Sturgeon and the SNP stood on a platform of anti-Westminster protest. More broadly, the SNP's raison d'être is to campaign for Scottish independence from the United Kingdom. So, politically, the SNP has been clear and open about its ultimate wish to break up the Union. The party's methods in 2015 matched its motives for the future. It is not clear that the same can be said about Cameron's own approach.

Did the warnings about the SNP dictating terms to Ed Miliband really work with the grain of Cameron's own political faith? When pressed, he says that his guiding creed is patriotism, and a deep belief in Britain as a country of enormous potential. It is tempting to speculate that the Prime Minister who could not sleep during the Scottish independence referendum because he was so anxious for the future of the Union must at some stage have inwardly flinched at being required to stoke anti-Scottish sentiment among the English. Yet he never tried to dissuade Crosby from the campaign strategy he had designed.[229] Perhaps a suppressed reflex of something approaching remorse was what lay behind his victory speeches, in Witney and outside No. 10, in which he declared his intention to heal the divisions, to make Britain 'One Nation' again. Why else promise to bring the country together?

In his speech at the CTF Partners summer party at the Science Museum in London, Lynton Crosby was modest enough to suggest that the campaign had been David Cameron's. In truth, it was his own leadership, not that of the Prime Minister, that was tested – and found to be more than adequate – in the intense pressure of the 2015 general election. Crosby was also candid enough to acknowledge that he may have failed if he had not found a way to animate the passions of the electorate.

'In politics, when reason and emotion collide, emotion invariably wins,' Crosby said. 'Our campaign sought to persuade through reason but then motivate through emotion. When one looks at the decimation of the Liberal Democrats and the stonewalling of Labour's advances, with many unexpected gains, one sees that reason prevailed and emotion did its work.'

ENDNOTES

1 Private information
2 Private interview
3 Private interview
4 Interview, Alan Sendorek, special adviser to the Prime Minister 2010–15
5 Private information
6 Private information
7 Private information
8 Private information
9 Private information
10 Private information
11 Private information
12 Private interview
13 Private interview
14 *The Guardian*, 16 March 2015
15 Quoted in *Daily Telegraph*, 21 November 2012
16 *The Observer*, 20 July 2013
17 Lynton Crosby, speech to CTF Partners summer party, 14 July 2015
18 Ibid.
19 Private interview
20 Private interview
21 Boris Johnson, *Daily Telegraph*, 4 March 2013
22 Private interview
23 Interview, Boris Johnson
24 Private interview
25 Private interview
26 Private interview
27 Private interview

28 David Cameron, speech to CTF Partners summer party, 14 July
    2014
29 Private interview, senior Tory, with the author, quoted in *Sunday
    Telegraph*, 17 May 2015
30 Private interview
31 Private interview
32 Private interview
33 Private interview
34 Private information
35 Private interview
36 Private interview
37 Private interview
38 Andrew Feldman, interview, *The Times*, 4 July 2015
39 Ibid.
40 Private interview
41 Interview, Craig Elder
42 *The Guardian*, 3 February 2015
43 *Daily Express*, 5 August 2013
44 *The Guardian*, 29 June 2014
45 Private interview
46 Private interview
47 Private interview
48 Private interview
49 *Daily Telegraph*, 31 October 2014
50 Private interview
51 Private interview
52 *The Guardian*, 4 June 2015
53 Private interview
54 Private interview
55 Private interview
56 Private interview
57 Interview, Grant Shapps
58 Private interview
59 Private interview
60 Ibid.
61 Interview, Boris Johnson
62 Interview, Grant Shapps
63 After the general election, Lynton Crosby presented findings of
    a post-polling day survey of 2,000 people to the new Cabinet. It
    found that voters most associated the Tories with being 'best able
    to manage the economy, spending and debt' (45 per cent agreed)
    and being able to provide 'strong and stable government after the
    election' (43 per cent). However, Crosby told ministers and MPs

that, to win voters' support, they must deliver on their promise to 'control and reduce immigration'. Increasing NHS spending, delivering an EU referendum and clearing the deficit were also priorities, but less popular than tackling immigration, which was backed by 39 per cent of voters surveyed.

64 Andrew Feldman, interview, *The Times*, 4 July 2015
65 Private interview
66 Private interview
67 Private interview
68 Private interview
69 *The Guardian*, 3 February 2015
70 Private information
71 Private interview
72 Private interview
73 Interview, Bob Roberts
74 Private information
75 Private interview
76 Private interview
77 Private interview, Cabinet minister
78 Tim Montgomerie, 'Con HQ announces first ten of forty target seat selections', ConservativeHome.com, 6 November 2012
79 Private interview
80 Private information
81 Private interview
82 *The Times*, 4 June 2014
83 Mark Wallace, 'The computers that crashed. And the campaign that didn't', ConservativeHome.com, 16 June 2015
84 Interview, Nick Clegg
85 Private interview
86 Lord Ashcroft Polls, 8 April 2015, http://lordashcroftpolls. com/2015/04/back-to-the-con-lab-battleground, accessed 12 September 2015
87 Mark Wallace, 'Is there a problem with the Tory ground war in the marginals? And if so, how big is it?', ConservativeHome.com, 10 April 2015
88 Private information
89 Mark Wallace, 'The computers that crashed. And the campaign that didn't', ConservativeHome.com, 16 June 2015
90 Interview, Craig Elder; he believes digital strategy should be about more than attaching shareable cute animal pictures to your brand
91 Ibid.
92 Private information
93 Private interview

94   Private interview
95   Interview, Alan Sendorek
96   Private interview
97   Iain Duncan Smith, interview with the author, *Sunday Telegraph*, 26 April 2015
98   *The Times*, 23 April 2015
99   Nicky Morgan, interview with the author, *Sunday Telegraph*, 19 April 2015
100 Private information
101 Private interview
102 Private information
103 Private interview
104 Private interview
105 Private information
106 Private interviews
107 David Cameron, interview with the author (unpublished extract), *Sunday Telegraph*, 29 March 2015
108 Private interview, Tory aide
109 Private interview
110 Private information
111 Private interview
112 Private information
113 Private interview
114 Private information
115 Private interview
116 Private interview
117 Jim Messina, interview, *The Spectator*, 12 May 2015
118 Andrew Feldman, interview, *The Times*, 4 July 2015
119 Private interview
120 Iain Duncan Smith, interview with the author, *Sunday Telegraph*, 26 April 2015
121 Ibid.
122 Private information
123 Private interview
124 Private information
125 Interview, Lynton Crosby
126 Private interview, shadow Cabinet minister
127 Ibid.
128 Private interview, Miliband aide
129 Private interview
130 Private interview
131 Private interview, shadow Cabinet minister
132 Private interview

133 Nigel Farage interview with the author, *Sunday Telegraph*, 12 April 2015

134 Raheem Kassam, interview, *The Guardian*, 11 June 2015

135 George Osborne, interview with the author (unpublished extract), *Sunday Telegraph*, 5 April 2015

136 Private information

137 Interview, Nigel Farage

138 Private information

139 Private information

140 Raheem Kassam, interview, *The Guardian*, 11 June 2015

141 Tim Carr, Iain Dale and Robert Waller (eds), *The Politicos Guide to the New House of Commons 2015* (Biteback Publishing, 2015), pp. 9–10

142 Private interview

143 Private interview

144 Private interview

145 Private interview

146 Private interview

147 Private interview

148 Private interview

149 Private interview

150 Private information

151 Private interview

152 Interview, Tom Baldwin

153 Private information

154 Private interview

155 Private interview

156 Private interview

157 Private interview

158 Private interviews

159 Private interview

160 Interview, Bob Roberts

161 Interview, James Stewart

162 Interview, Tom Baldwin

163 Interview, Nick Clegg

164 Private information

165 Private interview

166 Interview, Nick Clegg

167 Private information

168 Private interview

169 Private interview

170 Private interview

171 Private interview

172   Vince Cable, interview, *Mail on Sunday*, 26 April 2015
173   Private interview
174   Private interview
175   Interview, Nick Clegg
176   Private information
177   Ibid.
178   *The Guardian*, 24 June 2015
179   Nick Clegg, interview with the author (unpublished extract),
      Sunday Telegraph, 3 May 2015
180   Private interview
181   Interview, Nick Clegg
182   Private interview
183   Interview, Nick Clegg
184   *The Guardian*, 24 June 2015
185   Private information
186   *Profile*, BBC Radio 4, 15 October 2011
187   Ibid.
188   Ibid.
189   Private information
190   Private information
191   *Sunday Times*, 19 April 2015
192   Private information
193   Private information
194   Private information
195   Private interview
196   Private information
197   Ibid.
198   *The Spectator*, 13 June 2015
199   Private interview
200   Private interview
201   Private interview
202   *Sunday Times*, 10 May 2015
203   Private information
204   Private interview
205   Private interview
206   Private interview
207   Private interview
208   Private information
209   Interview, James McGrory
210   Private information
211   Private interview
212   Private interview
213   Private interview

214 Private information
215 Private interview
216 Private information
217 Private interview
218 Private interview
219 Private interview
220 Private interview
221 Interview, Lynton Crosby
222 Private information
223 Private information; CTF Partners' post-election study questioned 2,000 UK adults on 27–28 May online and was presented to the Cabinet and party MPs in July 2015
224 Interview, Martin Boon
225 Interview, Lynton Crosby
226 At the time of writing, the Electoral Commission had not published details of party spending during the election. Conservative strategists say Labour was outspending them in the final weeks of the campaign, but in a less targeted way. The Tories invested more resources earlier, in direct mail, for example, whereas Labour received donations from unions and others later in the campaign, leaving Miliband's team with little time to target precisely. There is some evidence for this in the different 'contact rates' voters reported to Lord Ashcroft, as discussed in Chapter 5.
227 Private information
228 Lord Forsyth, interview, *The Guardian*, 20 April 2015. Lynton Crosby regards this critique as illogical. He says: 'They can't blame the Tories for the fact that Labour lost Scotland to the SNP. You can't blame the Conservatives for the fact that there is another party who have an ambition to divide the country.'
229 Private interview

GENERAL ELECTION 2015 – THE RESULTS

Electorate: 46,425,386. **Turnout:** 66.1 per cent.
All figures are in comparison to 2010
(Respect's George Galloway won his seat in a 2012 by-election)

	PPCS	SEATS	GAIN	LOSS	+/-	VOTES	VOTE SHARE	+/-%
Conservative	647	331	35	11	+24	11,334,920	36.9	+0.8
Labour	631	232	22	48	-26	9,347,326	30.4	+1.5
SNP	59	56	50	0	+50	1,454,436	4.7	+3.1
Lib Dems	631	8	0	49	-49	2,415,888	7.9	-15.2
DUP	16	8	1	1	0	184,260	0.6	0.0
Sinn Féin	18	4	0	1	-1	176,232	0.6	0.0
Plaid Cymru	40	3	0	0	0	181,694	0.6	0.0
SDLP	18	3	0	0	0	99,809	0.3	0.0
UUP	15	2	2	0	+2	114,935	0.4	0.0
UKIP	624	1	1	0	+1	3,881,129	12.6	+9.5
Green	573	1	0	0	0	1,157,613	3.8	+2.8
Alliance	18	0	0	1	-1	61,556	0.2	+0.1
Ind (NI)	1	1	0	0	0	17,689	0.1	0.0
Others	680	0	0	0	0	270,723	0.9	-2.6
	3,971	650				30,698,210	100	

Abbreviations:
PPCs: prospective parliamentary candidates, SNP: Scottish National Party, DUP: Democratic Unionist Party, SDLP: Social Democratic & Labour Party, UUP: Ulster Unionist Party

The Conservatives won a twelve-seat majority with 37 per cent of the vote. This was achieved thanks largely to voters in England. In Scotland, the Conservatives won just 14.9 per cent of the vote, their lowest total since 1865. The Conservatives won twenty-seven seats from the Lib Dems and eight from Labour. The Tories lost one seat to UKIP compared with 2010 and ten seats to Labour (meaning a net loss of two seats to Labour).

The Conservatives targeted 100 key constituencies in England and Wales (out of 650 constituencies across the UK).

Just 901 voters in the seven most marginal Tory/Labour seats may have decided the outcome of the election. If these individuals had voted for Labour instead of the Conservatives, David Cameron would not have won Gower, Derby North, Croydon Central, Vale of Clwyd, Bury North, Morley and Outwood, or Plymouth Sutton and Devonport. These seats have combined majorities that would be wiped out by 901 voters switching from Tory to Labour.[1] This would have denied the Conservatives an overall majority in the Commons. Such calculations make for intriguing parlour games, and clearly over-simplify the picture, but the figures illustrate how critically important a few hundred voters in marginal seats can be.

The Conservatives concentrated their votes where it counted. The net increase in the number of seats the Tories won (8 per cent) was ten times the increase in the proportion of votes they won (0.8 per cent). Labour, however, piled up votes where they were not needed. The party increased its share of the vote by 1.5 per cent but lost twenty-six seats (10 per cent of its 2010 total) overall.

The seats-to-votes ratios varied widely for different parties. The Conservatives polled 34,244 votes for every seat won. Labour polled 40,290 votes per seat. The Liberal Democrats polled 301,986 votes per seat. The SNP won 25,972 votes per seat. UKIP won 3.9 million votes across the country and just one seat.

SELECT TIMELINE FOR THE 2015 GENERAL ELECTION

21 March 2012 – George Osborne delivers the 'Omnishambles' Budget, proposing to put VAT onto pasties and pies and increase the taxes that apply to caravans and churches.

3 May 2012 – Election held for Mayor of London. Boris Johnson wins a second term in City Hall after a campaign directed by Lynton Crosby.

2 October 2012 – Ed Miliband declares Labour are the true party of 'One Nation', claiming Disraeli's phrase as his new slogan, in a speech to party conference delivered entirely without notes, to widespread acclaim, even from senior Tories.

18 November 2012 – Crosby is hired by the Conservatives as a consultant to the party's general election campaign.

September/October 2013 – Candidates chosen for all of the Tories' forty 'attack' seats and the first 3,000 volunteers sign up to join Team 2015. Ed Miliband announces his policy to freeze energy prices at Labour's conference.

22 May 2014 – European Parliament elections. UKIP top the vote with 27.5 per cent, winning twenty-four MEPs. The Conservatives come third.

18 September 2014 – Scottish independence referendum. The 'No' to independence campaign wins by 55 per cent to 45 per cent for Alex Salmond's 'Yes' campaign. Salmond resigns and is later replaced by Nicola Sturgeon as SNP leader and First Minister of Scotland.

23 September 2014 – Miliband delivers his last Labour Party conference speech before the election, without a script for the third year in a row. He forgets to mention the deficit.

18 March 2015 – George Osborne delivers the coalition's last Budget.

23 March 2015 – Cameron tells the BBC he won't stand for election again as party leader in 2020, saying, 'Terms are like Shredded Wheat – two are wonderful but three might just be too many.'

26 March 2015 – The Sky News/Channel 4 election programme, *Battle for No. 10*. Cameron and Miliband appear one after the other in the first of the televised 'debates', with Jeremy Paxman interviewing both leaders and Kay Burley moderating questions from the audience. Cameron struggles with questions on food banks, while Miliband declares: 'Am I tough enough? Hell yes, I'm tough enough.'

30 March 2015 – Dissolution of Parliament for the general election.

2 April 2015 – The seven-way leaders' debate on ITV, involving Cameron, Miliband, Nick Clegg, Nigel Farage, Nicola Sturgeon, Natalie Bennett and Leanne Wood.

8 April 2015 – Ed Miliband launches Labour's 'non-dom' policy: a promise to abolish non-domicile tax status so that rich people who make their money in the UK cannot avoid paying their fair share of income tax.

9 April 2015 – Defence Secretary Michael Fallon claims Miliband would be willing to scrap Trident nuclear weapons and weaken Britain's defences to secure the support of the SNP in a hung parliament. Writing in *The Times*, he says: 'Ed Miliband stabbed his own brother in the back to become Labour leader. Now he is willing to stab the United Kingdom in the back to become Prime Minister.'

13 April 2015 – Miliband launches Labour's manifesto. A new Budget responsibility lock promises spending restraint to deliver a strong economic foundation. Other pledges include an NHS with time to care; controlled immigration; higher living standards for working families; and a country where the next generation can do better than the last.

14 April 2015 – David Cameron launches the Tory manifesto, promising to provide 'the good life' for people and families 'at every stage of life'. Pledges include taking family homes worth up to £1 million out of inheritance tax; a new 'right to buy' for housing association tenants; and thirty hours of free childcare for parents of three- and four-year-olds.

15 April 2015 – Nick Clegg publishes Lib Dem manifesto with pledges to cut tax and spend more on the NHS.

16 April 2015 – The so-called 'challengers' debate' broadcast by the BBC with opposition party leaders, excluding Cameron and Clegg.

25 April 2015 – Cameron appears to forget that he supports Aston Villa, not West Ham, during a speech on diversity in Croydon.

26 April 2015 – Cameron visits Yeovil and delivers his first passionate, 'pumped-up' speech, stepping up the tempo of his campaign.

29 April 2015 – Russell Brand publishes his interview with Ed Miliband on his 'Trewz' YouTube channel.

30 April 2015 – BBC *Question Time* election special, with Cameron, Miliband and Clegg.

3 May 2015 – Miliband unveils an 8ft 6in. slab of limestone engraved with his key election pledges. It becomes known as Labour's 'Ed Stone'.

7 May 2015 – Polling day. At 10 p.m., the broadcasters' official exit poll suggests the Tories will win 316 seats, far more than any opinion poll had indicated during the campaign.

8 May 2015 – David Cameron forms the first Conservative majority government since 1992, with 331 seats (including the Speaker). Ed Miliband, Nick Clegg and Nigel Farage announce their intentions to resign.

Endnotes

1   Source: http://diamondgeezer.blogspot.co.uk/2015/05/majority-2015.html?m=1, accessed 23 September 2015